LINCOLN CHRISTIAN
W9-BRR-216

Praise for the First Edition of *Hollywood Worldviews*

"Provocative and challenging. Even when I find myself disagreeing with Brian Godawa in his evaluation of a particular film, his cinematé and sophisticated point of view command attention."

Michael Medved, film critic and author of *Hollywood Versus America*

"This is an important book. Brian Godawa opens doors of understanding that we never knew were there. He gives us a grid through which we can clearly see what is going on philosophically and theologically within cinema art. Very simply, Brian has written the best book on the various worldviews behind popular Hollywood movies to date. I cannot recommend it enough."

David Bruce, webmaster, HollywoodJesus.com

"At last! A Christian book about Hollywood by a Hollywood Christian. With biblical balance and artistic insight, Brian Godawa cautions against both the legalisms of cultural anorexia and the naiveté of cultural gluttony. I'll never again watch a movie and be content to simply say whether or not I liked it!"

Greg Johnson, resident theologian, St. Louis Center for Christian Study, and author of *The World According to God*

"The greatest special effect in any movie is a great story. Brian Godawa, a screenwriter himself, understands this and understands the power in a good story's underlying assumptions. His fine book is a helpful guide for everyone who likes to go to the movies without checking their faith at the door."

Paul Sailhamer, seminar instructor, Faith Goes to the Movies

UPDATED AND EXPANDED

HOLLY WOOD WORLD VIEWS

WATCHING FILMS WITH WISDOM & DISCERNMENT

BRIAN GODAWA

FOREWORD BY
RALPH WINTER

IVP Books

An imprint of InterVarsity Press
Downers Grove, Illinois

InterVarsity Press
P.O. Box 1400, Downers Grove, IL 60515-1426
World Wide Web: www.ivpress.com
E-mail: email@ivpress.com

Second Edition ©2009 by Brian Godawa
First Edition ©2002 by Brian Godawa

All rights reserved. No part of this book may be reproduced in any form without written permission
from InterVarsity Press.

InterVarsity Press® is the book-publishing division of InterVarsity Christian Fellowship/USA®, a
movement of students and faculty active on campus at hundreds of universities, colleges and schools of
nursing in the United States of America, and a member movement of the International Fellowship of
Evangelical Students. For information about local and regional activities, write Public Relations Dept.,
InterVarsity Christian Fellowship/USA, 6400 Schroeder Rd., P.O. Box 7895, Madison, WI
53707-7895, or visit the IVCF website at <www.intervarsity.org>.

All Scripture quotations, unless otherwise indicated, are taken from the New American Standard
Bible®, copyright 1960, 1962, 1963, 1968, 1971, 1972, 1973, 1975, 1977, 1995 by The Lockman
Foundation. Used by permission.

Design: Cindy Kiple
Images: Punchstock

ISBN 978-0-8308-3713-7

Printed in the United States of America ∞

InterVarsity Press is committed to protecting the environment and to the responsible use
of natural resources. As a member of Green Press Initiative we use recycled paper
whenever possible. To learn more about the Green Press Initiative, visit <www.
greenpressinitiative.org>.

Library of Congress Cataloging-in-Publication Data

Godawa, Brian.
    Hollywood worldviews: watching films with wisdom and discernment/
    Brian Godawa.—Updated and expanded [ed.].
        p. cm.
    Includes bibliographical references and index.
    ISBN 978-0-8308-3713-7 (pbk.: alk. paper)
    1. Motion pictures—Religious aspects—Christianity. I. Title.
    PN1995.5.G65 2009
    791.4301—dc22
                        2009011675

P	18	17	16	15	14	13	12	11	10	9	8	7	6	5	4	3	2	1
Y	23	22	21	20	19	18	17	16	15	14	13	12	11	10	09			

928/

To the memory of
Francis A. Schaeffer and H. R. Rookmaaker,
who both taught me to see
the worldview behind the art

121265

CONTENTS

FOREWORD

Like Brian Godawa, I too love movies. I love the emotional journey that movies take me on. So different from books or music or theatre or art, all of which bring me joy or sadness or excitement, movies involve my senses and my thinking in a way that allows me to escape or go deeper into a place than I ever thought possible.

As a producer and lover of movies for many years now, and as a follower of Christ, I have not found many places where both of these "loves" can intersect (or collide sometimes). And not many places where deep dialogue can happen on postmodernism and Indiana Jones. Maybe that is why Brian and I became fast friends and why I like this book so much.

Hollywood and the study of the entertainment business, and its impact on our culture, has no lack of commentators. Brian makes his case for understanding the world of movies in a clear and easy way, and he has detailed his argument with many examples from movies. The wealth of examples not only enriches the reading but makes me realize that we have an embarrassment of rich movies and journeys to enjoy.

Reading this book is actually somewhat frustrating since I keep wanting to stop and rewatch the movies he references. That's because, whether or not I agree with his interpretation of any particular movie, he challenges me to go deeper—which only makes me love movies even more.

As an accomplished screenwriter, Brian gives a unique commentary to this subject. He knows how to tell a story and how to create a structure and flow to the writing. I find this book to be scholarly—it is well researched and documented like a textbook, but also approachable and readable. I just like to keep Wikipedia handy on those philosophy chapters. And for full disclosure, Brian has worked for me as a screenwriter. I love not only his skills as a writer but also his skill as a working "reporter" on what we filmmakers do and what it means. We continue to kick around ideas for future movies together.

It is interesting to make movies and then hear others talk about what the movie is about. As filmmakers, it is sometimes shocking and sometimes laughable to hear what reviewers say—too much analysis or misguided agendas or just over thinking can produce movie reviews that are way off. But sometimes a reviewer's comments can be startlingly insightful. That is what I find in reading this book—Brian's insights on how to see various movies keep me wanting more, tracking down more, watching more, enjoying more films.

Brian suggests that a good sermon is like a good movie. And for me, both must have three things: great content, flawless structure and some kind of engaging style.

I get asked two questions as a movie producer. First, what is a producer? (There are many books on this, and there's too much to say here.) And second, usually while working on a movie, I get asked, what is the movie about? Content is important to an audience—not that they want to hear a lesson or a sermon, but they want to know the narrative, what is the story? Is it worth my time? Will I enjoy it?

Developing movies at the studio is usually a process about the structure and the style, not about the content. The writer thinks deeply about this (usually) and so do the principal players (actors, director, producer) since that is how you are going to transmit the story.

But very few reflect about their own worldview or the roots of why this story is going to be told in this way. It just comes out in their art.

Brian's skill is helping us to view those underpinnings, to see how the story is built and how it impacts our larger cultural thinking. It is a fascinating process—what comes out of our movies that we can't control but describes who we are inside.

I hope that Brian updates this book every several years, or that we can talk him into a website or blog that applies this kind of thinking to the current crop of summer movies or Academy nominees. I taught a Sunday school class where we examined the Best Picture nominees against some of these same principles. It was the best attended class at the church—who doesn't want a homework assignment of watching some movies and then coming to class with the Bible to see if we can figure out what it all means. Well now you have no excuse—Brian provides the questions and topics at the end of each chapter.

I hope you enjoy the book as much as I do.

Ralph Winter
Producer *(X-Men, Fantastic Four, Wolverine)*

PREFACE

GOD LOVES MOVIES

God *loves* movies. Movies are visually dramatic stories, and in the Bible the dominant means through which God communicates his truth is visually dramatic stories—*not* systematic theology, or doctrinal catechism or rational argument. A survey of the Scriptures reveals that roughly 30 percent of the Bible is expressed through rational propositional truth and laws. While 70 percent of the Bible is story, vision, symbol and narrative.[1] Sure, God uses words, rationality and propositions to communicate his message. But modern evangelicalism has not always recognized how important visual imagery, drama and storytelling are to God.

VISUALLY

Movies are a visual medium. Cinematic composition, color, light and

---

[1] Of course, most of the propositional content and imagery is integrated with each other, so a strictly "scientific" separation is not possible. Both are necessary to God's revelation, but the sheer comparison of volume is revealing.

movement confer emotional states and embody symbolic meanings and ideas with deep effect. Consider the sense of awe at the majestic panoramic depiction of good battling evil in *The Lord of the Rings*. Remember the visual punch in the spiritual gut experienced through *The Passion of the Christ* as it incarnated the atonement imagery of Isaiah and the Gospels.

The thousands of miracles that God performed for his people in the Bible were not mere abstract propositions, but "signs and wonders," sensate visual displays of God's glory.[2] God's own temple was designed by him to be a visually rich engagement of the senses as his people worshipped him, surrounded by colors, images, pictures and statues of visual beauty (Ex 25; 28; 1 Kings 6; 2 Chron 3; 4) New covenant sacraments are visual *experiential* pictures of grace that are not reducible to abstract propositions.

And then there are dreams and visions: God's form of television and movies. Joseph's dreams of fat and skinny zombie cows, Ezekiel's *Close Encounters* with spinning wheels, Nebuchadnezzar's *Terminator* statue, as well as other visions given to dozens of Old *and* New Testament saints are all stunning high-definition, Dolby Surround Sound feasts for the senses as well as the spirit. God loves movies. He produced a lot of them.

God also uses visual images to reveal *himself*. The burning bush is just a trailer for upcoming releases. From the Old to the New Testament, God's favorite visual images to use for his presence seem to be thunder, lightning, clouds, smoke and fire. Tent pole spectacular! And no blue screen CGI!

DRAMATIC

Movies are all about drama. Drama is relationship in action. It is existential rather than intellectual. As we follow characters working through their moral dilemmas and personal journeys, so we learn through them. It is one thing to rationally explain the concept of forensic justification, but the power of seeing Jean Valjean being forgiven in *Les Misérables* embodies that truth existentially like no theological exposition could.

Rather than merely give sermons or lectures, God often had his proph-

---

[2]See Heb 2:4; Deut 6:22; Dan 4:1-3; Acts 14:3; 2 Cor 12:12.

ets give plays. Ezekiel played the role of an action hero in a war epic (Ezek 4:1-3) but also stretched his acting chops in a more indie style, art-house performance (Ezek 4:4-8). And there were plenty more episodes of the Ezekiel show.[3]

Jeremiah could have been nominated for an Emmy or an Oscar because so many of his prophecies were theatrical performances.[4] Isaiah broke the social taboos of modesty with R-rated shocking performance art as he walked around naked as a *visual* "sign and token" of Israel's shame (Is 20:2-4).

In the New Testament, God uses the Lucas-like special visual effects of a picnic blanket from heaven filled with unclean animals to persuade Peter of the new covenant inclusion of Gentiles. God, it seems, is the original Cecil B. DeMille. Mere words were not enough for him. He wanted drama. He wanted lights, camera, action!

Several books of the Bible are deliberately structured according to theatrical conventions. The books of Job and Jonah are depicted in dialogues reminiscent of ancient plays, including prologues, epilogues and several acts. Job's friends function as the chorus of ancient theatrical performances. The book of Mark structurally resembles a Greek tragedy.[5] God loves the visual, and God loves drama. But even more, he loves visually dramatic *stories*.

STORIES

Movies are first and foremost stories. And so is the Bible. The Bible is the story of God's redemptive activity in history. It communicates doctrine and theology mostly through story. Storytelling draws us into truth by incarnating worldview through narrative. Jesus taught about the kingdom of God mostly through parables—sensate, dramatic stories. He chose stories of weddings, investment bankers, unscrupulous slaves and buried treasure over syllogisms, abstraction, systematics or dissertations. He could do abstraction; he preferred not to.

---

[3]See also Ezek 5:1-4; 12:1-11, 17-20; 37:15-23.
[4]See Jer 13:1-11; 19:1; 17:19-27; 27:1-14; 32:6-15; 43:8-13; 51:59-64.
[5]"Theater," in *Dictionary of Biblical Imagery,* ed. Leland Ryken, James C. Wilhoit and Tremper Longman III (Downers Grove, Ill.: InterVarsity Press, 1998), p. 856.

Indeed, stories and parables may be a superior means of conveying theological truth than propositional logic or theological abstraction. As N. T. Wright suggests, "It would be clearly quite wrong to see these stories as mere illustrations of truths that could in principle have been articulated in a purer, more abstract form."[6] He reminds us that theological terms like *monotheism* "are late constructs, convenient shorthands for sentences with verbs in them [narrative], and that sentences with verbs in them are the real stuff of theology, not mere childish expressions of a 'purer' abstract truth."[7]

Kenneth E. Bailey, an expert on Middle Eastern culture, explains that "a biblical story is not simply a 'delivery system' for an idea. Rather, the story first creates a world and then invites the listener to live in that world, to take it on as part of who he or she is. . . . In reading and studying the Bible, ancient tales are not examined merely in order to extract a theological principle or ethical model."[8] Theologian Kevin Vanhoozer agrees that doctrinal propositions are not "more basic" than the narrative; to the contrary, they fail to communicate what narrative can. He writes in his book, *The Drama of Doctrine*, "Narratives make story-shaped points that cannot always be paraphrased in propositional statements without losing something in translation."[9] If you try to scientifically dissect the parable you will kill it, and if you discard the carcass once you have your doctrine, you have discarded the heart of God.

Because of our modern Western bias toward rational theological discourse, we are easily blinded to the biblical emphasis on visually dramatic stories. We downplay the visual, while God embraces the visual as vital to his message. We elevate rational discourse and put down dramatic theater as too emotional or entertainment-oriented, while God elevates drama as part of our *imago Dei*. We consider stories to be quaint illustrations of abstract doctrinal universal truths, while God uses sen-

---

[6]N. T. Wright, *The New Testament and the People of God* (Minneapolis: Fortress Press, 1992), p. 77.

[7]Ibid., p. 78.

[8]Kenneth E. Bailey, *Jacob and the Prodigal: How Jesus Retold Israel's Story* (Downers Grove, Ill.: InterVarsity Press, 2003), p. 51.

[9]Kevin J. Vanhoozer, *The Drama of Doctrine: A Canonical-Linguistic Approach to Christian Theology* (Louisville, Ky.: Westminster John Knox Press, 2005), p. 50.

sate, dramatic stories as his dominant means of incarnating truth. God *loves* movies.

AND SO DO I

I am a screenwriter. I've been at it for many years, winning various screenwriting honors and making a few movies along the way. I write stories that move me, like the feature film *To End All Wars;*[10] stories that intrigue me, like the supernatural thriller *The Visitation,* which is based on bestselling author Frank Peretti's novel; stories that make me laugh with ironic truth, like *Change Your Life,* a comedy about multilevel marketing; and stories that illuminate history and draw controversy, like my PBS documentary *Wall of Separation.* So what I have to say about the craft and industry of filmmaking comes from my experience as a writer in the business.

Any movie that gets made is the result of a collaboration of hundreds of people. And they are all responsible in differing degrees for the final result of the film: its look; its feel; its visual, audible and dramatic impact. From the set designer to the cinematographer to the actors to the key grips and gofers, a movie would not be what it is without everyone involved in the process. Dozens of these individuals affect the content, from the writer to the director to the producer to the executives overseeing the project; all are profoundly part of the process, but they all serve the story—because the story is king. In this sense, all those participating in the production of a movie are storytellers, not merely the writer.

It is this primary importance of the story that originally drew me to the movies. There's just something about a good story that makes me sit up and listen: the captivation of narrative, the magnetism of drama, the curiosity of interesting characters and the meaning of it all. It's no wonder Jesus used parables and stories to make his points and explain the unexplainable nature of God's kingdom to his followers. Drama brings to life the issues of life.

---

[10]*To End All Wars,* starring Kiefer Sutherland, is based on Ernest Gordon's *Through the Valley of the Kwai* (New York: Harper, 1962), the true story of Allied POWs who suffered in the Burma-Siam prison camps under the Imperial Japanese during World War II and were forced to build a railroad through hundreds of miles of man-eating jungle.

Great movies are like incarnate sermons. Watching sympathetic heroes work through their experiences often has more impact on my life than a rigorously reasoned abstract argument. Watching Eric Liddell run for God in *Chariots of Fire* proves to me that living for God without compromise is worth far more than what the world provides. Reliving the dilemmas of Captain John Miller and his men in *Saving Private Ryan* reminds me to be grateful for those who sacrificed for the precious freedom I enjoy. Movies like these force me to reevaluate my life so that I don't squander it on self-seeking pettiness. I remember some movies better than most sermons, probably because they put flesh onto the skeleton of abstract ideas about how life ought or ought not to be lived.

That's why I got into movies, and that's why I write about them now. From the funniest comedy to the saddest tragedy, movies capture the imagination, but they also convey the values and worldviews that we hold dear (as well as some we detest). My goal is to help the viewer discern those ideas that drive the story to its destination and see how they influence us to live our lives—to understand the story *behind* the story. But we must be careful in our discernment *not* to reduce a movie merely to its worldview, as if knowing the idea is enough to understand it. As indicated above, it is "entering into" the story where one comes into true contact with that worldview, not through mere rational analysis. This book is not a call to praise or condemn films simply because of their "message." Rather, by learning to be more aware of worldviews, we will be more equipped to appreciate the finer elements of what is going on in our movie-watching experience.

Another danger of reducing a movie to its worldview alone is the potential of failing to see the value of other elements that contribute to the whole of a movie. Cinematography, music, acting and other aesthetic aspects all contribute richly to the experience of cinema. The lack of space and time to cover such elements is, in my opinion, a limitation of this book. In fact, an entire book could be written on each of these aspects. On the other hand, this kind of specialized focus avoids the shallow brevity that often results from an all-encompassing survey.

I would like to thank the following for their help with hammering out this manuscript: my lovely wife, Kim, for all her patience and support;

my patron producer and fellow Schaefferian, Jack Hafer; my Christlike producer, Ralph Winter; my graceful theologian, Ken Gentry; my transcendentally nimble philosopher, Aaron Bradford; my amusing and forbearing editor, David Zimmerman; my writing pal and sister-in-law, Shari Risoff; my movie buddies, Eric and Laura Baesel; a mighty warrior of the pen, Tal Brooke; a mighty CRI editor and movie buff, Melanie Cogdill; CRI's research monster, Stephen Ross; the storymeister, Jim Womer; my lifelong friend, Rich Knox; and as always—Joe. And a very special thanks to Internet Movie Database <www.imdb.com> for its indispensable information on movie stats.

INTRODUCTION

"Movies corrupt the values of society."
"Movies have too much sex and violence."
"Movies are worldly and a waste of time."
"Movies are dangerous escapist fantasies."

Those are just a few of the refrains repeated by many of today's culturally concerned Americans. Our cultural psyche has been damaged by Hollywood's defiant decadence and its relentless pushing of the envelope of common decency. But such sentiments suffer from a diluted mixture of truth and error. Not only do they miss the positive values that do exist in many movies, but also those who would completely withdraw from culture because of its imperfection suffer a decreasing capacity to interact redemptively with that culture. They don't understand the way people around them think because they are not familiar with the "language" those people are speaking or the culture they are consuming. A communication barrier results, and these cultural abstainers often end up in irrelevance and alienation from others. I call these artistic teetotalers cultural anorexics.

But the cultural anorexics also endanger their own humanity. The arts (of which movies are a part) are a God-given means of expressing our humanity. The creation of art, though flawed or imperfect, reflects the creativity and beauty of our Creator. To reject any of the arts in toto is to reject the *imago Dei*, the image of God in humanity. Even though we are fallen, with our art partaking of this fallenness, we are still created in the image of God, and therefore our creations continue to reflect our Maker. As Francis Schaeffer was fond of pointing out, that *imago Dei* comes through even if the artist tries to suppress it. This is so because all truth is, in one sense, God's truth, no matter who is saying it, whether it be a prophet, infidel or donkey.

Sometimes the most egregious lies are expressed through so-called Christian culture. For instance, dramatic pulpit oratory too often is infected by heresy, and public testimony too often panders to sensationalism. Christian movies, though well intentioned and sincere, often suffer from heavy-handedness in their desire to convert the unbeliever through art. Rather than being true to the ambiguities and difficulties of reality, rather than wooing the viewer with the right questions, an emphasis on clearly expressed answers often results in preachiness and a tendency toward platitudes. Authenticity and integrity can suffer because of manipulation. Which is more to be avoided: a pagan movie that rings true or "Christian" propaganda that rings false?

But another individual occupies the opposite end of the spectrum, and this one I call the *cultural glutton*. This is the person who consumes popular art too passively, without discrimination. Here are some of the expressions common to the cultural glutton:

"I just want to be entertained."

"You shouldn't take it so seriously."

"It's only a movie."

"The sex and violence don't bother me."

Cultural gluttons prefer to avoid analyzing movies beyond their entertainment value. They just want to escape and have fun for two hours in another world. When challenged by cultural critics to discern the messages within the movies, these moviegoers balk at such criticism as being too analytical or "reading into things." And many filmmakers mouth agreement with them.

One of Samuel Goldwyn's most famous sayings is "If you want to send a message, use Western Union." The meaning of this maxim is that movies are for entertainment, not the transmission of personal, political, social or religious views. And many share this viewpoint. No less a screenwriting icon than William Goldman (screenwriter of *The Princess Bride* and *Misery*) has pronounced, "Movies are finally, centrally, crucially, primarily *only* about story."[1]

Conventional wisdom and popular idols notwithstanding, nothing could be more of a half-truth. While it is true that story is the foundation of movies, an examination of the craft and structure of storytelling reveals that the drawing power of movies is not simply that they are "good stories" in some indefinable sense but that these stories are *about something*. They narrate the events surrounding characters who overcome obstacles to achieve some goal and who, in the process, are confronted with their personal need for change. In short, movie storytelling is about *redemption*—the recovery of something lost or the attainment of something needed.

I propose an amendment to Goldman's thesis that would complete the thought more accurately: movies may be about story, but those stories are finally, centrally, crucially, primarily, *mostly* about redemption.[2]

WORLDVIEWS

Much has been written in recent years on the concept of worldviews and how they influence our lives. James Sire, in his classic introductory text on worldviews, *The Universe Next Door*, defined a worldview as "a set of presuppositions (assumptions which may be true, partially true or entirely false) which we hold (consciously or subconsciously, consistently or inconsistently) about the basic makeup of our world."[3] He added that worldviews all tend to have rock-bottom answers to at least seven basic questions: (1) What is really real? (2) What is the nature of external reality, the world around us? (3) What is a human being? (4) What happens to a person after death? (5) Why is it possible to know anything at all? (6)

---

[1]William Goldman, *William Goldman: Four Screenplays* (New York: Applause, 1995), p. 2.
[2]Storytelling may have many functions, such as presenting historical information, providing moral teaching and offering a ritual or spiritual explanation. Depending on the kind of story, movies certainly may fulfill other purposes, but the redemptive aspect is, I believe, the dominant one.
[3]James W. Sire, *The Universe Next Door: A Basic Worldview Catalog* (Downers Grove, Ill.: InterVarsity Press, 1997), p. 16.

How do we know what is right and wrong? (7) What is the meaning of
human history?[4] David Noebel, in *Understanding the Times*, categorizes
worldviews as frameworks of interpreting reality through ten integrated
disciplines: theology, philosophy, ethics, biology, psychology, sociology,
law, politics, economics and history.[5] That is, every worldview is a system of beliefs that seeks to address each of these elements of our
existence.

One of the simplest ways of understanding a worldview is as a belief
system or web of beliefs that contains a creation-Fall-redemption motif.
This approach has grown out of the writings of Dutch Christian philosopher, Herman Dooyeweerd.[6] In this view, every worldview has some understanding of the original state of reality (creation), what went wrong
with that original state (Fall) and how to recover or return to that original state (redemption).

For many years, these definitions of worldview have maintained a
metaphysical bias. They have all tended to stress worldview thinking in
terms of cognitive *concepts* about the world, rational *propositions* about
reality, abstract *ideas* about truth. Because of this bias toward philosophical rationality, few of them have incorporated the most ancient understanding of worldview as a story that gives meaning to existence through
narrative.[7]

Yet, if we look closer at the creation-Fall-redemption approach, for
example, we will discover that it is not merely a list of metaphysical concepts, it is a narrative: a progression or course of events with characters
and plot—in other words, a worldview is a *story*. Humanity's existence
begins in one state (creation), something happens to change it all (Fall),
which sets human beings on a search to fix things by finding their way

---

[4]Ibid., pp. 17-18.

[5]David Noebel, *Understanding the Times: The Collision of Today's Competing Worldviews*
(Manitou Springs, Colo.: Summit Press, 2006).

[6]Herman Dooyeweerd, *In the Twilight of Western Thought: Studies in the Pretended Autonomy of Philosophical Thought* (Nutley, N.J.: Craig Press, 1972).

[7]In a more recent book, James Sire expands his understanding of worldview to include
this element of story, as well as a few others, including orientation of the heart, a devo-
tional commitment to the "really real" and the nature of behavior over mental assent.
See James Sire, *Naming the Elephant: Worldview as a Concept* (Downers Grove, Ill.:
InterVarsity Press, 2004).

back to that original state (redemption). Creation, Fall, redemption—beginning, middle, end of story. In postmodern parlance, a worldview could also be considered a *metanarrative*. Metanarratives are "over-stories" or big picture stories that give meaning to the little pictures of our own lives and experiences. In this sense, as New Testament scholar N. T. Wright explains, "All worldviews are at the deepest level shorthand formulae to express stories."[8] Stories are the primary way in which we think and organize our understanding of reality. More will be said about story in the chapter "Stories and Mythology."

Let's look at a couple examples of this narrative expression of worldviews. Monists believe that everything in the universe is ultimately one in essence (creation). Humanity is without peace because we falsely perceive distinctions among things (Fall). This perception of distinction is itself alienation. Humanity's need is to change this perception so that we see all things as ultimately one. When we do so, we find the harmony we lack in our lives (redemption).

The rationalist or modernist believes that our problem stems from irrationality (Fall). If we would only align ourselves with logical principles (creation), we would redeem ourselves from the irrationality of emotion and religious faith (redemption).

The Christian worldview sees humanity as created in the image of God (creation). But we are also sinful and alienated from our Maker as well as from our fellow human beings, exposing us to the inevitability of God's eternal wrath (Fall). Redemption in Christianity is found in the substitutionary sacrifice of the innocent (Christ) in place of the guilty (sinners), which pays the penalty of sin (justice) and reconciles the sinner to God and to others (mercy).

The Lion, the Witch and the Wardrobe, C. S. Lewis's classic adapted by Andrew Adamson, Ann Peacock, Christopher Markus and Stephen Mc-Feely, is an example of the Christian worldview. The world of Narnia was once an idyllic land (creation), until the White Witch came and made it everywhere winter and never Christmas, freezing her enemies in stone (Fall). But when Aslan comes he restores the Deep Magic by sacri-

---

[8]N. T. Wright, *The New Testament and the People of God* (Minneapolis: Fortress Press, 1992), p. 77.

ficing himself on the stone altar (substitutionary atonement), which leads
to the overthrow of the White Witch's forces and melts the snow and
frees the people from stone (redemption).

The Golden Compass, the adaptation of Philip Pullman's trilogy, *His Dark Materials*, is an upside-down version of Narnia that presents an atheistic world-view. In this view the universe is originally harmonious without religion (creation), until God, the ultimate enemy, and "The Magisterium" of religious people "tell people what they cannot do," which blinds and enslaves people (Fall). Redemption then comes from "killing God" and freeing one's self from the "tyranny" of such religious "control."[9]

**HISTORICAL FILMS
—FICTION**

Dances with Wolves
Last of the Mohicans
Saving Private Ryan
The Patriot
Gladiator
The Last Samurai
Apocalypto
The Lost City
Trade
The Da Vinci Code

The redemption in a particular world-view or belief system is its proposal for how to fix what is wrong with us. And redemption includes values about the way people ought or ought not to live and behave in this world. If a story is about a character who learns that lying hurts others and that family is more important than career (as in *Liar Liar* with Jim Carrey), then that story's redemptive message is that people's alienation is solved through honesty and family. We *ought* to make family and honesty more important than career and success. If a story is about clever, suave criminals getting away with a crime (as in *Ocean's 11*), the story's redemptive message, immoral though it may be, fits the perception of criminals: crime pays, and hipness is more important than obeying the law.

---

[9]*The Golden Compass* is a self-contradictory attempt to use the transcendent categories of fantasy that point toward deity (such as prophecies, good and evil, spirits, and magic) to promote an antitranscendent (imminent) worldview that denies such transcendent categories. Supposed "good guys" are running around telling the Magisterium (the "bad guys") what they shouldn't do, namely, telling people what they shouldn't do. The obvious contradiction is obviously not apparent to the storytellers. For more detail on this self-contradiction in secular and humanist movies, see the section in chapter six on "Humanism in the Movies."

I will show in the following chapters that most movies follow a main character who seeks a specific goal and in so doing learns something about himself or herself and the world in a way that inevitably results in this person's redemption—or lack thereof.[10]

SUSPENSION OF DISBELIEF

We are all aware of the age-old question of whether art mirrors or influences society. Luminaries from both sides of the aisle have weighed in on the reflection/infection debate. And this debate will probably rage on till the Final Judgment. In his book *Hollywood Versus America*[11] film critic and Hollywood boogeyman Michael Medved argued that filmmakers *intend* to influence the public through the values and characters they portray in television and film. His thoroughly documented opus concluded that entertainment reinforces certain values over others, namely those that reflect the current fashion of the creative community.

He pointed out the hypocrisy of those in the dream business who proclaim that movies don't influence belief or behavior while charging millions of dollars for advertising and product placements in movies and receiving awards and prestige for promoting trendy social agendas in their movies. His thesis, which still holds true today, is that many movies do not reflect the dominant values of the American public and often self-consciously defy financial interest; therefore they can only be deliberate attempts by those involved to influence public opinion. Witness the unprecedented success of Michael Moore's docuganda[12] *Fahrenheit 911*, or the success of companies like Participant Productions whose agenda-

---

[10]Some critics of this view claim that redemption is an arbitrary theme. One could just as easily say that all movies are about sex; any movie that doesn't deal with sex is about the suppression of sex. But sex as an underlying theme is a Freudian novelty; a theology of storytelling comes from a more objective standard: the Bible, as well as all of recorded ancient history. As I will discuss in later chapters, the nature of storytelling as narrative with a purpose and a view toward redemption is a presupposition of the Christian worldview. God, the author of history, tells fictional and nonfictional stories to show the meaning behind life and the possibility of redemption. Humankind, made in God's image, has told stories in this way since creation.

[11]Michael Medved, *Hollywood Versus America* (New York: HarperCollins, 1992).

[12]Propaganda masquerading as documentary.

driven movies such as *Syriana, Charlie Wilson's War, North Country,* and *Good Night, and Good Luck* reflect their stated purpose of "entertainment that inspires and compels social change."

But even in spite of this agenda-driven contingent, it is important to understand that Hollywood is not a monolithic culture of antitraditional values. All too often Christians and other religious people create a straw man caricature of Hollywood as a conspiracy of malevolent personalities attacking tradition. Yes, there are plenty of those kind of people in the business. But there are also plenty of others who are different. There are also those who simply want to make and sell whatever makes money, and there are those who believe in creating uplifting entertainment as they see it. The problem is that Hollywood is like any other subculture: it may follow trends and have certain tendencies, but it is a wildly diverse place and full of complexities and people who do not fit the stereotypes. As the reader will see in this book, the moment one generalizes a value in one movie to all of Hollywood, they miss the bigger picture, by neglecting to see the two other movies that promote the opposite value.

And it goes deeper than that. For I hope to illustrate that even most movies are not wholly evil or wholly good. Most movies are a mixed bag of values and ideas, some good, some bad, but most worth engaging in and discussing. What commonly occurs is Christians demonizing movies like the Harry Potter series for its occultism or anti-authority values, but failing to see that these movies also uphold other good values like courage, loyalty and sacrifice. Such knee-jerk reactions and gross over-simplifications are what steer us out of the cultural conversation.

But it is also true that much entertainment meets an already existing demand in the audience. The public is not always consistent with its own claim of traditional morality. A herd instinct still guides the masses toward titillation of already darkened impulses. Actions *do* speak louder than words, and even though "family friendly" movies have a much larger audience than envelope-pushing R-rated movies, R-rated movies still make millions and millions of dollars a year, testifying to a significant interest in their darker material.

It is the position of this book that movies *both* reflect and influence society. An Oliver Stone film like *JFK* or the anti-Christian *Da Vinci Code* may be obvious in its intent to propagandize, but it is no less a reflection of what a certain segment of the population already believes. *Hannibal*, the sequel to *Silence of the Lambs*, may push the moral envelope with a sympathetic cannibal as hero, but millions went to see it knowing full well what they were in for. A movie like that doesn't make well over $160 million at the box office by scandalously breaking new moral ground with an unwilling public. The ground is already tilled in the hearts of the people, or they wouldn't want to see it. The success of *Hannibal* reflects a society already fascinated with evil.

HISTORICAL FILMS—NONFICTION

Schindler's List

Chariots of Fire

Braveheart

Rob Roy

Amistad

To End All Wars

Hotel Rwanda

North Country

The Last King of Scotland

United 93

Charlie Wilson's War

Good Night, and Good Luck

The Changeling

The Downfall

Cinderella Man

While it is true that some movies may be more influential than others, it is incumbent upon moviegoers to understand what they are consuming and the nature of their amusement. It is not the least bit ironic that the word *amusement* means "without thought" (its original usage was "to delude or deceive"). Sadly, this is all too often what happens when the lights go down and the curtains go up. We suspend our disbelief and, along with it, our critical faculties.

By knowing something of the craft of storytelling, of its structure and nature, the average moviegoer might be less inclined to treat his or her viewing as mere entertainment and see another side of the movie equation: a means of communicating worldviews and values with a view toward redemption. This knowledge need not spoil the joy in entertainment or justify total withdrawal from culture. Rather, it can deepen one's appreciation and sharpen one's discernment, helping the reader strike a balance between two extremes: cultural anorexia and cultural gluttony.

AUTHORIAL INTENT AND READER RESPONSE

My personal involvement in movies dictates the focus of this book. I have decided to concentrate primarily on American mainstream movies made within the last twenty or so years. Older classics have much to offer in the way of analysis, but space is limited, so they are for another to explore. This book contains few references to foreign and art-house films because these are not as widely viewed within the mainstream.

My goal in this book is to increase art appreciation, but I am limiting that artistic education to the story. There is much more to be learned about creative communication through a film's acting, art direction, cinematography and soundtrack, but that is beyond the scope of this book. I want to inform the reader of the nature of storytelling and analyze how worldviews are communicated through most Hollywood movies. As readers sharpen their understanding of movies, they will be more capable of discerning the good from the bad and avoid the extremes of cultural desertion (anorexia) and cultural immersion (gluttony).

FAIR WARNING

The reader should be aware that on the following pages I reveal important plot twists and character revelations about specific movies. Regrettably, this is unavoidable because much of the worldview and philosophy of a film is wrapped up in these twists. But be encouraged—good stories are often not hindered by such foreknowledge. If you demand total innocence regarding the plots of movies you intend to see, then skip over discussions of those movies as you encounter them in the text.

Well, here it is: Movie Appreciation 101. What follows are the confessions of a filmmaker: how we storytellers try to influence you, the audience, with our worldviews.

ARE YOU A CULTURAL GLUTTON OR A CULTURAL ANOREXIC?

Ask yourself these questions to challenge your personal growth.

Cultural Glutton

1. Do you watch every movie that interests you without considering beforehand whether its subject matter is appropriate?

2. Do you think movies and television are only entertainment without any real messages?

3. How many hours a week do you spend on entertainment? Now compare that with how many hours a week you read the Bible or other spiritual growth material.

4. How many times have you enjoyed a movie that you later came to realize was offensive to your beliefs or worldview?

Cultural Anorexic

1. Do you generalize all movies as "worldly" or consider any depiction of sin as wrong without concern for context?

2. Are you unable to appreciate anything good in a movie because of some bad you see in it?

3. Do you consider art and entertainment to be wastes of time and therefore spend all of your leisure time on "spiritual" activities?

4. How many times have you been incapable of interacting with those around you because you were out of touch with their cultural experience?

ACT ONE

STORYTELLING IN THE MOVIES

1

SEX, VIOLENCE & PROFANITY

As I speak about movies at churches and Christian schools around the country, I find that the first and foremost concern in many Christians' and culture critics' minds is the issue of sex, violence and profanity in the movies. It is difficult for many people to appreciate whatever good is in movies if they have to wade through a cesspool of sin to find the jewels. Since this is their first and foremost concern, we'll address it first and foremost—and biblically.

On one level the concern about artistic vice is entirely legitimate because of the preoccupation that many films seem to have in integrating the evil that people do into their stories. Many studies have linked media consumption with degenerate social behavior. Statistics show that Americans absorb into their minds through the media thousands of violent acts, vile obscenities and acts of immoral sexuality every year. But the part of the puzzle not typically addressed is the context out of which these sinful acts pour forth. And it is perhaps here that the most damage *or good* can be done to the individual and society.

Although violence and sexual immorality are results of the Fall in Eden, not all accounts of sex and violence are intrinsically immoral. It is the *context* through which these misbehaviors are communicated that dictates their destructive or redemptive nature. It is not merely the detailed acts of violence portrayed in teen slasher series like *Friday the 13th, Halloween* or *Hostel* that make them detrimental to the minds of youth. It is that these acts exist within a nihilistic view of the world, with murder demythologized through diabolical detail and the existential association of sex with death. The devaluing of human life is realized through evil as entertainment. On the other hand, films like *Schindler's List, Braveheart, Letters from Iowa Jima* and *The Last King of Scotland* portray equally graphic brutality, but their context is ultimately redemptive. That is, the depiction of man's inhumanity toward man repulses, rather than entertains, and points toward redemption from such evil. Similar extremities of violence can issue from different contexts and produce opposite results.

The ultimate sourcebook for most media watchdogs is the Bible. And it ought to be—without its definition of a universal objective morality, we have no absolute reference point for right and wrong. Without God's definitions of good and evil, there can be no ultimate value difference between the diabolical acts of Hannibal Lecter and the innocent ones of Forrest Gump. The Bible alone provides a justifiable objective standard for making moral judgments that transcend the whims of personal opinion.

But we must be careful in our appeal to the Good Book when analyzing the morality of stories. For in its pages are detailed accounts and descriptions of every immoral act known to humanity. A cursory perusal of these depictions of vice is enough to make any concerned reader blush. But it only proves that sex and violence are not always literary taboo in Holy Writ. In fact, the depiction of evil is treated as the necessary prerequisite to understanding redemption.

EXAMPLES OF VIOLENCE

Let's take a look at the following interesting passage from a script and examine it in light of moral scruples. The first is a scene from a period piece that takes place in a distant exotic land. Think *Gladiator* meets

Indiana Jones. Ehud, our swashbuckling hero, is about to give a "message" to the evil villain, King Eglon, who is oppressing Ehud's people like some kind of Darth Vader:

> Ehud made himself a sword which had two edges, a cubit in length, and he bound it on his right thigh under his cloak. He presented the tribute to Eglon king of Moab. Now Eglon was a very fat man. . . . Ehud came to him while he was sitting alone in his cool roof chamber. And Ehud said, "I have a message from God for you." And he arose from his seat. Ehud stretched out his left hand, took the sword from his right thigh and thrust it into his belly. The handle also went in after the blade, and the fat closed over the blade, for he did not draw the sword out of his belly; and the refuse came out. . . . Now Ehud escaped while they were delaying, and he passed by the idols and escaped to Seirah.

What script is this from? A Jerry Bruckheimer or Michael Bay action movie? The next installment of *Die Hard?* Obviously not. The informed reader already knows this is a passage from the Bible—Judges 3:16-26, to be precise. God, as the sovereign author of human history, wrote this script, and it's loaded with lies, espionage, intrigue, murder and an explicit grotesque image of a man's intestinal excrement spilling out over a plunged weapon. And it all ends with an escape scene reminiscent of many action films today. I could go on, but you get the picture. Parental discretion advised.

The polemical point of the book of Judges was to show how necessary it was for Israel to have a godly king by depicting how evil they had become when "everyone did what was right in his own eyes" (Judg 17:6; 21:25)—a situation not unlike today, in our world of moral relativity and terrorism. This same book earlier described the prophetess Deborah singing a praise and worship song (Judg 5:24-27) about Jael driving a tent peg through the skull of the wicked ruler Sisera (Judg 4:17-22)! I'd like to see congregations across the land sing *that* hymn in church, complete with a chorus about Sisera bowing at her feet and falling dead.

But that is child's play compared to the story of the Levite and his concubine in Judges 19. This Bible narrative contains some of the most gruesome imagery and hideous acts of evil in all of Scripture. Here we have the Levite bringing his unfaithful concubine back home. On their journey they stay in the house of an old man in the city of Gibeah, where a gang of sexual perverts seek to rape the visitor. Instead, the old man, in a perverse act of hospitality, offers his virgin daughter and the visitor's concubine in the Levite's place. The perverts gang rape and abuse the concubine all night, until she lay dead on the doorstep. Whereupon the loving Levite, in a twisted symbolic gesture, takes a knife and cuts her body up into twelve pieces. This event is so abhorrent, the Scriptures conclude, "Nothing like this has ever happened or been seen from the day when the sons of Israel came up from the land of Egypt" (Judg 19:30). As a matter of fact, if the book of Judges were to be filmed, it would easily be rated NC-17. Indeed, nothing like this has ever been seen on a Bible flannel graph or on a church video.

EXAMPLES OF SEX

How about this steamy sex-scene dialogue?

> How beautiful are your feet in sandals,
>> O prince's daughter!
>> The curves of your hips are like jewels,
>> The work of the hands of an artist.
> Your navel is like a round goblet
>> Which never lacks mixed wine;
>> Your belly is like a heap of wheat
>> Fenced about with lilies.
> Your two breasts are like two fawns,
>> Twins of a gazelle. . . .
> Your stature is like a palm tree,
>> And your breasts are like its clusters.
> I said, "I will climb the palm tree,
>> I will take hold of its fruit stalks."
>> Oh, may your breasts be like clusters of the vine,
>> And the fragrance of your breath like apples,
> And your mouth like the best wine!

Is this some description of Monica Belluci or Halle Berry in a sexy thriller? On the contrary, it's from Song of Solomon 7:1-3, 7-9.

And Solomon does not merely dwell on married love in his portraits of sexuality in Scripture. He also pictures a vividly sensual scene of adul-

terous seduction in Proverbs 7, complete with the detailed smells, sights
and sounds of the moment: sensually exotic linens on the bed, sweet-
smelling perfume and lustful whispers of enticement. It's enough to
make a reader's erotic imagination spin wild. Solomon does this in order
to lead the reader vicariously into a realistic experience of the surprise
that occurs when the adulteress's apparently sweet bed of "myrrh, aloes
and cinnamon" turns out to be an entrance to the "chambers of death."
This is something we can see in the Bible or in the movie *Fatal Attraction,* but I suspect neither will be available in the church library's video
section any time soon.

Sexually explicit imagery is found throughout Scripture. The *Dictionary of Biblical Imagery,* pointing out translations appropriate for some
Song of Solomon passages, explains that the image of the "garden" used
in Proverbs 5:15-19 and Song of Solomon 4:12-15 is a reference to the
woman's sexual organ. In addition, according to the *Dictionary,* one of
the "tamed" English translations of Song of Solomon 5:4-5 reads truer to
the original Hebrew as the following:

> My lover thrust his hand through the hole,
> and my vagina was inflamed,
> I arose and opened for my lover.[1]

And the Bible is not one-sided in its portrayal of sexuality. Regarding
Song of Solomon 5:14:

> In the midst of the one descriptive song of the man, the woman says,
>
> > His arms are rods of gold
> > set with chrysolite.
> > His body is like polished ivory
> > decorated with sapphires. (Song of Solomon 5:14 NIV)

Once again the English translations are reticent and here intentionally
obscure the more explicit Hebrew text. It is not his body that is like a slab
of ivory, but rather his sexual organ, which is like a tusk of ivory.[2]

---

[1]"Sex," in *Dictionary of Biblical Imagery,* ed. Leland Ryken, James C. Wilhoit and Tremper Longman III (Downers Grove, Ill.: InterVarsity Press, 1998), p. 777.
[2]Ibid., p. 778.

Sex

Adultery (Judges 19:22-25; 1 Samuel 2:22; 2 Samuel 11; Proverbs 2; 5; 7)

Incest (Genesis 11:29; 19:31-36; 35:22; 38:16-18)

Masochism and satanic worship (1 Kings 18:25-28)

Orgies (Exodus 32:3-6)

Prostitution (Genesis 38:12-26; Judges 16:1)

Rape—even gang rape (Genesis 34:2; Judges 19:22-25; 2 Samuel 13:6-14)

Seduction (Proverbs 7)

Violence

Annihilation of entire cities (Genesis 19:23; Joshua 6:21; 8:22-26; 10:34-42)

Bludgeoning of a thousand men to death (Judges 15:15-16)

Burning victims alive (Numbers 16:35; Joshua 7:25; Judges 9:49; 15:6; Daniel 3:22)

Cannibalism (2 Kings 6:28)

Cutting off of thumbs (Judges 1:6-7)

Decapitation (1 Samuel 17:5; 31:9; 2 Samuel 16:9)

Disemboweling (Judges 3:21-22; 2 Samuel 20:10; 2 Chronicles 21:19; Acts 1:18)

Dismemberment (1 Samuel 15:32-33)

Genocide (1 Samuel 22:19; Numbers 31:17; Deuteronomy 2:34; 3:6; Joshua; Matthew 2:16)

Gouging out of eyes (Judges 16:21)

Hanging (Joshua 10:26-27; Esther 9:25; Matthew 27:3-5)

Human sacrifice (2 Kings 3:27; 16:3; 17:17, 31; 21:6; 2 Chronicles 28:3)

Murder after murder after murder (Genesis to Revelation)

Stabbing (Judges 3:16-26; 2 Samuel 2:23; 3:27; 20:10)

Stoning (Numbers 15:36; Joshua 7:25; 1 Kings 21:13; Acts 7:54-59; 14:19)

Striking between the eyes (1 Samuel 17:49)

Suicide (1 Samuel 31:4-5; 2 Samuel 17:23; 1 Kings 16:18; Acts 1:18)

Lawlessness

Arson (Numbers 11:1; Judges 9:49; 15:5; 18:27; 20:48; 2 Kings 25:9)

Blasphemy (Exodus 32:4; 2 Kings 18:4, 28—19:5; Job 2:9; Isaiah 36:14-20)

Destruction of public property (Joshua 6:34; 8:19; 11:11; Judges 1:8; 16:30-31)

Revenge (Genesis 34:25; Judges 15:7-8; 2 Samuel 3:27; 13:23-29; Mark 6:19-24)

Theft (Genesis 31:19, 34-35; Joshua 7:11; Judges 17:2; 18:14-27; John 12:6)

Voyeurism (2 Samuel 11:2)

Vulgar insults (1 Kings 12:10; Galatians 5:12)

Figure 1. Sex, violence and lawlessness depicted in the Bible

Some Christians through history have sought to avoid the sexual imagery in Song of Solomon by interpreting it as an allegory of God's love for his people. But they overlook the fact that even if this love poem were mere allegory, *it is still sexually erotic imagery* which is being used of God's "intercourse" with his church.

While biblical passages like the ones discussed above do not justify pornography or obscene entertainment, their erotic visual stimulation, verbal seduction and physical consummation could arguably warrant the label "Under seventeen not admitted unless accompanied by an adult."[3]

EXAMPLES OF PROFANITY

What about vulgar language? Does the Bible contain foul-mouthed dialogue like that found in the movies? Is there any place at all for recounting the profanities that spew from the lips of depraved human beings? The answer may be upsetting to some—profanity actually has its place in the Holy Scriptures.[4]

In 1 Kings 12 the irresponsible King Rehoboam is approached by the people of Israel, who ask for a lighter yoke to bear than the one Rehoboam's father gave them. Rehoboam avoids wise elderly counsel and tells the people by way of analogy, "My little finger is thicker than my father's loins! Whereas my father loaded you with a heavy yoke, I will add to your yoke" (1 Kings 12:10-11).

Now there are two meanings to this statement. First of all, the Hebrew word for "loins" *(motnayim)* is usually a reference to the middle part of the man's body as his seat of strength. Thus, Rehoboam is more than likely referring to the nature of bodily weakness under a heavier yoke. Solomon's burden on the people was nothing compared to what Rehoboam is going to give them.

---

[3]John Stuart Peck, a Greek and Hebrew scholar as well as a producing artistic director of an Ontario theater company, writes of the need for Christians to produce "erotic" art that maintains artistic fidelity to biblical sexuality. "There is artwork about sex [in the Song of Solomon], and, furthermore, there are points in chapters 4 and 7 that are so potentially explicit that most translations muff them. Nevertheless, we would not call these passages pornographic or obscene. We could call them 'erotic.'" John Peck, "Sex in Art—An Erotic Christian Imagination?" *Cornerstone* 30, no. 121 (2001): 15. The article is an edited and enhanced version of a speech he delivered in November 1998 at Regent University, Virginia <www.regent.edu/acad/schcom/csfc/journal/peck.html>.

[4]I am using the dictionary definition for *profanity* as meaning "abusive, vulgar, or irreverent language" *(American Heritage Dictionary,* 3rd ed.).

However, *motnayim* has in some places been used as a reference to the male generative organ.[5] The language of the Bible is filled with alliterative wordplays and poetic analogies. With this context in mind, Rehoboam appears to be making a double entendre with the pinkie and the penis—a common male insult of powerlessness since the beginning of time (especially from the likes of the "young men" with whom Rehoboam counseled). Even if one considers the "safe" English translation of the word as "loins," the harshness of the insult is no less clear.

Here, as elsewhere, the Scriptures are not gender-exclusive in their revelation of coarse or derogatory language used by sinners. As the *Dictionary of Biblical Imagery* reveals, "Crude metonymy for women as sexual objects appear in Judges 5:30 (the NIV translates, 'girl,' but the Hebrew is coarse slang; cf. Ecclesiastes 2:8, where women are referred to as 'breasts')."[6]

But there is even more explicit vulgar language elsewhere from the pen of Paul the apostle. In the book of Galatians, Paul is criticizing the Judaizers who sought to enforce circumcision as a necessity for the justification of the believer. These legalists sought to put Gentiles under the yoke of Jewish ceremonial law that had already been abrogated by Christ's death (Eph 2:11-16). In short, the Judaizers were teaching that Gentiles had to be circumcised to be saved. This was so serious an issue to the apostle that he used the strongest language possible to negate it: "You have been severed from Christ, you who are seeking to be justified by law" (Gal 5:4). He uses the very notion of "severing" used in circumcision as a wordplay on their own spiritual condition.

But here's the plot twist: in order to express God's animosity toward those of the "false circumcision," Paul says, "I wish that those who are troubling you would even mutilate themselves" (Gal 5:12). The Greek word for "mutilate" here is *apokopto,* which means "to cut off."[7] This is

---

[5]R. Laird Harris, Gleason L. Archer and Bruce K. Waltke, eds., *Theological Wordbook of the Old Testament* (Chicago: Moody Press, 1980), 1:536-37.

[6]Ryken, Wilhoit and Longman, *Dictionary of Biblical Imagery,* p. 778. The Hebrew word for "many concubines" used in Ecclesiastes 2:8 is *shiddah,* which translates as "many breasts."

[7]Robert L. Thomas, ed., *New American Standard Exhaustive Concordance of the Bible* (Nashville: Holman, 1981), p. 1634.

a nice English translation of saying, "I wish they would just go all the way and cut off their penises." This harsh dialogue not only uses vulgarity to make a point, but it also carries a mocking to it. It's a case of employing coarse sarcasm to express a deadly truth.

Another Greek profanity that the apostle Paul used to shock his readers into spiritual seriousness was *skybalon*. In Philippians 3:8, he describes all the righteous achievements of his life as being *skybalon* compared to knowing Christ Jesus his Lord. The *Dictionary of Biblical Imagery* states that *skybalon* "forcefully expresses Paul's extreme attitude toward his past human attainments. The glories of gaining and serving Christ make Paul's religious prestige seem like mere excrement!" But then the dictionary adds this illuminating little sentence: "Several other coarse English colloquialisms would more closely suggest the negative inflections *of skybalon*." Now, I wonder which "English colloquialisms" those might be? Might they have "four letters"? *Skybalon* is, in fact, the Greek equivalent of a much harsher word than excrement.[8]

EXAMPLES OF BLASPHEMY

For those who accept some bad language or cursing in movies as true to reality, a common exception is the use of the Lord's name in vain, or blasphemy. They reason that violation of the third commandment is not an acceptable sin to portray.

Yet various acts of blasphemy are described explicitly in the Bible. *Blasphemy,* defined as "impious, and irreverent speech against God, . . . is always in word or deed, injury, dishonor and defiance offered to God."[9] Biblical incidents such as the golden-calf debacle (Ex 32), the brazen serpent scandal (2 Kings 18:4) and the Baal prophets' contest with Elijah (1 Kings 18:20-39) were in effect acts of blasphemy.

Blasphemous speech or behavior is a foul stench in the nostrils of God and is therefore deserving of wrath, but no more wrath than any other

---

[8]"Dung," in *Dictionary of Biblical Imagery,* ed. Leland Ryken, James C. Wilhoit and Tremper Longman III (Downers Grove, Ill.: InterVarsity Press, 1998), p. 222.

[9]T. Ress, "Blasphemy," in *International Standard Bible Encyclopedia,* ed. James Orr (Rio, Wis.: Ages Software, version 8.0, 2000), p. 457.

sin. And that is all the more reason to depict it in a truthful light. That's exactly what the Bible does when it records blasphemies from the tongues of men and angels.

We need not look far to uncover the first blasphemy recorded in the Bible, as the serpent prods Eve to defy God: "You surely will not die! For God knows that in the day you eat from it your eyes will be opened, and you will be like God, knowing good and evil" (Gen 3:4-5). This bald accusation that God is childishly selfish and jealous of humanity's potential is pure blasphemous defiance.

There are other famous recorded instances of blasphemy in the Scriptures: Job's wife pleading with her husband to "curse God and die" (Job 2:9); King Sennacherib calling Yahweh an impotent, lying deity (Is 36:14-20); Peter denying Christ (Mt 26:74); the spectators at the cross taunting Jesus (Mt 27:40); and those who, as quoted by Paul, were saying, "Jesus is accursed" (1 Cor 12:3). Would any of those Christians, offended at hearing blasphemy in a movie, be consistent and yell, "Foul! Thou art foul!" when a Christian quotes these blasphemous passages from the Bible?

VICE AND JESUS

When confronted with this plethora of sex and violence, one may be tempted to qualify such depictions by an appeal to its journalistic style of reporting history. Is the historical documentation of sex and violence the same as fictional stories containing sex and violence? Well, let's ask Jesus.

In his parables Jesus used fictional accounts of beatings, murder, dismemberment and torture as metaphors and images of the kingdom of God.

Who can ignore the gore and brutality depicted in the book of Revelation? In this imaginative vision, given to John by Jesus himself, we are swept along with special effects that outdo those of George Lucas's Industrial Light and Magic and with horror imagery that makes Stephen King nightmares look like children's bedtime stories. (Incidentally, King and other horrormeisters draw a good portion of their fantastical imagination from Judeo-Christian spiritual imagery.) And most Bible scholars agree: prophetic literature, such as the book of Revelation, communicate eternal truth through violent images of imagination and metaphor.

Revelation	Imagery
9:1-11	Genetically mutated monsters chasing and tormenting screaming people
9:13-18	Armies of bizarre beasts wreaking death and destruction on the masses
12:3-4	A demonic dragon chasing a woman with the intent to eat her infant child
11:7-13	A beast dragging rotting corpses through the streets for three days while people party over them
19:17-18	Birds eating human and animal remains
17:1-5	A harlot having sex with kings and merchants
20:13-14	Dead people being reanimated and thrown alive into a lake of fire to be tormented forever

Figure 2. Violent imagery in Revelation

Scripture	Parable	Fictional Sins Described
Matthew 22:1-13	The king's wedding feast	Beatings, murder, war, arson
Matthew 18:23-35	The unforgiving servant	Choking, torture in prison
Matthew 24:45-51	The faithful and unfaithful slaves	Beatings, drunken parties, *Hannibal*-like bodily dismemberment
Matthew 18:6	Millstone metaphor	*Godfather*-style drowning
Matthew 18:7-9	Analogy of sin's seriousness	Gouging out of eyes, cutting off of hands (reminiscent of *Seven*)
Matthew 7:24-26	House built on sand	Destruction of private property

Figure 3. Parables and metaphors of Jesus that portray sinful behavior

WHORES, SLUTS AND ADULTERESSES: METAPHORS FOR AN UNFAITHFUL PEOPLE

God often used socially uncomfortable drama as a means of communicating truths to people. He commanded Hosea to marry a prostitute named Gomer in order to dramatically communicate the nature of Israel's faithless relationship to her spiritual husband, God (Hos 1). God commanded Isaiah to walk around naked for three years to emphatically declare the shame of what would happen to the Egyptians and Ethiopians (Is 20:2-4).[10] The shame of the nakedness was precisely God's point in this ancient performance art. Imagine the reaction by the religious mainstream of Isaiah's day, clucking their tongues, pronouncing their anathemas and proclaiming his immodesty as a violation of social decency, resulting in, of course, a boycott.

Some of the most frequent metaphors that God uses to depict Israel's faithless wandering from Yahweh are those of adultery, prostitution and sexual promiscuity. Over and over again, the abomination of idolatry is graphically depicted as immoral sexual intercourse with false gods. Explicit sexual immorality appears to be one of God's favorite dramatic metaphors for insulting Israel about its spiritual apostasy.[11]

Jeremiah has God picturing Jerusalem not merely as an adulteress and a prostitute servicing her clients on the hills and in the fields, but as a "lustful" horse neighing after others, which brings the response from God of "stripping off her skirt" to expose her naked genitals to everyone—an image he uses elsewhere as well.[12] He reiterates Israel's harlotries "on every high hill and under every green tree," and then depicts

---

[10]Some scholars question whether this nakedness is stark or modestly limited. It is possible that the command to Isaiah to take off his sackcloth did not necessarily entail removing his tunic underneath (his underwear). Conservative commentators Keil and Delitzsch say, "With the great importance attached to the clothing in the East, where the feelings upon this point are peculiarly sensitive and modest, a person was looked upon as stripped and naked if he had only taken off his upper garment. What Isaiah was directed to do, therefore, was simply opposed to common custom, and not to moral decency." C. F. Keil and F. Delitzsch, *Isaiah,* Commentary on the Old Testament (Albany, Ore.: Ages Software, version 1.0, 1997), 7:294. But even granting this interpretation, we see that he nonetheless violated the social customs of modesty.

[11]Ex 34:15-16; Lev 17:7; Deut 31:16; Judg 2:17; Is 50:1; 54; Jer 3:2-8; Ezek 16; 23; Hos 1:2; 9:1.

[12]Jer 13:22, 25-27; Is 47:1-3, Hos 2:3 and Nahum 3:5-6.

Judah as a sister who follows her into adultery and has sex with stones and trees (Jer 3:1-9). Not very G-rated imagery there. Boy, God sure has an "active imagination," as they say.

Imagine the ironic humor of a Christian crusader against R-ratings trying to preach a sermon to his church on Sunday from Ezekiel 16 in the Holy Bible. In that chapter alone, God allegorizes Israel as a child born of pagan parents, whom God waits for until she grows up and her naked breasts form and she becomes mature enough to marry God. But Israel's slip into idolatry with Egyptian and Assyrian gods is then portrayed as playing the harlot with every horny "passer-by who might be willing" to have sex with her (Ezek 16:15, 26, 28). He pictures idol worship in the very distasteful image of a woman having sex with a metallic dildo (Ezek 16:17), an obvious reference to the phallic nature of many of the gold and silver idols of the day. And if that isn't bad enough, then she "spreads her legs" to every passer-by (Ezek 16:25), first for the Egyptians (Ezek 16:26), then for the Philistines (Ezek 16:27), then the Assyrians (Ezek 16:28), and don't forget the Chaldeans (Ezek 16:29). And to top it all off, God mocks Israel not simply for being a prostitute but for being a *stupid* prostitute: if you're going to be an immoral sex addict, at least do it right and get paid (Ezek 16:34). God even goes so far as to pictorialize his punishment of Israel in shockingly graphic terms:

> I will gather all your lovers with whom you took pleasure, even all those whom you loved and all those whom you hated. So I will gather them against you from every direction and expose your nakedness to them. . . . I will also give you into the hands of your lovers, and they will . . . strip you of your clothing, take away your jewels, and will leave you naked and bare. They will incite a crowd against you and they will stone you and cut you to pieces with their swords. They will burn your houses with fire and execute judgments on you in the sight of many women. Then I will stop you from playing the harlot, and you will also no longer pay your lovers. (Ezek 16:37-41)

Imagine that same moral protestor exegeting Ezekiel 23 for his congregation only a few weeks later as he preaches through the Bible. Here God reiterates Israel's spiritual harlotry in the terms of a story of two sisters, adding Samaria in complicity with Jerusalem (Ezek 23:4). Now

God describes Israel yet again as a whore, giving it to every horseman of the pagan nations of Assyria and Egypt. What's more, he describes the men grabbing their "virgin bosom[s]" (Ezek 23:3, 8) and "pour[ing]out their lust on her" (Ezek 23:8). And what do you think they might be "pouring"? But if that isn't enough, sister Samaria lusts after pagan paramours whose "flesh like the flesh of donkeys and whose issue is like the issue of horses" (Ezek 23:20). Exegete that.

And please explain to the younger people in the congregation what God means when he says that Israel is having so much adulterous sex that she is sexually worn out and yet still surprises God with her perseverance by having more sex with partying drunks (Ezek 23:42-44)!

Could a "G-rated" Christian teach his kids in Sunday School about Nahum 3, another prophecy describing Israel's unfaithfulness as "the many harlotries of the harlot, the charming one, the mistress of sorceries, who sells nations by her harlotries and families by her sorceries" (Nahum 3:4). God then graphically depicts his punishment of her as lifting up her skirt to expose her naked genitals in disgrace to the surrounding nations (Nahum 3:5). And then he throws feces on her to make her a vile spectacle (Nahum 3:6). Yes, you read that right. *Scripture* says God would throw feces on Israel. Or as the apostle Paul would probably say: *skybalon*. The Bible certainly isn't the prettiest of family-friendly programming.

Lest anyone think the New Testament is more puritanical, the book of Revelation brings back the symbolic image of a "great harlot" (most likely Israel) doing the deed with the kings of the earth so thoroughly and repeatedly that she is described as drunk with adultery (Rev 17:2). How would VeggieTales animate that for their next kid's Bible film?

Shocking metaphor and explicit drama are common means by which God communicates when people have become thickskulled, dull of hearing or wicked of heart. One might say, with tongue firmly planted in cheek, that God was the original Shakespeare.

THE TRUE, THE HONORABLE AND THE PURE

Some Christians sincerely concerned with obeying the Bible will often find passages that in their eyes appear to discredit the depiction of immorality in art. One such common passage is Philippians 4:8:

Finally, brethren, whatever is true, whatever is honorable, whatever is right, whatever is pure, whatever is lovely, whatever is of good repute, if there is any excellence and if anything worthy of praise, dwell on these things.

Readers of Bible passages like this one often misunderstand the language to be expressing a "hear no evil, see no evil, speak no evil" approach to spirituality. But ignoring the dark side is not at all what the verses are indicating.

It is not only true, honorable and right to proclaim that Jesus is the way, the truth and the life, but it is also true, honorable and right to proclaim that Satan is the father of lies (Jn 8:44) and that false prophets are his minions (2 Cor 11:14-15). It is not only pure, lovely and of good repute that Noah was depicted in the Bible as a righteous man, but it is also pure, lovely and of good repute that all the rest of the earth around him were depicted as entirely wicked (Gen 6:5). It is not only excellent and worthy of praise that Lot was revealed as a righteous man, but it is also excellent and worthy of praise that the inhabitants of Sodom were revealed as unprincipled men "who indulge[d] the flesh in its corrupt desires and despise[d] authority" (2 Pet 2:10).

If we ignore truth's darker side, we are focusing on half-truths, and there are no fuller, more complete lies than half-truths. Think of it this way: is it not true, honorable, right, pure and lovely that God drowned every person on the earth except for eight people (Gen 8)? Is it not of good repute, excellent and worthy of praise that God destroyed Sodom and Gomorrah and all their immoral inhabitants with fire and brimstone (2 Pet 2:6-9), and that God had the Israelites kill every man, woman and child of the Canaanites with the edge of the sword (Josh 6:21; 10:30, 37, 39)? To answer no to any of these questions is to ascribe dishonor, wrongness, impurity and unlovely behavior to God himself. The implication is unavoidable: the depiction of evil and its destructive ends can be just as true, honorable, right, pure, lovely, excellent and worthy of praise as can be the depiction of righteousness and its glorious ends.

Biblical storytelling is simply not a series of Precious Moments figurines or Thomas Kinkade paintings. We must face the fact that the

Scriptures depict sinful acts that are revolting to our sensibilities. The portrayal of good and the portrayal of evil are two sides of God's revelation to us of his one good and holy truth. This is *not* to say that God himself has a dualistic light side and dark side to his nature, or even that good cannot exist apart from evil, but rather that God has chosen to include depictions of both evil and good in his revelation of truth to us. So pointing out wrong is part of dwelling on what is right, exposing lies is part of dwelling on the truth, revealing cowardice is part of dwelling on the honorable, and uncovering corruption is part of dwelling on the pure.

SPEAKING OF THINGS DONE IN SECRET

Another concern that some Christians have with the cinematic depiction of deeds of the flesh is that it violates Paul's admonition that "it is disgraceful even to speak of the things which are done by [the sons of disobedience] in secret" (Eph 5:12). They read this to mean that we should not even *talk* about the evil that people do, let alone *watch* acts of depravity displayed before our eyes in movies.

I believe this viewpoint misunderstands the text. In fact, a closer examination of the context of Ephesians 5 will reveal that Paul is saying the exact opposite! Look at the verses before and after this verse. Ephesians 5:11: "Do not participate in the unfruitful deeds of darkness, but instead even expose them." Ephesians 5:13: "But all things become visible when they are exposed by the light, for everything that becomes visible is light."

Paul is not telling us to avoid talking about deeds of darkness because of their disgracefulness; rather, he is telling us to *expose* them by talking about them! By bringing that which is disgracefully hidden out into the light, we show it for what it really is. It is precisely because many sins are disgraceful that they are done in secret, so dealing openly with them exposes them as such, and this proper biblical use of shame aids us in the pursuit of godliness.

SETTING OUR EYES ON EVIL THINGS

Another verse often used to deny the validity of watching movies depicting sins comes from the Psalms:

> I will set no worthless thing before my eyes;
>   I hate the work of those who fall away;
>   It shall not fasten its grip on me. (Ps 101:3)

But again, the context of this Scripture carries a different meaning than what these well meaning Christians mean. The context of the Psalm is an expression of David seeking to avoid "dwelling" amidst wicked, "worthless" men and their evil ways, versus the godly, who "walk in a blameless way." Other Bible translations use the terms "wicked," "vile" or "base" for the Hebrew word translated "worthless" above. David is not saying that he will not look at an object or observe sinful behaviors; he is talking metaphorically about not desiring to live the lifestyle or achieve the goals of the wicked. A few verses later, he says, "My eyes shall be upon the faithful of the land." His contrast here is not between art that shows wickedness and art that does not; it is between the *goals* of the wicked and the *goals* of the righteous. It is the *intent* this Scripture is talking about.

By way of concession, I think it is safe to say that the goal or intent of pornography is worthless, wicked, vile and base, so we can certainly apply this Scripture to that kind of movie. But it is certainly not right to apply it to a movie like *The Passion of the Christ*, which depicts the worst, most heinous wickedness in all of history—the murder of the Son of God. Should we not set that movie of godly intent before our eyes?

MOVIES WITH SINFUL BEHAVIOR DEPICTED AS OPPRESSED BY CONVENTIONAL MORES

The Age of Innocence

Philadelphia

And the Band Played On

The Scarlet Letter

The People Versus Larry Flint

The Crucible

Wilde

American Beauty

Boys Don't Cry

Quills

Chocolat

Far from Heaven

Kinsey

Brokeback Mountain

V for Vendetta

Little Miss Sunshine

I Now Pronounce You Chuck and Larry

And lest we forget, if one claims that this verse commands the prohibition of "looking upon sins" depicted in stories, then one must black out a huge amount of the Bible itself, since the Scriptures are full of such depictions of sins, both venial and mortal.

EXPLOITATION AND EXHORTATION

Now, what is to be made of all this sex and violence permeating the defining moral standard of Western civilization, the Bible? Is this hypocrisy or self-contradiction? Does such ribald revelation of humanity's darker side in Scripture justify exploitation of our prurient baser instincts? Are Christians defenseless against unbelievers who claim the Bible is X-rated and compare it to pornography? May it never be! Having laid down a rationale for the depiction of depravity, let us now qualify that rationale with *context, context, context.* And context makes all the difference between moral *exhortation* and immoral *exploitation* of sin.

Exploitation, in this context, is the unethical or selfish use of something. Exploitation in movies would amount to an unethical use of sex or violence unintended by Scripture. But what is the intent and extent of Scripture's use of sex and violence? In all of the impropriety portrayed in the Bible we see several elements that make it very different in nature from the lurid celebration of wickedness seen in exploitative movies.[13]

1. Intent. Most biblical spectacle is not exploitative in its intent. It is historical reporting on the highest ground. The storyteller cannot stop the evil that people do, but he can use that evil against them through eyewitness testimony. The writers *expose* man's inhumanity to man for the purpose of moral instruction and with the intent of avoiding the doomed repetition of history. These stories are equivalent to the journalistic impact of photos of the Holocaust or the American Civil Rights movement victims. They uncover hidden corruption and expose evil to the light of day (remember Eph 5:11-13?), which can sometimes result in social changes of behavior, or at least an influential historical reminder for future generations. For example, the movie *United 93* could even be

---

[13]*Gratuitous* is another word often used in relation to sex and violence in movies. But gratuitous means "without good reason." So the goal is to see if the Bible, and by analogy cinema, has good reasons behind its portrayal of such sins.

interpreted as a how-to manual for American citizens dealing with terrorists.

But this veracity is also found in fictional stories aspiring to be true to the time period. *Apocalypto* is an example of a movie that is an entertaining chase film about a man running for his life and trying to save his family from the barbaric Mayans in ancient South America. The gruesome historical realities of Mayan human sacrifice displayed in the movie is a powerful moral corrective to the politically constructed fiction of the peace-loving indigenous natives of the Americas. Indeed, in a broader sense, it deconstructs the entire Rousseauean theory of the "noble savage" who is supposedly untainted by the "imperialistic Western civilization."[14] The violence of the film shatters that propaganda with a thundering punch in the political gut.

Blood Diamond, whose title embodies the very theme of the diamond trade being built upon the blood, sweat and tears of slavery, captures that reality with a powerful fictional tale told within an historically accurate setting. The movie not only includes the true horrors of modern slavery but also reveals the hidden facts of children soldiers in many third world countries. The viewer sees the violence that these forcefully recruited children engage in, even to the extent of killing their own families by the command of criminal gang leaders. Such horrors must be depicted to wake up the public to our apathetic and unengaged lifestyles. Many people, after watching that movie, committed to buying only "conflict free diamonds" from sellers who are not engaged in such atrocities.

On the other hand, slasher flicks like *The Texas Chainsaw Massacre*, *The Hills Have Eyes* and *Halloween* (2007) seem to focus on man's depravity, not as a moral corrective, but as a basis for creative exploration. Evil as

---

[14]Another movie that creatively deconstructs the noble savage myth is M. Night Shyamalan's *The Village*. People raised in a community that is cut off from the rest of society ultimately learn that man's evil nature is not part of civilization but part of his essential nature that resides in him no matter where he exists, whether jungle or city. *The New World*, Terrence Malick's interpretation of the story of Pocohantas, as well as the animated movies *Pocohantas* (1995) and *Tarzan* (1999), are movies that depict the noble savage fiction in a positive way, as the harmonious pagans, in tune with Mother Earth, being despoiled by the intrusion of European Western civilization.

entertainment in and of itself. These movies tend to reduce to a survival of the fittest ethic, kill or be killed—which is ultimately a nihilistic form of atheism. *Hostel* is a movie about tourists who are captured and taken to a secret hideout where rich people pay big money to torture and kill them. Despite the positive potential for this moral questioning of power and riches, this movie is so filled with detailed graphic gore that it displays more a fascination with evil (and to make money off of kids who love to watch evil) than an attempt to make the world a better place. Listening to the writer-director of this movie, Eli Roth, speak about his sentimental love of violence and gore only reinforces that moral tension.[15]

2. *Depiction.* True, evil is depicted in Scripture, but not always through intimate detail or excessive indulgence. Humankind's depravity is not emphasized more than our redemptive potential. Sin is a manifestation of the need for redemption, not an object of obsessive focus.

While the biblical text does not flinch at divulging David's adultery with Bathsheba or Shechem's rape of Dinah, it *does* avoid pornographic explorations of body crevices and private parts writhing in sexual ecstasy or pain. When David cuts off Goliath's head, we are not indulged in a slow-motion close-up of the sword piercing the neck and the carotid artery spurting blood as the eyes pop and the flesh rips. This kind of violence has the potential to become exploitative.

Of course, the nature of literature allows mystery and room for the imagination that avoids exploitation, and this allowance is not as easily achieved with the visual medium of cinema. But it can be done. Remember the fade-out that used to always follow the kiss? Alfred Hitchcock was famous for his suspenseful moral tales devoid of cinematic gore, and they are still among the finest films to watch. And fade-outs still exist in some Hollywood movies today—believe it or not. Narrative summary is the main technique that biblical writers use to avoid indulgence in the titillation of sin while addressing it honestly, and it remains for contemporary filmmakers to find new ways to break through the all-too-common exploitation of sex and violence with new means of subtlety and diversion.

---

[15]"Hostel Q&A," Creative Screenwriting Magazine podcast on iTunes. (Senior Editor Jeff Goldsmith interviews writer/director Eli Roth for *Hostel*.)

As a qualifying note, there can be value to showing certain details of depravity if it is done appropriately. As indicated in the Judges passages above, there are at times detailed descriptions in the Bible that turn the stomach, making this principle a gray area for debate. In the same way, the horrors of war simply could not be captured in the twenty-minute scene of Omaha Beach in *Saving Private Ryan* without showing the effects of military weaponry on bodies.

MOVIES THAT CELEBRATE VIOLENCE

Robocop

Last Man Standing

Walking Tall

The Punisher

Sin City

Smokin' Aces

Doomsday

Shoot 'Em Up

On the other hand, movies like *Kill Bill 1 & 2* engage in an orgy of sword violence choreographed like a beautiful dance, complete with dozens of severed arms and blood spewing arteries. The creator, Quentin Tarantino, has often expressed his love affair with violent cinema for violent cinema's sake. The line for the acceptable portrayal of evil must be drawn by the adult individual somewhere between the two extremes of dishonest avoidance of all iniquity and gluttonous imbibing in unnecessary detail of sex or violence.

3. *Consequences.* In the Bible sinful behavior always has consequences. Sin leads to destruction, not to freedom unfettered by moral restraint. In Genesis, Jacob's deception leads to paranoia and backfires against him. The sins committed in Sodom and Gomorrah lead to fire and brimstone. David's adultery leads to the loss of a son, and his violence leads to the inability to build God's temple. Movies such as *Unfaithful* explore this biblical narrative of adultery and other sexual perversity leading to destructive consequences. But this is a far cry from the manipulative attempts of movies, such as *American Beauty,* that legitimize destructive sexual behavior by portraying their deviants as poor victims of puritanical oppression. An increasing occurrence in more recent movies is a portrayal of the homosexual as a wise mentor or sympathetic sidekick who has the most humane life and a better understanding of love and romance than do heterosexuals. *Alexander* and *Brokeback Mountain* are examples of the mainstream attempt to tell a classic epic romance of

"eternal love" with two men in the place of a man and woman, as if they are morally equivalent.

Fight Club—a movie that on its surface appears to be an excursion into violence as a way of solving life's problems—is actually a moral fable about the negative consequences of pursuing that line of thinking. As the main character gets deeper into his friendship with a reckless man who lives dangerously, he soon discovers that the reckless man is merely a projection of his own dark side that is leading him to destruction, and the main character must stop him before he takes his depravity to its logical conclusion.

FILMS FEATURING HOMOSEXUALS AS SUPERIOR MENTORS OR HEROIC ADVOCATES

The Adventures of Priscilla Queen of the Desert

The Birdcage

As Good as It Gets

My Best Friend's Wedding

Chasing Amy

The Love Letter

Flawless (1999)

Bounce

The Next Best Thing

The Mexican

American Beauty

Bridget Jones's Diary

Billy Elliot

Mona Lisa Smile

Kinsey

I Now Pronounce You Chuck and Larry

Alexander

Brokeback Mountain

Milk

This kind of moral teaching through the negative consequences of actions is also the purpose of tragedies. Traditionally, tragedies contain sad endings rather than happy endings, not because they are trying to communicate despair but because they are trying to exhort us as to the consequences of certain common flaws in human nature. A hero's tragic flaw—such as ambition *(Macbeth)*, jealousy *(O)*, greed *(Wall Street)*, wrath *(Seven)*, glory *(Amadeus)* or revenge *(Man on Fire)*—is the cause of his downfall, thus illustrating the wages of sin and inspiring the viewers to live contrarily.

The danger, however, of focusing too exclusively on the wages of sin is that it can lead to the very exploitation of the sin that the story is trying to critique. An example of hypocritical moralism is *Borat: Cultural Learnings of America for Make Benefit Glorious Nation of Kazakhstan*. In this film, creator Sacha Baron Cohen pre-

MOVIES WITH NEGATIVE CONSEQUENCES OF SIN

Fatal Attraction

Damage

Anna Karenina

The End of the Affair

The Talented Mr. Ripley

Eyes Wide Shut

The Golden Bowl

Dinner with Friends

Unfaithful

Broken Flowers

Wedding Crashers

Keeping Mum

Little Children

Premonition

Knocked Up

The Painted Veil

tends to be a racist, sexist, anti-Semitic bigot from Kazakhstan. He goes out into the real world as this character and films the reactions of Americans to him in a reality TV approach. On the one hand, he exposes incipient racism, sexism, anti-Semitism and other bigotries to ridicule. He includes in his mockery the politically correct cowardice of Americans unwilling to challenge such hatred in the name of tolerance and multiculturalism. Unfortunately, he does so by lying to people and exploiting them, such as the Third World community where he shot his Kazakhstan hometown scenes. He deceived the town and paid only pennies for their location, while mocking their ignorance and unethically making millions of dollars off of them. Hardly an example of loving your neighbor. More like a Pharisee, trumpeting others' bigotries, while engaging in his own.

4. *Context*. Immoral deeds in the Bible are always contextually presented as immoral. As already pointed out above, evil is not glamorized as entertainment, and sin is not presented as an "alternate lifestyle." There is always a call to redemption, the hope for a better humanity, not the nihilistic negation of "This is real life, baby. Get used to it." There is no sense of catharsis, the rationalization of purging evil through acting it out that is sometimes used by artists to justify excessive brutality and evil in films. Noted film director Martin Scorsese has disclosed such dark intentions: "Maybe we need the catharsis of bloodletting and decapitation like the ancient Romans needed it, as ritual but not real like the Roman circuses."[16]

Gory teen slashers and horror movies such as the *Saw* franchise are

---

[16]Quoted in Michael Medved, *Hollywood Versus America* (New York: HarperCollins, 1992), p. 199.

not the only films that can fall into the category of cathartic saturation in blood. Many "shoot-'em-up" action movies can degenerate into dehumanization. Some action movies push the envelope in their pursuit of justice and personal redemption by focusing too heavily on finding new ways people can be beat up, shot up or carved up, resulting in what some argue is exploitation.

Revenge movies such as *V for Vendetta* and *The Brave One* have their heroes satisfy their sense of justice outside of the law or through vigilante means without repentance and could also arguably be called exploitation.

GRATUITOUS GORE IN FILM

Scream

I Know What You Did Last Summer

From Dusk till Dawn

John Carpenter's Vampires

The Devil's Rejects

Hostel

House of Wax

Grindhouse

Saw II-IV

Movies that portray villainous or criminal characters as heroes, such as the *Pirates of the Caribbean* and the *Ocean's Eleven* franchises, could also be considered exploitative when they encourage the audience to root for criminal behavior. Usually this is justified by making the villain a worse criminal than the hero.

But be careful. Just because a villain gets away doesn't always mean the story is glorifying villains or saying that crime pays. Sometimes, it is a broader moral statement of warning. These stories are cautionary tales that warn us of the deceiving nature of evil and of how evil can triumph if good men don't take a stand or learn their lesson. In *Lord of War*, Nicolas Cage plays Yuri, a Ukrainian immigrant arms dealer during the 1980s and 1990s. It's a black comedy of how the dismantling of the end of the Cold War provided arms for sale that Yuri exploits for a profit. In fact, that's

MOVIES THAT FEATURE VIGILANTE VIOLENCE

The Crow

A Time to Kill

L.A. Confidential

Get Carter

In the Bedroom

Paparazzi

Walking Tall

Four Brothers

V for Vendetta

Shoot 'Em Up

Hannibal Rising

The Brave One

what's wrong—he only cares about profit, selling his guns to anyone who will pay, good or bad, one side or the other. He has no allegiance but to money, and he fuels civil wars, genocidal dictators and other atrocities around the world, but he sleeps at night because he rationalizes everything in a way that real world arms dealers currently do. He is contrasted with the olden days where the CIA would only fund the side they wanted to win, because they believed in them. Yuri represents the modern international capitalist who has no values but what money can buy.

MOVIES WITH A VILLAIN AS HERO

Hannibal

Gone in Sixty Seconds

Swordfish

American Outlaws

Bandits

Heist

The Score

Ocean's Eleven

Ocean's Twelve

Paparazzi

V for Vendetta

Matador

Inside Man

Pirates of the Caribbean 1-3

Paparazzi

Four Brothers

Hannibal Rising

The Bank Job

In Bruges

Sometimes stories in which people do the right thing can end up being immoral stories. The context can turn what is otherwise good moral behavior into ultimately immoral values. *The Bridges of Madison County*—the tear-jerking romance adapted by Richard LaGravenese from Robert James Waller's popular novel—is the story of a small-town married woman (played by Meryl Streep) who has a short adulterous affair with a dashing, globe-trotting photographer for *National Geographic* (played by Clint Eastwood). She feels the stultifying pressure of her traditional role as mother and wife and is tempted to leave her traditional family behind to travel the world with this fast-living man of passion and freedom. At the end she chooses the right thing—to stay with her family and husband. She realizes that the fantasy will not deliver the ultimate romantic satisfaction she longs for any more than does her current situation. Here is a story that accepts the covenant a woman has made with her spouse and children as a higher responsibility than the fleeting effect of hormones.

The downside of this portrayal is that the woman never confesses to her husband and clings to her tryst of infidelity all her life as her one true experience of real love, in contrast to her boring, conventional married life. Rather than rekindling lost love in her flesh-and-blood husband, she retreats psychologically into her fantasy of unfaithfulness. *Bridges* proposes doing the moral thing on the surface, but its context encourages clinging to immoral feelings in the heart, something Jesus roundly condemned in the Sermon on the Mount (Mt 5). And this same exact theme is repeated over again in movies like *Girl with a Pearl Earring*, *Beyond Borders*, *Neverland* and *Lost in Translation*.

Like *The Bridges of Madison County*, some movies deal honestly with the real temptation of adultery, but differ with that movie in how they conclude with the hero choosing to rekindle his or her marriage instead of pining over wanting someone else. Examples of this biblical kind of repentance are *Spanglish* and *Shall We Dance?*—movies with characters who are tempted by adultery but return to their wives and find renewed value, appreciation and love.

CAUTIONARY TALES TO INSPIRE CHANGE

The Usual Suspects

Primal Fear

American Psycho

Saw

Capote

Lord of War

Thank You for Smoking

United 93

The Omen

28 Weeks Later

Mr. Brooks

Context is everything. So in a sense, this final idea of context is a summary of the other three points. The three things to remember when deliberating about the appropriateness of sex, violence or profanity in a movie is *context, context, context!*

DRAWING THE BALANCE

By differentiating between exploitation and exhortation, the greatest story ever told expresses standards of morality without compromising its honesty about the human condition. However, after trying to establish some guidelines for the definition of exploitation, we must face the reality that the lines will not be the same for everyone. What is exploitation for one person is often moral exhortation for another. This is not to say that all morality is relative. But it *is* to say that we should discuss our opinions with others in an open dialogue and with enough humility to recognize when we may be wrong—and to change our views, if needed. One of the purposes of the arts is to stimulate discussion of values and beliefs, to engage in soul-searching discourse with one another.

Leland Ryken's *The Liberated Imagination* does a great job of helping the adult individual understand the nature of modern art and guiding adults to draw their own lines of balance. On the difficulty of dealing with realism in the arts and biblical allowance, he concludes,

> Whenever we find ourselves wondering about the legitimacy of Christian contact with modern art, we should stop to consider that we cannot run away from our own society, that we must face its art and values, and that the Bible itself insists on our contact with realism in art. We are left walking a tightrope between the extremes of total rejection and total affirmation.[17]

A sense of balance is what a Christian needs. People who are inclined either to immerse themselves in modern art or to avoid it completely probably need to check their inclination.

Christians tend to be either cultural anorexics or cultural gluttons— either avoiding all movies or watching too many of them. We must face our selfish tendency to rationalize our own prejudices. As pointed out earlier, one person's sense of exploitation may simply illustrate his own prudery, while another person's tolerance may actually be her own indulgence in besetting sin. Hopefully, through the exchange of opinions with an open mind and a humble disposition, we can use movies and their contrast of humanity's lighter and darker sides as a means of understanding and interacting redemptively with ourselves and the world around us.

WATCH AND LEARN

Watch one of the following movies with a select group of friends and discuss it.

1. Sexuality. *The Golden Bowl.* While it does not contain explicit sex

---

[17]Leland Ryken, *The Liberated Imagination: Thinking Christianly About the Arts* (Wheaton, Ill.: Harold Shaw, 1989), pp. 255-56.

scenes, it is a moral tale about adultery. Discuss how adultery is examined and how it communicates the destructive nature of infidelity.

2. Profanity. *Magnolia*. While there is a lot of harsh language and cussing in this movie, it also contains strong redemption that is connected to God's providence. Discuss the various story threads in the movie and what the redemption is. Was the harsh grittiness necessary?

3. Violence. *To End All Wars*. While this is a true story about men being tortured as POWs, it contains a strong gospel atonement theme. Discuss whether you believe the violence was necessary to communicate the power of the redemption.

2

STORIES & MYTHOLOGY

Every story is informed by a worldview. And so every movie, being a dramatic story, is also informed by a worldview. There is no such thing as a neutral story in which events and characters are presented objectively apart from interpretation. Every choice an author makes, from what kinds of characters she creates to which events she includes, is determined by the author's worldview. A worldview even defines what a character or event *is* for the writer—and, therefore, for the audience. And the worldview or philosophy of a film is conveyed much in the same way as stories of old would convey the values and beliefs of ancient societies—through dramatic incarnation of those values. In a sense, movies are the new myths of American culture.

Christopher Vogler, accomplished educator of writers and a student of the famous mythologist Joseph Campbell, explains the nature of myth:

> What is a myth? For our purposes a myth is not the untruth or fanciful exaggeration of popular expression. A myth, as Joseph Campbell was

fond of saying, is a metaphor for a mystery beyond human comprehension. It is a comparison that helps us understand, by analogy, some aspect of our mysterious selves. A myth, in this way of thinking, is not an untruth but a way of reaching a profound truth. Then what is a story? A story is also a metaphor, *a model of some aspect of human behavior.*[1]

In the PBS series *The Power of Myth* we get the nod from Campbell himself about just what story does for us:

BILL MOYERS: So we tell stories to try to come to terms with the world, to harmonize ourselves with reality?
JOSEPH CAMPBELL: I think so, yes.[2]

Psychoanalyst Bruno Bettelheim agrees. Writing in *The Uses of Enchantment* (his classic on the meaning and importance of fairy tales), he says, "Myths and fairy stories both answer the eternal questions: What is the world really like? How am I to live my life in it? How can I truly be myself?"[3]

Since the beginning of time, humankind has used story to convey the meaning and purpose of life. Within its various forms (myth, fable, parable, allegory), and within its development from oral tradition to codification, storytelling has through the eons been the backbone of civilizations. It has maintained ritual, systematized beliefs and taught dogma. In essence, story incarnates the myths and values of a culture with the intent of perpetuating them. Moses' Pentateuch tells the story of the redemption of the Hebrews. The Babylonian *Epic of Gilgamesh* tells the heroic redemption of its principal character, Gilgamesh. Homer's epic poem *The Odyssey* is the tale of the redemptive journeys of Odysseus.

We now live in a world permeated with science and technology, but does that make us any less storytellers or any less myth-oriented in our lives? Our culture still thrives on storytelling in many manifestations, in-

---

[1]Christopher Vogler, *The Writer's Journey* (Studio City, Calif.: Michael Wiese Productions, 1992), p. vii. The emphasis is mine.
[2]Joseph Campbell with Bill Moyers, *The Power of Myth* (New York: Doubleday, 1988), p. 4.
[3]Bruno Bettelheim, *The Uses of Enchantment: The Meaning and Importance of Fairy Tales* (New York: Random House, 1989), p. 45. Unfortunately, Bettelheim's analysis of fairy tales suffers the excesses of a myopic Freudianism.

cluding news, books, music and movies, to name a few. The very nature of moviemaking and moviegoing itself incarnates the sacred transmission of myth, much as occurred for the ancients. As author Geoffrey Hill proposes in his treatise on the mythic power of film, *Illuminating Shadows:*

> As ironic modern worshippers we congregate at the cinematic temple. We pay our votive offerings at the box office. We buy our ritual corn. We hush in reverent anticipation as the lights go down and the celluloid magic begins. Throughout the filmic narrative we identify with the hero. We vilify the antihero. We vicariously exult in the victories of the drama. And we are spiritually inspired by the moral of the story, all while believing we are modern techno-secular people, devoid of religion. Yet the depth and intensity of our participation reveal a religious fervor that is not much different from that of religious zealots.[4]

While the interpretation of *all* moviegoing as religious liturgy may be strained, it is certainly a caution to the viewer to avoid an identification with the cultural glutton who, through lack of discernment, often falls prey to such manipulation. Perhaps Hill's thesis better serves the argument that no story exists neutrally as raw entertainment without reference to cultural beliefs and values. Neglecting the importance of the worldview behind a movie denies as well the influence our stories have on the human psyche, collective *and* individual.

COMIC-BOOK SUPERHEROES

An example of mythological adaptation in our secular society can be found in comic-book heroes. Speaking as long ago as 1963, famous anthropologist Mircea Eliade stated, "The characters of comic strips present the modern version of mythological or folklore Heroes."[5] In *Hancock*, starring Will Smith as a homeless superhero, we hear it from the lips of a superhero herself, "In the past, we were gods and angels. Now, we're superheroes."

The proliferation of comic books adapted into movies signals a contemporary hunger for hero worship, the desire for redemption through

---

[4]Geoffrey Hill, *Illuminating Shadows: The Mythic Power of Film* (Boston: Shambhala, 1992), p. 3.

[5]Mircea Eliade, *Myth and Reality* (New York: Harper & Row, 1963), pp. 184-85.

the salvific acts of deity. In all these comic-book-based stories there is a projection of superpowers onto individuals much in the same way that the gods were projections of pagan hope. Watching *X-Men*, for instance, with all its superheroes and supervillains in our contemporary world, brings to mind the pantheon of Greek gods from Mount Olympus battling it out over mortal human beings. Each god in the pantheon had a special power: Hermes, the messenger of the gods, could run with fleet-winged feet; Hephaestus was the god of fire. Likewise, each of the mutant X-Men has a power that enables him or her to battle evil or do evil: Mystique can change her shape to appear to be something else; Storm can call forth the powers of nature; Magneto has powers of magnetism. The spiritual aspect of these abilities has been secularized, reinterpreted through evolutionary myth as the result of genetic mutation, but the metaphor remains the same.[6] As Francis Schaeffer has pointed out, the gods of Greece and Rome were actually "amplified humanity, not divinity,"[7]so modern day comic-book heroes are amplified humanity within our secular scientific worldview.

The gods of yore also had amplified weaknesses as well. They would get jealous of another god and wipe out whole populations; they would have sibling rivalry with their divine brothers or sisters; and they would brood, pout and even pull pranks on humans. In like manner, modern-day superheroes have similar struggles. *Hancock*, mentioned earlier, is about a homeless, alcoholic, down-and-out slob of a superhero who is melancholic because he is separated from his true love. *My Super Ex-Girlfriend* is about a guy who falls in love with a woman and finds out she is actually a superhero. Unfortunately, she is also a jealous and paranoid lover with mood swings and supertantrums of Olympic proportions. *The Incredibles* is

---

[6]*Fantastic Four* (2005) is another example of the evolutionary metanarrative in comic-book heroes. The four heroes get their powers by coming into contact with a cosmic storm cloud that is described as the beginning of the source of life on earth billions of years ago. This is the "scientific" theory currently in vogue, made popular by Carl Sagan, that believes earth was "seeded" with life by a meteor or other source from another galaxy. But it is also a version of "punctuated equilibrium," made popular by evolutionary theorist Stephen J. Gould, that asserted evolution occurred in leaps and bounds (rather than gradual mutations) by the addition of bursts of energy into the otherwise closed system of our geosphere.

[7]Francis Schaeffer, *How Should We Then Live?* (Westchester, Ill.: Crossway, 1982), p. 85.

SUPERHERO MOVIES

Superman

Superman Returns

Batman Begins

The Dark Knight

Dick Tracy

Teenage Mutant Ninja Turtles

The Shadow

Judge Dredd

The Phantom

The Punisher

Spawn

Steel

Blade

Mystery Men

X-Men

Spider-Man

Daredevil

Catwoman

Hellboy

Fantastic Four

The Incredible Hulk

Ghost Rider

Wolverine

Watchmen

Ironman

Green Lantern

Pixar's animated story about a family of superheros who bicker and argue and need to learn how to get along. *Mystery Men* shows superhero wannabes struggling to balance their efforts to save the world with their unsatisfying family and work lives.

The story of Superman is a classic American tale that many say embodies a mythical retelling of the life of Christ. Eliade opines of Superman's preternatural identity hidden behind his Clark Kent humanity, "This humiliating camouflage of a Hero whose powers are literally unlimited revives a well-known mythical theme. In the last analysis, the myth of Superman satisfies the secret longings of modern man who, though he knows that he is a fallen, limited creature, dreams of one day proving himself an 'exceptional person,' a 'Hero.'"[8]

Superman Returns, written by Dan Harris and Jerry Siegel, returns to the comic hero's religious mythology. Superman is likened to deity throughout the film. The recurring thematic phrases "I have sent you my only son" and "The son becomes the father and the father becomes the son" refer to Superman's metaphorical link with his father, Jor-El (an obvious derivative of a name for God in Hebrew: *El*). While not exactly orthodox Christian doctrine, this relational incarnation is certainly derived from Jesus' own words, "For God so loved the world, that He gave His only

---

[8]Eliade, *Myth and Reality,* p. 185.

begotten Son" (Jn 3:16), and "He who has seen Me has seen the Father" (Jn 14:9).

A bad guy compares Superman to Prometheus and the gods, and ultimate bad guy Lex Luthor responds jealously, "The gods are selfish beings, who don't share their powers with mankind," thus expressing the spiritual hubris similar to the original sin in the Garden. In response to Lois Lane's claim that "the world doesn't need a savior and neither do I," Superman flies her up into the stratosphere, where we hear the prayer-like cacophony of billions of people in need of his saving powers ringing in his ears. Like an omniscient deity, Superman compassionately replies to Lois, "Every day I hear people crying for one."

Beowulf, written by Neil Gaiman and Roger Avery, is a subversion of the hero myth itself. It is an antihero myth. While telling the tale of the great warrior Beowulf seeking to destroy the monster Grendel in an ancient land, it shows how people's idolization of heroes as mythic in their deeds and character is sheer hogwash. Beowulf's own glory and honor are haunted in his soul because he knows that they only come to him because he gave in to the temptation of his flesh to adultery (sleeping with a "demon"). So, while everyone speaks of his greatness, he can barely live with himself, because the dragon that taunts his kingdom is a direct result of his own actions ("the sins of the fathers"). Heroes, he sighs, are just as fallible as everyone and undeserving of the worship they receive.

GRAPHIC NOVELS

An extension of the superhero comic books that Hollywood has capitalized on bigtime are graphic novels. Graphic novels tend to be gritty, dark, R-rated comic books that will extend to the length of one hundred to four hundred pages. They are often serialized in comics, but are then published as a complete bound novel when completed. In graphic novels the heroes are more antiheros, in that, unlike traditional superheroes, they are deeply flawed, even to the extent of sometimes being criminals themselves. Whereas traditional superheroes are amplified humanity in virtue or ability, the modern hero is more like amplified humanity of the dark side. Some of them are more modern heroes in that they are often ordinary people doing extraordinary things rather than extraordinary people doing extraordinary things.

Of the graphic novels turned into movies, some of the antiheroes are a murdered ghost seeking vengeance *(The Crow)*, a mob hit man trying to protect his son's innocence *(Road to Perdition)*, a family man haunted by his criminal-assassin past *(A History of Violence)*, a psychologically tortured clairvoyant detective *(From Hell)*, a demon from hell *(Hellboy)*, a series of criminals and corrupt cops who try to do the right thing for once *(Sin City)*, an alienated cop in the process of a divorce *(30 Days of Night)*, and a psychologically disturbed bipolar *(Batman: The Dark Knight)*. Other graphic novels translated into graphic movies are *V for Vendetta* and *300*.

On the downside, the dark world of these graphic novel movies can feed nihilistic violence in immature youth. On the upside, they portray heroes that are broken and, in that sense, more human like the rest of us. We sympathize with them because their sin haunts them even as they seek to do right. As Paul the apostle writes,

> For we know that the Law is spiritual, but I am of flesh, sold into bondage to sin. For what I am doing, I do not understand; for I am not practicing what I would like to do, but I am doing the very thing I hate. But if I do the very thing I do not want to do, I agree with the Law, confessing that the Law is good. (Rom 7:14-16)

The Dark Knight is the most successful movie adaptation of a graphic novel. If Superman represents the goodness of divinity in its purity, then Batman represents the dark side of that divinity as an angst-ridden, deeply flawed hero in a morally confused postmodern world. Christopher Nolan's *The Dark Knight* also proves that superhero movies are not all light entertainment, but can be among the most soul-searching, thought-provoking metaphysical explorations into the meaning of life and morality. The Batman, a scientific crime fighter, as opposed to a supernatural superhero, seeks to maintain a moral code while fighting the ultimate agent of chaos, the Joker. But in this morally ambiguous universe, that moral task appears impossible, and no one is clean, not even the Batman. He must torture a terrorist in order to save innocent lives, violate his jurisdiction by entering foreign countries to snatch criminals and illegally wiretap an entire city to catch the Joker—all timely issues of justice that reflect the very ones debated in America's War on Terror (an obvious metaphor of the movie). In a way, *The Dark Knight* subverts the superhero paradigm by asking the question of whether so much power should be vested in the hands of individual men. It challenges our notions of our moral views of the world and our own goodness. But at the end, in a Christlike substitutionary atonement, the Batman takes the blame for crimes he did not commit in order to protect a positive legacy of law enforcement for the people. The Batman is rejected by the very world he has saved.

One of the strongest examples of the postmodern "anti-superhero" trend is found in Zach Snyder's *Watchmen,* a cinematic translation of comic-book cynicism. In this dark tale superheroes are psychologically damaged idealists, disillusioned with their goals of truth, justice and the American way—to the point of accepting political lies and the murder of millions of innocent New Yorkers in order to achieve the "higher goal" of utopian peace (doing evil that good may result). The only remaining idealist, who still believes in the power of "truth" and wants to fight evil with uncompromising moral zeal, is Rorschach, who must be killed in order to protect the truth from being discovered. A final scene hints at the reality that the dark side of human nature is never obliterated; the cycle of violence is threatened all over again.

Is this a tragedy or a celebration of despair? Given a lack of theological context, this otherwise biblical revelation of sinful nature can arguably become a nihilistic complaint of hopelessness.

WESTERNS

Another popular source of American mythology is the Western genre. Values like rugged individualism, the pioneer spirit, vigilante justice, outlaws as heroes, restlessness of spirit and love of outdoors run deep in many Americans' hearts and in many American Westerns. A typical Western movie reinforces the image of the lone, righteous man facing a savage world, carving his way through a harsh, rugged terrain, burly outlaws and wild Indians in order for civilization to find its roots. With a six-gun on his hip and a warrior code of honor, the cowboy hands out posse justice to outlaws who endanger the growth of the village. Morality is a law of the jungle, solved by survival of the fittest.

The anti-Western is an overturning of the mythology of the Western by showing the dark side of the aforesaid values. Movies like *Wyatt Earp*, *Ravenous*, *Unforgiven* and *3:10 to Yuma* are anti-Westerns that show the values of the American West to have been founded on questionable or even immoral premises. In David Webb Peoples's Oscar-winning *Unforgiven,* the characters struggle with the reality of killing people and the romantic hype that surrounds unrealistic heroes and villains through dime-store fiction novels. It shows that shooting men dead is not as easy and without spiritual consequences as most Westerns would make us believe. Ironically, its star, Clint Eastwood, is himself one of the spaghetti Western icons whom this movie deconstructs. In the end, the "hero" must become villainous himself in order to defeat the villains, blurring the line between the white hats and the black hats, between good guys and bad guys.

3:10 to Yuma, written by Halsted Wells, depicts Ben Wade, the proverbial consummate outlaw who lives by no code but the lawless West. He's slick, he's romantic, and even heroic in his personality. As Wade is captured and then escorted cross-country to prison by a ragtag group of deputized men, he confronts his doppelganger opposite: a loser rancher family man trying (yet failing) to be a hero to his own son. As Wade is faced with this irony, he discovers the humanity and love he could never have in that simple rancher, a modern man of the new world. Wade sees in him true heroism and courage in facing the impossible with honor. In this story, the civility that tends toward weakness also achieves the grace and love that the untamed Wild West cannot achieve. *3:10 to Yuma* subverts the Western myth.

Mythology is far from dead, even in a modern technological and secularized world. And movies are one of the most effective means of communicating mythology because they are a story-centered medium that captures and reflects our deeply held beliefs.

MYTHOLOGY, PAGANISM AND CHRISTIANITY

Joseph Campbell has become a saint to many in Hollywood, thanks to the evangelistic efforts of such apostles as George Lucas and Christopher

Vogler. Campbell's approach to mythology is akin to Jung's concept of the archetypes residing in the individual and collective unconscious.

Like Carl Jung, Campbell believed that the individual unconscious mind of each person is an extension of the unified "collective unconscious"—an amalgamation of all of humankind's ancestral experience. Our minds share in the pool of all human psyche throughout the ages, like many individuals sharing in the same dream. His monism concludes, "The essence of oneself and the essence of the world: These two are one."[9]

According to Campbell, all religions and mythologies are but local manifestations of the single truth of what he calls the "Monomyth" of the hero. The Monomyth, in its most basic form, consists of the hero's journey from separation to initiation to return (remember the definition of *worldview?*),[10] and it embodies redemption in a way we will discuss in the next chapter on story structure. Campbell attempts to prove his thesis with an eclectic recitation of many of the world's stories, from creation myths to flood legends and heroes of faith.

Vogler puts it simply: "All stories consist of a few common structural elements found universally in myths, fairy tales, dreams, and movies. They are known collectively as The Hero's Journey."[11] It is difficult to deny this common thread among diverse cultures, and the Christian need not fear facing such facts. After all, the meaning of so-called facts is in the interpretation, and the interpretation is in the worldview.[12] So how does the Christian deal with such mythical similarities among cultures?

Christians need not deny a Monomyth that is reinterpreted through different traditions. We need to only understand it in its true nature from God's own revelation. After all, God is the ultimate Storyteller, and the Scriptures say that he has placed a common knowledge of himself in all people through creation and conscience (Rom 1:18-20; 2:15). This explains the true genesis and nature of the Monomyth. In running from God, heathen humanity distorts that Monomyth of knowledge inside

---

[9]Joseph Campbell, *The Hero with a Thousand Faces* (Princeton, N.J.: Princeton University Press, 1973), p. 386.

[10]Ibid., p. 30.

[11]Vogler, *Writer's Journey,* p. 3.

[12]Campbell's individual interpretation is founded on relativistic monism, which does not comport with Christianity.

itself. Thus all religions and rituals have the scent of an original truth that has been turned into the stench of a lie:

> Even though [human beings] knew God, they did not honor Him as God or give thanks, but they became futile in their speculations, and their foolish heart was darkened. Professing to be wise, they became fools, and exchanged the glory of the incorruptible God for an image in the form of corruptible man and of birds and four-footed animals and crawling creatures. . . . They exchanged the truth of God for a lie, and worshiped and served the creature rather than the Creator, who is blessed forever. Amen. (Rom 1:21-23, 25)

It should not surprise or scare us that all cultures have creation myths, flood legends and similar ritualistic concepts. We should expect it. And we should not tremble at modern scholarship that sees historical fabrication in mythical origins. Just because there is similarity in myth between Christianity and other religions does not mean that Christianity is on an equal playing field with these religions or subordinate to a more generic Monomyth. Christianity is itself the true incarnation of the Monomyth in history, and other mythologies reflect and distort it like dirty or broken mirrors.

In addition to providing this true underlying mythology of reality, Christianity alone provides the justification for storytelling. Robert W. Jenson, in an article explaining "how the world has lost its story," points out that the very precondition for the intelligibility of storytelling is itself a "narratable world."[13] That is, the biblical notion of linear history, with an author, characters and a purposeful goal, was the philosophical foundation of the search for meaning in a narrative of life. Storytelling is meaningless gibberish unless reality itself is narratable. And reality is unnarratable in a universe without a transcendent narrator.

Author Daniel Taylor comments on this legacy of Western culture's biblical heritage of living in a narratable world. In order to tell a story with plot and characters that are not in utter chaos, one must already believe that reality is explainable, he says, and "that belief depends on a

---

[13]Robert W. Jenson, "How the World Lost Its Story," *First Things* 36 (October 1993): 19-24.

number of supporting beliefs: that reality is at least in part knowable; that there are meaningful connections between events; that actions have consequences; that humans do most things by choice, not by irresistible compulsion; that we are therefore responsible; and so on."[14]

We are creatures of story, created by a storytelling God, who created the very fabric of our reality in terms of his story. Rather than seeing our existence as a series of unconnected random events without purpose, storytelling brings meaning to our lives through the analogy of a carefully crafted plot that reflects the loving sovereignty of the God of the Bible. As Taylor concludes:

> Stories link past, present, and future in a way that tells us where we have been (even before we were born), where we are, and where we could be going. . . . Our stories teach us that there is a place for us, that we fit. They suggest to us that our lives can have a plot. Stories turn mere chronology, one thing after another, into the purposeful action of plot, and thereby into meaning. . . . Stories are the single best way humans have for accounting for our experience.[15]

God is such a creative author that he embodies both myth *and* history into his own narrative of redemption. As C. S. Lewis put it:

> The heart of Christianity is a myth which is also a fact. . . . By becoming fact, it does not cease to be myth: That is the miracle. I suspect that men have sometimes derived more spiritual sustenance from myths they did not believe than from the religion they professed. To be truly Christian we must both assent to the historical fact and also receive the myth (fact though it has become) with the same imaginative embrace which we accord to all myths. The one is hardly more necessary than the other. . . . We must not be ashamed of the mythical radiance resting on our theology. We must not be nervous about "parallels" and "Pagan Christs": they ought to be there—it would be a stumbling block if they weren't. We must not, in false spirituality, withhold our imaginative welcome.[16]

---

[14]Daniel Taylor, *The Healing Power of Stories: Creating Yourself Through the Stories of Your Life* (Dublin: Gill & Macmillan, 1996), p. 140.

[15]Ibid., pp. 1-2.

[16]C. S. Lewis, *God in the Dock: Essays on Theology and Ethics*, ed. Walter Hooper (Grand Rapids, Mich.: Eerdmans, 1970), pp. 66-67.

J. R. R. Tolkien was the master storyteller who led C. S. Lewis to Christ with this kind of myth-become-fact reasoning. In Tolkien's famous lecture "On Fairy-Stories" he speaks of approaching the "Christian story" with joy because the nature of fantasy and even happy endings (which he calls "eucatastrophe") gives us a "sudden glimpse of the underlying reality or truth" of the ultimate happy ending: the resurrection of Christ and the believer's sharing in that resurrection.

> The Gospels contain a fairy-story, or a story of a larger kind which embraces all the essence of fairy-stories. They contain marvels—peculiarly artistic, beautiful and moving: "Mythical" in their perfect, self-contained significance; and among the marvels is the greatest and most complete conceivable eucatastrophe. But this story has entered History and the primary world: the desire and aspiration of sub-creation has been raised to the fulfillment of Creation. The Birth of Christ is the eucatastrophe of Man's history. The Resurrection is the eucatastrophe of the story of the Incarnation. This story begins and ends in joy. It has pre-eminently the "inner consistency of reality." There is no tale ever told that men would rather find was true, and none which so many sceptical men have accepted as true on its own merits. For the Art of it has the supremely convincing tone of Primary Art, that is, of Creation. To reject it leads either to sadness or to wrath.[17]

See the chapter "Jesus" for a detailed analysis of Christ myths.

DEMYTHOLOGIZATION

One modern mythology is the naturalistic worldview, with its agenda of demythologization. Since naturalists believe there are no true spiritual realities, only natural phenomena, they assume that there must be a natural explanation behind every myth or religious belief. According to the naturalist, primitive peoples create myths and religious symbols for natural phenomena they do not understand. For instance, if a culture does not understand thunder, it reinterprets thunder to represent a deity in order to make sense of it. The goal of the naturalist, then, is to discover what natural experiences cultures had that drove them to create such mythology.

---

[17]J. R. R. Tolkien, "On Fairy-Stories," in *The Monsters and the Critics and Other Essays,* ed. Christopher Tolkien (London: George Allen & Unwin, 1983), pp. 155-56.

A.I.: Artificial Intelligence, Steven Spielberg's adaptation of Stanley Kubrick's original film concept, is an evolutionary tale that demythologizes humankind's quest for meaning and significance in transcendent notions like religion. This homage to Kubrick is the story of a little robot boy, David (played by Haley Joel Osment), on a quest to become human. While the blatant references to Pinocchio throughout the film emphasize David's quest as a metaphor for our own dilemma of humanity, there is a quantum leap of difference between the original and the modern deconstruction of that myth.

The original *Pinocchio* was a morality tale, a purely allegorical story about good behavior and good choices being the defining characteristics of a child worthy of love. In today's climate of scientism, many believe that it is possible for consciousness to emerge out of mechanical complexity. In this context the Pinocchio quest is no longer a metaphor but a literal ethical question: what makes us different from any highly complex mechanical device? If we can create artificial intelligence, how is our intelligence any less "artificial"? *A.I.* attempts to answer this question with the simple maxim that to love and be loved is what makes us human.

Following in the footsteps of the lead characters in *Frankenstein* and *Blade Runner,* the robot boy David is not merely searching for the Blue Fairy to make him human; he is also searching for his creator. But his creator cannot help him. The scientist who manufactured David represents the view that the abstract ability to seek after what one cannot see is what makes us human. We create myths or fairy tales in order to give meaning to our lives. Mythology here is the symbolizing of what we do not understand into larger-than-life, transcendent images. Thus David remembers that the first thing he saw upon his "birth" was an angelic figure with wings. We discover later that this apparent religious image was in fact the logo of the corporation that created him.

In this movie, religion and myth are reduced to natural explanations. There is no spiritual or transcendent aspect to our existence. Even the terms for the robots ("mechas") and humans ("orgas") reflect this reduction of life forms to mechanical or organic complexity. David seeks after the Blue Fairy to make him a real boy, which we all know is not going to happen because the Blue Fairy is a Disney construct. But this abstract belief compels him onward, with religious fervor, to find the myth as truth.

By finding and deciphering the abstract literary clue left at Dr. Know's vending machine (a *Wizard of Oz* symbol), David is able to find his maker at "the end of the world, where the lions cry," which is the mythical poetic way of describing the scientific creator's lair in the flooded remains of Manhattan city. So David's ability to find meaning in myth, to symbolize what he does not understand into mythological constructs, to seek after that which cannot be seen, is what makes David "human" to the scientist. Humanity's spiritual quest is unveiled as an imminent symbol-creating enterprise rather than a transcendent symbol-discovering enterprise.

But David is not satisfied. In fact, he is in despair. So he casts himself into the sea in angst-ridden resignation. At the bottom of the ocean he stumbles upon Coney Island, now underwater from the risen seas, and prays to the Blue Fairy statue he finds in Pleasure Island Park to make him a real boy. The statue, by now an obvious icon of the Virgin Mary, does not "answer" his prayers, and he remains in unbroken devout gaze and unsatisfied longing until his batteries run out. This is a visual reference to the filmmaker's perception of humanity's tenacious, yet ultimately vain, religious quest. And that vanity of religion is further emphasized when David finally touches the Blue Fairy, that symbol of divinity, at the end of the movie, and it crumbles into dust. Earlier, David's robotic partner, Gigolo Joe, had explained in the front of a church that sooner or later the women who go there become dissatisfied with their spiritual quest (God's love) and end up in his physical arms for "real" affection and love.

Two thousand years later, when all of humankind has died out and only machines remain, some highly advanced robots, looking very much like the popular conception of alien beings, are able to "resurrect" David (recharge his batteries) and even give him for one day his dream of "resurrecting" his original organic "mother" from her DNA in order to experience her love (more religious concepts naturalized). At the end of the day, when his mother is about to go to sleep and awaken nevermore, she tells David that she loves him and has always loved him. This finally satisfies David, and he is able to lie down and die with her in happiness, knowing that he is now human because he has loved and been loved. This final shot of him closing his eyes and being able to die is very important because early in the movie it was established that David did not close his eyes to sleep because he didn't have to sleep. The fact that he now closes his eyes is the evidence that he has become human and can die in peace as a human, having found his meaning.

Some may find in *A.I.* an analogy to the Judeo-Christian notion of God creating human beings as creatures whose humanity is defined in being loved by their Creator as well as others. In the first scene of *A.I.* the scientist speaking to his class of students makes this very comparison of God creating Adam to love and be loved. But with all its religious imagery and references, *A.I.* is more fittingly a humanistic interpretation of our personal quest for meaning being found in loving and being loved by other people (because *there is no transcendent reality*), as well as our manufacturing of myth (including God) as a means of explaining what we do not scientifically understand. *A.I.* is a deconstruction of religious belief into mythical construct,[18] and it revisits the evolutionary conclusion that consciousness naturally emerges out of the inherent properties of matter, that humanity can actually be achieved by a highly complex machine.

Other movies try to demythologize religion as the misunderstood worship of aliens who visited Earth in the ancient past. The parallels with Genesis, Eden, the forbidden fruit, and the ascension and return of Christ are obvious in the recent "re-imagining" of *Planet of the Apes*. Movies such as *Stargate*, *Alien vs. Predator* and *Indiana Jones and the Kingdom of the Crystal Skull* depict the pyramids of ancient Egyptian religion *(Stargate)* or the ziggurats of South American religion *(AvP* and *Indiana Jones)* as a result of "primitive" man being influenced by aliens who visited our planet eons ago in their "chariots of the gods."

---

[18]Even in the final scene, in which David does meet the Blue Fairy, she is really an illusion constructed by the advanced robots to meet David's desire in his own terms rather than in terms of "reality."

While there may be some truth to the natural origins of some religious beliefs, demythology, as an absolute interpretation of history, suffers from its own mythological bias. Screenwriter David Franzoni explained when he was writing the screenplay for *King Arthur* that his script "aims more for history than myth."[19] And the movie gives the impression that it is a more historically accurate depiction based on new archaeological evidence. What Franzoni does not mention is that there is no certifiable history of King Arthur, and the new evidence is quite ambiguous. All we have are medieval romances, Welsh legends and other academic speculations of his exploits. To say that one will "aim more for history than myth" is really to say that one will aim more for one myth or legend over other myths or legends. The art of demythologizing is itself a mythology that believes there are no preternatural or transcendent mysteries to life, so it interprets what it cannot understand or does not know in terms of its own naturalistic cause-and-effect bias. This is not to say that all myth and history are equal in factual value, but it is a strong challenge to those who neglect to understand that even historical accounts are filtered through the historian's bias.

MYTH AND MEANING

From the Greek tragedies of Euripides to the bawdy comedies of Shakespeare, both ancient and classical writers suffered no shame in telling a good story with the intention of proving a point or illustrating how they believed we ought to live in this world. Storytelling from its inception was expected to be more than entertainment.

Through their craft, the first storytellers were expected to teach the culture how to live and behave in their world. The rejection of "messages" in movies as "preachy" or "propaganda" is a recent phenomenon that results from the splitting of reality into secular/sacred distinctions, as if a story about human beings relating to one another could exist in a vacuum, without reference to values or meaning. All movies inherently

---

[19]Quoted in John Soriano, "WGA.org's Exclusive Interview with David Franzoni," WGA <http://www.sois.uwm.edu/xie/dl/Movie%20Project%20Team%20Folder/Movie%20 Project%20Team%20Folder/Writers/David%20Frazoni-%20Gladiator.pdf>. The interview has been removed from WGA.org since publication of the first edition of this book.

contain messages in the very nature of their storytelling. Characters making choices that result in consequences is a "message" about how the storyteller thinks the way the world works.

Joseph Campbell was worried about the thoughtless irresponsibility of modern movie narrative. He called our storytellers to return to one of the primary functions of myth: its pedagogical nature, teaching how to live a human life under any circumstances.[20] This return to the craft as high priesthood is a recognition of the privilege and responsibility that storytellers have in "making and breaking lives" by the power of their medium and its message.[21]

DEMYTHOLOGIZATION
Stargate
Cast Away
A.I.
Planet of the Apes
Alien vs. Predator
King Arthur

True, some movies are more obvious or blatant than others in their message, and some are simpler or less focused than others, but all of them communicate values and worldviews nonetheless. This is a matter of degree, not of essence. Often the very movies that people think are not meaningful are actually loaded with powerful messages and worldviews.

Just Friends is a romantic comedy about an obese high schooler, Chris, who grows up, gets hot and successful, comes back home ten years later, and tries to bed the only woman he loved in high school, Jamie, who was only interested in him as friends. This story has all the typical crass jokes of men trying to get women to sleep with them, but the point of it all is to mock such juvenile immaturity in males. Because Chris has become promiscuous and selfish, he tries to catch Jamie for all the wrong reasons. It is not until he sees himself in another selfish, womanizing user, who is trying to bed Jamie as well, that Chris takes responsibility for his immaturity. Chris wins Jamie but never has sex with her. Instead, his return to her involves the desire to marry and have children with her, so there is a rather conservative moral to the story. A promiscuous man learns that true love is possible only by repenting from the irresponsible pursuit of using women. Like Proverbs 7 explained earlier, *Just Friends* mocks the immoral lifestyle by showing the dead end of it all.

---

[20]Campbell, *Hero*, p. 31.
[21]Ibid., p. 8.

Rather than spurning mythology as something that only so-called primitive societies have, we ought to recognize that the heart of movie storytelling (modern mythology) is the communication and reinforcement of worldviews and values. And so we ought to judge movies in this light, even getting involved ourselves in creating and telling stories that express redemption for a lost world.

WATCH AND LEARN

1. With a friend or two, watch the movie *Cast Away*. Look for and discuss the symbolic references to the development of humankind in the experience of Chuck on the island. Look also for Chuck's ultimate reconnection with civilization. What do the symbols of the volleyball, time, the angel wings and the whale represent? Discuss the kind of character that Chuck is at the beginning and then how he has changed after his journey. Imagine yourself in his shoes, and discuss what aspects of your life you would change if you had the same experience. Discuss what you think the movie was saying about what is really valuable in life.

2. Watch the movie *Spitfire Grill* with some friends, and discuss the elements of the Christ story that you see in the movie.

3. Consider a comedy movie that you never thought was meaningful beyond a bunch of jokes and gags. Now rewatch that movie, and discuss the journey of the main character. What was he or she like at the beginning of the movie? What did this person learn or not learn? How did the character change, or how did the character change others, by the end of the movie? If you were to see the movie as a parable, what would be its main message?

3

REDEMPTION

One of the most frustrating replies to hear when asking people what they thought of a movie is "I liked it" or "I didn't like it," *accompanied by an inability to explain why.* But with an elementary understanding of the structure of storytelling, an informed moviegoer can watch a film and enjoy the story while also engaging his or her critical faculties to understand what the movie is trying to say about the way in which we ought or ought not to live.

We have already established that stories do not exist in a vacuum of mere entertainment. Movies communicate prevailing myths and cultural values. And this cultural effect is far deeper than the amount of sex and violence in the story. It extends to the philosophy behind the film. The way we view the world and things like right and wrong are embedded in the redemptive structure of storytelling itself.

It is not necessary that audiences are consciously aware that a message or worldview is being communicated. The composition of a story leads a viewer through emotional and dramatic experiences to see things in the way the storytellers want the viewer to see. This is similar to the visual form, color and composition used by a painter to guide a viewer's eyes and mind to see and feel what the painter wants him to see and feel.

Now let's take a look at these structural elements, with movies to illustrate each one.[1] We will examine two films that are similar in theme but opposite in their worldview as well as being opposite in genre: *Amadeus,* the Oscar-winning tragedy about the man who killed Mozart (in the movie, though not in reality); and *The Truman Show,* the Jim Carrey comedy vehicle about an innocent and naive young man who discovers that his life is a TV show for the world.

THEME

The first element to consider when analyzing a movie is its theme. Every good movie has a theme. Some may call it "the moral of the story"; others may call it "the message"; but the theme is what the story is ultimately all about. You can state a theme propositionally as a premise that leads to a conclusion. It can usually be stated in terms of "x leads to y"[2] or some other prescriptive equivalent, such as "Fear of differences in others leads to alienation" *(Shrek)* or "Greed leads to self-destruction" *(Indecent Proposal* and *A Simple Plan).*

Other examples of themes include the following. *Traffic:* in the war on drugs, no one gets away clean, not even the good guys. *Babe:* biology can be transcended by personal choice (a pig proves that it *can* be a sheepdog). *Fatal Attraction:* infidelity turns against itself. *Dead Poets Society:* conformity kills the spirit, but individuality frees it. *Terminator* and *Jurassic Park:* unfettered technology turns against humanity.

The theme is the purpose or moral of the story, and it is incarnate in the plot. Aristotle described plot as the inevitable or probable sequence of events.[3] If we claim that a sequence of events is inevitable from a char-

---

[1] A dominant influence on my summary of storytelling structure in this chapter is John Truby's lectures called "Great Screenwriting Class." And the source for much of Truby's teaching was Joseph Campbell's insights into the heroic Monomyth. Campbell, of course, was simply drawing from the commonality of all world religions (which, as discussed in chapter one, are merely distortions of the true Christian Monomyth). John Truby's "Great Screenwriting Class" tapes, as well as other helpful tapes on genres, can be purchased at <http://www.truby.com/>.

[2] Lajos Egri, *The Art of Dramatic Writing: Its Basis in the Creative Interpretation of Human Motives* (New York: Simon & Schuster, 1960), pp. 1-32.

[3] Aristotle, *Aristotle's Poetics,* trans. James Hutton (New York: W. W. Norton, 1982), p. 53.

acter's beginning behavior, then we are making a moral claim about the world. X leads to y. If we behave in such a way, such an end will result. Our story fleshes out our theme.

Amadeus, written by Peter Shaffer, is the story of Antonio Salieri, the court composer of Austrian Emperor Joseph II. Salieri is a man who from an early age desired to glorify God by composing great music. But he soon realizes that God has instead chosen the childish infidel Wolfgang Amadeus Mozart for divine creativity. Salieri is so angered at God's seeming capriciousness that he eventually decides to get revenge on God by destroying Mozart. His attempts land him in an insane asylum. The theme: true freedom is found in accepting one's fate or destiny from God; trying to control one's destiny leads to slavery.

The Truman Show, written by Andrew Niccol, is about a naive young man named Truman, who dreams of leaving his small, idyllic town of Seahaven to see the world and find his true love. Every attempt he makes to leave is blocked until he discovers that his entire life has been a TV show controlled by a godlike television producer named Christof. Truman must confront his inner demons as well as the producer of the show to free himself from external controls and choose his own destiny in life. The theme of *The Truman Show* is that true freedom is found in controlling one's own destiny. God's sovereign control of our lives leads to slavery; human autonomy leads to freedom.

As you can see, both stories—*Amadeus* and *The Truman Show*—deal with the theme of God's sovereignty and human freedom, yet they arrive at opposite conclusions.

Many movies contain several themes. Some may be more general than others. For example, an additional theme of *The Truman Show* is the notion that media in America have become an all-consuming substitute for living real life. But even this theme serves the bigger theme of life as autonomous freedom.

THE HERO

With theme established, let's look at the basic structure of the story. Most moviegoers are familiar with the idea that stories have heroes and villains. Simply put, the hero is the main character, the one whom the story is about. The hero of *The Truman Show* is obviously Truman. *Amadeus* has a unique take on the hero because, in a sense, the villain is the hero. Salieri is the one trying to fight God and kill Mozart, and these facts make him the villain. But Peter Shaffer turns the perspective around and shows us the story through the villain's eyes as if he were the hero. So, to Salieri, God is the villain.

THE HERO'S GOAL

The hero always has a goal, a strong desire that drives the story. Without a goal, there is no story. And the hero is usually driven to the point of obsession with this goal. Salieri's goal is glory and greatness through musical perfection, which he will offer back to God in thanks. From his youth, he sets out to achieve that goal by studying music with all his heart. Truman's goal is to leave the small town he was brought up in and go to a distant, exotic location like Fiji. But Truman also has a secondary goal of finding the girl with whom he fell in love in an earlier time of his life.

THE ADVERSARY

The adversary is the external opponent of the hero and the hero's goal. I use the word *adversary* rather than *villain* because the word *villain* often conjures up the stereotype of Snidely Whiplash versus Dudley Do-Right, and this viewpoint can miss the finer distinctions and subtleties of more complex characters.[4] In essence, the adversary represents the contrasting belief system to that of the hero, resulting in a story that is ultimately a clash of worldviews. An adversary may be an individual, like Scar in *The Lion King,* or a force, like chance in *Forrest Gump,* or nature, as in *The Perfect Storm.* An adversary can be black-and-white evil, like a James Bond nemesis, or a complex character with positive virtues, like Sally Field's character in *Mrs. Doubtfire* or the math professor trying to help the genius Will in *Good Will Hunting.*

The adversary in *The Truman Show* is Christof, who is ultimately a symbol for God. It is no coincidence that his name suggests "Christ-off" and that he speaks to Truman ("True Man") at the end as God might

---

[4]Writers often call the hero "protagonist" and the villain "antagonist" for the same reason of avoiding extremes and stereotypes.

speak, "from the heavens." His desire is for Truman's good, but he ultimately keeps Truman from going to Fiji, which is Truman's goal.

On an earthly level, Salieri's adversary is Mozart, but really Mozart becomes the tangible symbol for Salieri's ultimate adversary, God. Salieri simply cannot accept that God chooses a pagan like Mozart to produce divine music and relegates a devout believer like himself to the ash heap of mediocrity.

CHARACTER FLAW

The hero wants something badly to begin with. That desire is the goal. The adversary blocks the hero from achieving that goal, but an internal opponent also holds him back: the character flaw.

At the beginning of the story, the hero sees life in the wrong way, and by the end of the story, he learns the right way to behave or think within life. This progression of change is what is referred to as the "character arc," the process by which a character changes his paradigm, seeking a *want* but discovering a *need* and responding to that need appropriately or not. If the character learns to respond appropriately, you have a comedy or drama; if the character does not respond appropriately, you have a tragedy.

In *The Truman Show,* Truman desires to leave his small town and go to Fiji. But his inner flaw is his own innocence and trust of others, which blinds him to the fact that his life is controlled by others, not himself. He also has a fear of water, which is a secondary flaw that keeps him from achieving his goal of leaving Seahaven.

In the beginning of *Amadeus,* Salieri wants to glorify God with great music. But his flaw is that he wants glory out of it for himself. He tries to make a bargain with God on his own terms, vowing that if God will make him famous, he will give God his chastity in return. What he offers is hardly an altruistic exchange, and it's hardly a humble approach to try to bargain with one's Maker.

THE APPARENT DEFEAT

The key to the middle of the story is that everything the hero does is blocked by the adversary and the hero's own internal flaw. There is wide latitude here for plot complications and reversals, betrayals and so on.

But the important point of the storytelling is to exhaust every possible option that the hero has to achieve her goal, with failure at every turn. There is often a moment of partial victory, like a few wins in a sports season of losses, that gives the hero new hope of achieving the goal. But ultimately every option is played out, and the hero cannot achieve what she wants. She may get close, but she cannot get all the way.

Somewhere near the end of this line, the hero faces what is called an "apparent defeat," wherein all the attempts to achieve the goal are frustrated to the point of total futility. Nothing the hero has done works; there are no other options, and the hero is left with no hope of ever achieving her goal.

Then the hero often has a "visit to death" or enters "the gauntlet." "Running the gauntlet" is an old phrase used to describe a form of punishment in which men armed with sticks or other weapons arranged themselves in two lines facing each other and beat the person forced to run between them. The gauntlet can be physical, as it is in *The Truman Show,* where Truman has to battle a sea storm that embodies his worst phobias about water. Or it can be metaphorical, as in *Amadeus,* where Salieri is reading Mozart's compositions and has to "face the music"— Mozart's music, that is—by concluding that he can never achieve this kind of brilliance and beauty and is doomed to a life of mediocrity.

FINAL CONFRONTATION

The gauntlet usually ends in a final confrontation between the hero and the adversary. This is sometimes called the "obligatory scene" in which the hero and adversary meet face to face, and their worldviews come into conflict. It does not always have to be a physical fight; it can be a verbal face-off. The final confrontation is often where the adversary explains his rationale for opposing the hero. Better movies will make this rationale as realistic as possible so as not to create cardboard villains. The adversary's rationale represents the worldview that the writer or storyteller does not want us to accept.

The final confrontation for Truman actually occurs after the sea storm when he hears the godlike voice of Christof from the heavens trying to persuade him not to leave. Their interchange looks and sounds very much like a man quarreling with his Maker, as in Job, only with quite opposite results.

Salieri's final confrontation is his attempt to "write Mozart to death." By pushing Mozart in his sickness, Salieri hopes to drive him to his grave and then perform at Mozart's funeral the very requiem he is transcribing, claiming the authorshipof this great and glorious musical perfection for himself. We hear Salieri's rationale throughout the entire film because he is telling us from his "confession" with the priest in the asylum.

SELF-REVELATION

The hero has a moment in the film, usually near the end, when he learns where he was wrong in what he had desired all along. He realizes that what he *wanted* was not what he *needed*. This is the view of the way we should or should not live that the storyteller is trying to convey to the audience. This moment is the character revelation of the hero, and it represents the theme or moral. It is often closely connected to the final confrontation, either as a result of that confrontation or as the means by which the hero can win the battle.

At the end of *The Truman Show* Truman almost drowns and experiences his own revelation when his boat hits the end of the sky, revealing the dome he has lived in all along. While debating with Christof, he realizes that he must walk away through the little door, into a cold, cruel world. But it is far better to live life free with danger than to live by some other's idea of protection, such as that of a benevolent deity.

In *Amadeus,* Salieri fails to face his self-revelation of God's sovereign control and attempts suicide. After he fails at this as well, he finally goes insane in his willful defiance, calling himself the patron saint of mediocrity and "blessing" the other mental patients around him.

RESOLUTION

The resolution (also called the dénouement) is a short epilogue to the story showing what results from the hero's change or lack of change. If she has chosen redemption, she has at least begun the restoration of what was lost. She recovers a harmony in her being and life that exemplifies the redemption.

In *The Truman Show* the resolution is left open. In a sense, it doesn't matter how his life ends after his final decision to change, because to the storytellers the point is that it is better to be free with danger and uncertainty ahead than to be protected under the control of a deity.

In *Amadeus,* Salieri's insanity is the result of his rejection of redemption, his refusal to submit to God. Because he does not accept his self-revelation, the story is a tragedy, a parable showing us the negative results of a life that defies God. And a life that defies God defies redemption.

REDEMPTION: WHAT IT'S ALL ABOUT

The reason for walking through these elements of the craft of storytelling used in movies is to illustrate how the essence of storytelling in movies is about redemption. A movie takes a hero with an inner flaw, who desires something and has a plan to get it. But he is blocked by an adversary until he almost fails but finally finds a solution. This process of goal, flaw, failure and self-revelation is the process of paradigm change or conversion in an individual.

CHRISTIAN REDEMPTION

Tender Mercies

The Mission

Shadowlands

The Addiction

Les Misérables

To End All Wars

The Lion, the Witch and the Wardrobe

Man on Fire

Amazing Grace

Premonition

Constantine

Spitfire Grill

A Christian testimony of redemption follows the same structure that a movie does. We, as individuals, have a *goal* for what we want in life to give us significance, fame, money, what have you. But Satan is our *adversary,* and our *character flaw* of sin keeps us from achieving that significance. We think that our control is our salvation, but we are wrong. We are the problem, not the solution. We get to the point in life where our constant attempts at achieving our goal are blocked to the point of *apparent defeat.* We get to the end of ourselves in a *final confrontation* when either we realize that we cannot achieve our misguided worldly goals or we achieve them and realize that they do not bring the significance we seek. And we finally have a *self-revelation* that what we wanted in life is not what we needed. Our alienation is caused by our own inner faults, our sins. We change our minds (repentance), which results in a changed life, our *resolution*. This is the common personal story of Christian conversion. This is the structure of redemption in stories.

CAVEAT EMPTOR: DIFFERENT KINDS OF REDEMPTION

Many films today operate within a humanistic framework of the world. This kind of redemption usually reduces to self-actualization or redemption through self-righteousness. Man is the measure of his own potential. In *Dead Poets Society* the redemption asserted, by the schoolteacher Keating, is that since we are food for the worms and there is no afterlife, we must "seize the day" by casting off social and moral restraint to find one's self or potential. Many of the "save the kids" movies about rescuing youth at risk are often unfortunately reducible to self-salvation.

Another popular form of redemption is called "existentialism." This is the view that humanity exists in an ultimately irrational universe without meaning that leads to despair (angst). The way of redemption is through the acceptance of responsibility for creating ourselves through personal choice or commitment. *Forrest Gump* is the popular form of this redemption. This existential redemption will be explored in more detail in chapter four.

Another increasingly popular redemption in film is Eastern mysticism. Mysticism takes many forms, of which the two strongest are monism and dualism. Dualism is the *Star Wars* variety of redemption—the dark and light sides of the Force. *Ghost* offers a dualism in which the bad people get sucked into spiritual punishment and the good people, who embrace their light side by letting go of their control over others, enter Nirvana. This kind of dualism is salvation by good works. *Phenomenon*, *Powder* and *I Heart Huckabees* are strong examples of the monistic view of redemption, the belief that enlightenment comes through experiencing a oneness with all things. This monist enlightenment will be discussed in detail in chapter six.

Story Element	*Amadeus*	*The Truman Show*	**The Apostle Paul's Testimony (Acts 26)**
Theme	Submission to God leads to freedom; personal control leads to slavery.	Submission to God leads to slavery; personal control leads to freedom.	Submission to God leads to freedom; self-righteousness leads to slavery.
Hero	Salieri	Truman	Saul
Goal	To glorify God with famous musical compositions	To leave Seahaven and find the mysterious woman he fell in love with	To attain the hope of the promise made by God to the forefathers by persecuting Christians
Adversary	Mozart (God)	Christof (God)	Christians (God)
Flaw	Vainglory. He bargains with God on his own terms.	Innocence—he trusts people too easily. Also, fear of water.	Self-righteousness
Apparent Defeat	Salieri reads Mozart's music written on first pass and realizes that he does not have greatness in himself.	The big storm at sea, which is the final and most difficult barrier for Truman to face.	The Christian church grew faster than Paul could persecute them.
Final Confrontation	Salieri tries to "write" Mozart to death.	Truman debates with Christof, who is in the sky.	Damascus road experience—God wins.
Self-Revelation	He cannot win against God.	His life has been controlled by another. He must give up his security if he is to have freedom from another's control.	He has actually been fighting against the very God he claimed to serve. His self-righteousness blinded him.
Resolution	Salieri refuses to submit and goes insane.	Truman walks out of his TV world through the stairway into freedom and uncertainty.	Paul ends up on trial for convincing people of the very thing he was trying to stop. But he is free from slavery to sin.

Figure 4. Elements of three stories

Another kind of redemption is the Christian notion of substitutionary sacrifice, faith, repentance and forgiveness. Every once in a while movies like *Chariots of Fire* come along and portray Christian redemption in their characters. Some of these will be discussed in chapter eight, but suffice it to say that they all illustrate Christian redemption through motifs that encompass facing one's own moral guilt, the need for repentance, the cleansing power of forgiveness, the undeserved nature of grace, the substitutionary nature of atonement and freedom through dying to self. And there are many other elements of the Christian worldview, including loving one's neighbor, truth, justice, mercy and so on, all of which point toward or illustrate our inner need for redemption.

SAVE THE KIDS SELF-SALVATION
Lean on Me
Dangerous Minds
Pay It Forward
Coach Carter
Gridiron Gang
Take the Lead
Freedom Writers
The Emperor's Club
Music of the Heart
Akeelah and the Bee
Finding Forrester

As a further qualification, not all stories of redemption are complete and deeply woven philosophies. Often they point to simple values like self-worth based on self-acceptance and not peer approval *(Toy Story),* coming-of-age based on awareness of mortality and not sexuality *(My Dog Skip),* the dangers of trusting technology *(Terminator 2, Jurassic Park),* or the blessings of a loving diverse family *(The Incredibles, Meet the Robinsons)*. But even these values are ultimately about how we ought or ought not to live in this life, that is, redemption.

JOIN THE REVOLUTION

And so the story goes. Movies are finally, centrally, crucially, primarily, *only* about story. And those stories are finally, centrally, crucially, primarily, *mostly* about redemption. With the proper tools in hand, one can accurately and objectively discern the messages, worldviews and philosophies of life promoted in the movies. The enjoyment of entertainment need not result in thoughtless abdication of one's critical faculties to the manipulation of emotion. When asked what you think about a movie, you can now avoid the generic responses "I liked it" and "I didn't like it" and offer a more informed response that articulates the redemption portrayed in the story. Movies are, after all, not *only* movies.

WATCH AND LEARN

1. Write out on a pad of paper the nine basic elements of story structure from this chapter. Then watch three films: a romantic comedy, a serious drama and an action movie. Afterward, fill in what you think fulfills each element for each movie.

2. Based on the character growth of the hero, write out the theme of each movie in the form of a moral, and consider how the movie makes its argument to prove that moral. In what way do you agree or disagree with that theme? How might you have done it differently?

ACT TWO

WORLDVIEWS IN THE MOVIES

4

EXISTENTIALISM

Many people consider philosophy to be irrelevant to our everyday lives: it is something practiced by academic eggheads in remote ivory towers, but certainly not something that results in practical living or "real life."

Contrary to this negative perception, the late Francis Schaeffer often pointed out that philosophy, though considered irrelevant by many people, was often a pertinent driving force of culture. The ideas generated by academic thinkers filter down through the high arts into the popular arts and are thus consumed by the masses, often without self-conscious recognition of their philosophical nature.[1]

People may not call their philosophical beliefs by their academic names of metaphysics (reality), epistemology (knowledge) and ethics (morality), but they operate upon them nevertheless. When a person says that someone ought not to butt in line at a movie theater (ethics) because everyone knows (epistemology) that "first come, first served" is the way the world works and that "what goes around, comes around" (metaphys-

---

[1]Francis Schaeffer, *The God Who Is There* (Downers Grove, Ill.: InterVarsity Press, 1968), pp. 13-48.

ics), then knowingly or unknowingly she is expressing a philosophy. When a kid watches the animated movie *Shrek,* he probably doesn't know about Carl Jung's theories of psychological types and the collective unconscious, but he is ingesting them nonetheless through those characters and that story adapted after the Jungian model.[2]

Everybody operates upon a philosophy in life, a worldview that defines for them the way the world works and how they know things and how they ought to behave. So philosophy is ultimately a practical reality for all of us. In this sense, *everyone is a philosopher;* some are just more aware of it than others.

One of the dominant influences on movies today is the philosophy of existentialism. In order to understand this influence, it is helpful to see the philosophy in its historical origins and context. In *Postmodern Times: A Christian Guide to Contemporary Thought and Culture,* Gene Edward Veith Jr. gives a brief outline to historical stages of thought in our Western civilization in order to show us how we got where we are now. He explains that the "premodern" phase, which included the Greek, Roman and early Christian empires, was marked by a recognition that reality was created and sustained by a supernatural realm beyond the senses. People believed in the supernatural and considered themselves subservient to it.[3]

By the 1700s, with the rise of the Renaissance culminating in the Enlightenment, society became "modern." That is, it began to see religion as ignorant, magical interpretations of a universe that is actually generated and sustained by naturalistic, machinelike laws, understood without any relation to deity. *Enlightenment* was the self-designation by this generation of humanists, who perceived the previous medieval era to be the "Dark Ages" precisely because religion was the dominant worldview, the "queen of the sciences." So their prejudices produced the oppressive

---

[2]The screenwriters admit *Shrek*'s Jungian ideas: "The book is very clever, because it knowingly used Jungian symbolism to tell the story," said Ted Elliott. "That was the most important thing that we wanted to take from the book—that *subversiveness*" ("Movie News—June 1, 2001," <www.videomoviehouse.com/June-01-2001.php>, emphasis mine).

[3]Gene Edward Veith Jr., *Postmodern Times: A Christian Guide to Contemporary Thought and Culture* (Wheaton, Ill.: Crossway, 1994), pp. 27-32.

term "Dark Ages," which served to demonize their enemies. The so-called Age of Reason was marked by naturalistic science and autonomous reason as absolute tools for truth. Man was the measure of all things, and reason was his god.[4]

Voices of dissent against the juggernaut of Enlightenment tradition were raised in the Romanticism of the early nineteenth century. And Romantic ideas became the seeds of our current postmodern condition. As Veith explains,

> Whereas the Enlightenment assumed that reason is the most important human faculty, romanticism assumed that emotion is at the essence of our humanness. The romantics exalted the individual over impersonal, abstract systems. Self-fulfillment, not practicality was the basis for morality. . . . Romantics criticized "civilization" as reflecting the artificial abstractions of the human intellect. Children are born free, innocent, and one with nature. "Society" then corrupts them with the bonds of civilization. . . . Romanticism cultivated subjectivity, personal experience, irrationalism, and intense emotion. . . . The romantics drew on Kant, who argued that the external world owes its very shape and structure to the organizing power of the human mind, which imposes order on the chaotic data of the senses. Some romantics took this to imply that the self, in effect, is the creator of the universe.[5]

Within this romantic milieu, existentialism was born.

A NECESSARILY OVERSIMPLIFIED BRIEF INTRODUCTION TO EXISTENTIALISM

Existentialism is a worldview that has many heads. So many varieties exist that it would take a book to define them all. There are even religious forms of existentialism to which some Christians lay claim. Famous translator and historian of existentialist philosophy Walter Kaufmann sums it up:

> Existentialism is not a school of thought nor reducible to any set of ten-

---

[4]Man as the measure of all things was a concept originated by the ancient Greek philosopher Protagoras. In some ways, the Enlightenment was similar to the Renaissance, which heralded a return to the classical Greek forms and principles of thought.
[5]Veith, *Postmodern Times,* pp. 35-36.

ets. . . . The refusal to belong to any school of thought, the repudiation of the adequacy of any body of beliefs whatever, and especially of systems, and a marked dissatisfaction with traditional philosophy as superficial, academic, and remote from life—that is the heart of existentialism.[6]

Though some of the best-known modern thinkers who have espoused existentialism are Jean-Paul Sartre, Albert Camus and Karl Jaspers,[7] its roots can largely be traced back to two men: Søren Kierkegaard (1813-1855), a Christian, and Friedrich Nietzsche (1844-1900), an atheist. We will address some of the specific beliefs of these men later in relation to particular films. For now I would like to focus on three emphases of the existential worldview in films today: (1) chance over destiny, (2) freedom over rules and (3) action over contemplation.

CHANCE OVER DESTINY

Existentialism accepts the Enlightenment notion of an eternally existing materialistic universe with no underlying meaning or purpose. While it does not deny the laws of nature, it sees these laws as order without purpose or meaning. This is what "the death of God" concept means—God does not "die" in the traditional sense, rather he ceases to be relevant because, without meaning behind the universe, the concept of God is unnecessary.[8]

The universe may be uniform, but its uniformity appears to our human perspective as a product of chance. And chance ultimately defies any notion of destiny or a fixed purpose toward which things are headed. Within our human perspective, *anything,* in this sense, is ultimately possible.

With the advent of quantum physics, the notion of chance as the underlying reality of our mechanistic universe has become even more fashionable. The uniformity of nature then becomes something that the mind

---

[6]Walter Kaufmann, *Existentialism from Dostoevsky to Sartre* (1956; reprint, Cleveland: World, 1970), back cover.

[7]In his *Existentialism,* Kaufmann adds to this list Dostoevsky, Rilke, Kafka and Heidegger.

[8]For an excellent summary of existentialism see James W. Sire, *The Universe Next Door: A Basic Worldview Catalog* (Downers Grove, Ill.: InterVarsity Press, 1997).

imposes on a chaotic universe. Since this universe has no inherent meaning, we lead ourselves to despair (angst) if we try to find any meaning within it. The mechanical cause-and-effect universe does not fit our human desires and thus appears to us as absurd.

Forrest Gump and its predecessor *Being There* are both popular movies that communicate the idea of a chance world in which events occur without purpose. The use of mentally challenged men in both films is a metaphor for chance itself. They have no "intelligent design" to their lives, and yet both of them become important figures in history without even realizing it.

In *Being There* Chance the gardener (a name chosen without coincidence) influences the president of the United States because Chance's simple-minded regurgitations of television platitudes are misinterpreted by accident as profound mysteries of genius. *Forrest Gump* has basically the same effect, with a simple-minded Forrest changing American history without even knowing it in a virtual exploration of the dual opposites of chance and destiny.

The title for the movie *Being There* is an English translation of the German word *dasein,* used by German existentialist Martin Heidegger (1889-1976) to define a human being as a field of probability, as opposed to the rationalist view of us as clear and distinct entities. At the last shot of *Being There,* just when we think there is some rational explanation for why this simple man has attained such status and impact on the world, he walks away from us on the surface of a lake—an allusion to the concept that mindless chance does in fact mysteriously guide the universe, like a god.

Lawrence Kasdan's *Grand Canyon* is another strong picture of a chance-ruled universe. In the very first scene Steve Martin's character, a Hollywood director of mindless, violent action movies, tells Kevin Kline's character, Mack, "Nothing can be controlled. We live in chaos, the central issue in everyone's life." This sets the stage for the rest of the movie, which is filled with the random evils of life. Police search helicopters and siren-screaming ambulances (symbols of the chaos) are ubiquitously in the background. The film concludes with one character's personal vision of standing on the edge of the Grand Canyon, where "we realize what a big joke we all are, our big heads thinking what we do is going to matter all that much." His conclusion is that we are all like gnats that land on the rump of a cow chewing its cud next to a road you ride by at seventy miles an hour. A pretty concise summary of the existential dilemma of meaninglessness (absurdity).

As in Heidegger's "being unto death," Sartre's "nausea" and Kierkegaard's "crisis of dread," these characters, through their near-death experiences, face the anxiety of their meaningless existence. And this is what the existentialist term "dread" (angst) means. It is not merely fear itself or a specific fear, even of death, but rather the general, overwhelming revelation of the meaninglessness of our existence. A specific encounter with death merely triggers this self-revelation.

The characters at moments wonder if all the chance happenings are miracles or messages from somewhere, maybe even sent by angels. But no answer is forthcoming from the supernatural. God is silent, because he is dead. They struggle with trying to make sense out of the pain and suffering in their lives but can ultimately find no rational answer. Fate and luck are ultimately what they believe in, condemning them to freedom in a random universe. Only by making individual choices to love other human beings do the characters find personal redemption in the midst of chaos. It is through their choices that they free themselves.

The existentialist writer Albert Camus wrote of the Greek myth of Sisyphus, condemned to endlessly rolling a stone up a hill, only to have it roll back down again. He says of this quest that "his passion for life won him that unspeakable penalty in which the whole being is exerted in accomplishing nothing."[9] That realization of insignificance becomes an important impetus for the existentialist storyteller.

Written by Zach Helm, *Stranger Than Fiction* embodies the eternal struggle of the existentialist to find meaning in an absurd universe of natural law and freedom from controlling destiny. Harold Crick (played by Will Ferrell) is an IRS auditor whose life has become a monotonous repetition of the same thing over and over (Sisyphus, anyone?). One day he hears a voice narrating his life with extraordinary accuracy, as if it

---

[9]Albert Camus, *The Myth of Sisyphus and Other Essays* (New York: Random House, 1955), p. 89.

were a novel. And only he can hear the voice. He visits a professor of literature (Dustin Hoffman), who tries to figure out if Harold's story is a comedy or a tragedy. When Harold discovers that the voice is that of a famous tragedist, Karen Eiffel (played by Emma Thompson), he realizes that the new novel she is writing is somehow the life he is living. But when the narrator reveals that he is going to die in a freak accident (chance), he has an existential crisis of dread. He watches nature documentary programs on TV that reinforce his dilemma. The documentary speaks of a seagull being attacked by fiddler crabs, "The wounded bird knows its fate. Its desperate attempts to escape only underscores the hopelessness of its plight"—illustrating Harold's own dread to a T.

The lit professor tells Harold to accept his death because it results from an act of self-sacrifice, which makes it a tragedy, and tragedy is more noble and gives meaning to life. When Harold finally accepts the despair of his own mortality and proceeds to do the noble act that results in his death, the author changes her mind and decides to keep Harold alive because the kind of person who would do that kind of selfless act should be kept alive. At the end of the movie, the author, Karen, narrates her conclusion that reads like a manifesto of existentialist experience where meaning is found in mundane moments of pleasure amid a world of pain.

> Sometimes, when we lose ourselves in fear and despair, in routine and constancy, in hopelessness and tragedy, we can thank God for Bavarian sugar cookies. And fortunately, when there aren't any cookies, we can still find reassurance in a familiar hand on our skin, or a kind and loving gesture, or a subtle encouragement, or a loving embrace, or an offer of comfort, not to mention, hospital gurneys, and nose plugs, and uneaten Danish, and soft-spoken secrets, and Fender Stratocasters, and maybe, the occasional piece of fiction. And we must remember that all these things, the nuances, the anomalies, the subtleties, which we assume only accessorize our days, are in fact here for a much larger and nobler cause. They are here to save our lives.[10]

---

[10]It is possible to interpret the author, Karen Eiffel, as a symbol for God. In this interpretation, Harold is like a person who is living without God, and through the realization of his mortality, he discovers God and God's influence on his life. He then reacts against the idea that God is in control, but ultimately resigns himself to God's sovereignty be-

There is some measure of truth to the claim that we cannot control the world around us. Many things that happen in life, especially tragedies, appear to be "without purpose." The real irony, however, is that films expressing the notion of a chance universe in fact follow specific, predetermined rules of structure for storytelling.

Structure within a story means that everything that occurs within the story follows a preexisting plan, that is, an order with a purpose. One of the rules in effective filmmaking is that everything that happens in a movie has to have a purpose. From what a person eats to what is going on in the background, everything is precisely ordained by writer and director to communicate character, plot and theme. There can be no arbitrary events. Anything that does not advance the story must be thrown out.

In this way, the act of storytelling itself denies the notion of a chance universe without purpose. In order to communicate an idea about mindless indeterminacy, a writer would have to intelligently determine all the instances of "chance" occurrence in his story. He would be assuming as true what he is trying to prove false. So a determined universe is inescapable in the art of story. Yet a determined universe makes freedom, history and change philosophically impossible. Proposing that both chance and destiny are ultimately true is contradictory and self-refuting. So where's the balance? What kind of determination is true? The answer is in the storytelling.

The biblical view of destiny is that a personal God (as opposed to impersonal fate) created the universe, sovereignly controls and providentially destines all things that come to pass without forcing human beings against our wills or negating our responsibility (Rom 9). Storytelling reflects the Christian God and his providential determination of the free

---

cause he realizes God knows better. God then gives him back his life, and he is more appreciative of all the experiences he has. The reason I do not consider this the intention of the writer of the movie, Zach Helm, is for two reasons. First, the only real reference to God is a negative one. The supposed "god" figure herself, Karen, explains in a TV interview that she doesn't believe in God. Also, the literary professor reflects the current postmodern theory of stories that are about stories, not about something "higher" or transcendent. (See the chapter on postmodernism in this book.) Karen Eiffel is a distinctly human author writing a story about humans that reflects an imminent universe of stories, not a transcendent one. Also, Karen is a means to the end of Harold's happiness, which is the human-oriented philosophy of this story.

acts of human beings. A screenwriter providentially creates characters based on the kind of story he or she desires to tell. Authors determine every single word, every single act, good and evil, of all their characters, down to the jot and tittle, sometimes working for hours on just the right turn of a phrase or subtle plot twist. Even events that seem like chance occurrences in a movie, like a freak car accident or the lucky throw of dice, are deliberately written in by authors to direct the story exactly where they want it to go. Yet when an audience watches the movie, we see characters freely acting and morally accountable for their actions in a world where some things appear to happen by chance. Our knowing that the characters and their stories are predestined by an author does not make them any less valuable or their stories any less meaningful.

But this apparent opposition of free will and chance are shown by the end of the story to be parts of the ultimate self-revelation of the main characters and others—and that revelation was what the storyteller "predestined" in his orchestration of all the events. There is a plan to it all, even if the characters don't know it at the time. Thus storytelling reflects the ultimate storyteller of all history, God himself. In this way art becomes an apologetic for the truth of the Christian faith.

Premonition is a movie that deals positively with destiny. In the story, Sandra Bullock plays Linda, a woman who wakes up on alternate days into alternate realities: one, where her husband Jim is dead from a car accident, and one, a week before the accident. As she struggles with her sanity over this premonition of the future, she seeks to figure out what she can do to stop his accidental death. When she discovers that her husband was planning an affair with an office colleague, she then struggles with whether she wants to stop his death or not. A priest tells her that her problem is not these freak experiences but her lack of faith in something that gives her life meaning (God) and of something to fight for (her marriage). She chooses to fight for her husband, and her movement toward him rekindles his love for her. She is unable to change God's will, so her husband does get killed, but she learns to repent, heal and love in the face of the reality of death. In *Premonition*, destiny is not some unfair bondage to be freed from but rather the boundaries within which we can find faith, hope and love.

FREEDOM OVER RULES

The existentialist's distaste of systems and schools of thought is closely tied to the doctrine of the individual's personal freedom as opposed to external rules. If there is an underlying order to the universe, then we would all, by virtue of being part of that order or design, be automatons of fate. Law, be it nature or logic, is universal and unchanging. So true freedom, according to this worldview, necessitates that humans be unfettered by any external or internal laws or rules. This is what Sartre meant when he coined the phrase "Existence precedes essence"—we exist without any prior essence or fixed meaning.[11] Therefore, we human beings ought to create our own essence or meaning within that void by our free choices.

Sartre said we are "condemned to be free" because we want to have rules or order to give our lives meaning, yet there are none, and this is unsettling to the core of our being. Thus we are solely responsible for whatever happens in our lives. With absolute freedom comes absolute responsibility. Because we create our own lives by our own choices, we cannot blame what happens to us on anyone or anything else but ourselves. Responsibility for our actions is not the same idea for an existentialist as it is for a classical or Christian thinker.

In the existential view, since the universe is absurd, we cannot comfort ourselves by conformity to some external order like religion or philosophy. We must create our own meaning internally, create ourselves, create our own essence. Another way of saying this is that individual choice is our "self-creation." All external absolutes, all systems of order—be they moral, political or religious—are simply systems of slavery created by others, denying the individual's ultimate autonomous freedom in a chance universe. It is not just that religions or politics abuse people; it is that the very existence of a system of beliefs implies an imposition of some on others and is therefore intrinsically oppressive.

If we vie for the safety of conformity to others' standards, we have exerted what Sartre called "bad faith,"[12] or as scholar Walter Kaufmann

---

[11]Alasdair MacIntyre, "Essence and Existence," in *The Encyclopedia of Philosophy,* ed. Paul Edwards (New York: Macmillan, 1972), p. 60.

[12]Jean-Paul Sartre, *Essays in Existentialism* (New York: Citadel, 1993), pp. 147-86.

translated it, "self-deception."[13] Since we are left to our own devices in order to define ourselves and create our essence, then we must look within ourselves to our personal intuition, our personal experience to make "good faith" choices.

Besides the "controlling" nature of morality and social norms, the ultimate controller of all things is God. So it is no surprise that atheistic existentialism stresses "the death of God" and that religious existentialism stresses the "wholly otherness" of God. A "wholly other" God is a God who exists on a plane irrelevant to our rational scientific world, a God who can be encountered only by an irrational "leap of faith."

Freedom from God's "loving control" is an existentialist theme explored in movies such as *The Truman Show* and Steve Martin's *Shopgirl*. In *Shopgirl* Claire Danes plays a young woman who has to decide between a wealthy, fun older man uninterested in commitment (Steve Martin) and a young poor peer (Jason Schwartzman). At first, she goes with the older man and experiences the fun, but the narration tells us she is seeking for some "omniscient" person to come down into her life and give her meaning and intimacy to quiet her loneliness (shot from a heavenly "God's-eye view" through a sun roof).

She thinks the older man with his maturity can do this, but of course he cannot connect with her as she needs. Claire ultimately realizes she can "hurt now or hurt later," and finally chooses the young man who has by now transformed into more of a gentleman who has concern for making her happy. This is more than a love story about maturity and age-appropriate relationships. It is an existentialist parable about the human quest for transcendence in deity, but the ultimate inability of finding personal connection in that deity. God is like a nice rich old man, who is comforting in his control, but who is distant and not very personal, whereas our fellow humans are full of faults, but at least up close and personal.

A good example of a film about freedom over rules is *Pleasantville*, written and directed by Gary Ross. It's the story of two 1990s Gen-Xers (brother and sister) who find themselves magically transported into the

---

[13]Kaufmann, *Existentialism*, p. 222.

world of an old black-and-white TV show called *Pleasantville*. The obvious intent of the filmmakers here is to attack traditional morality as embodied in the 1950s *Ozzie and Harriet* mentality, which is portrayed as oppressive to the individual's freedom. "Black-and-white people" (a symbol of black-and-white morality) discover joy and turn into color when they make personal choices against society's norms. Most of these choices wind up being for premarital and adulterous sex, an expression of freedom through immorality.

In one scene a girl plucks a "colored" apple off a tree to eat—a symbolic pointer to the Fall in Eden as a positive growth for humanity. By choosing to eat the fruit, Adam and Eve were actually taking an enlightened step of maturity, making their own moral choices rather than following the rigid "traditional morality" imposed by God.

Pleasantville does not merely attack morals but also offers the proposition that *all* external norms are oppressive and that redemption is found in people making their own internal, individual choices. The promiscuous sister finds her redemption, after turning half the schoolgirls into happy whores, by choosing to hunker down and bury her head in books to secure a real education. The key to her redemption lies not in making a moral decision but in making her own decision apart from any external rules.

The absoluteness of "personal choice" is a theme in the film *Citizen Ruth*, written by Alexander Payne and Jim Taylor. Laura Dern is Ruth, a pregnant, drug-addicted, unwed mother who is fought over by both pro-life people and pro-choice people to either save or abort her baby. The conclusion of the story is that she walks away from both camps because each violates her freedom to direct her own life. All external value systems err in imposing obligations to any code of behavior, liberal *or* conservative. The absolute authority to choose lies in the individual.

A good example of a movie that counters the exaltation of autonomous freedom and rejection of traditional values is *Blast from the Past*, written by Bill Kelly and Hugh Wilson. This fish-out-of-water fairy tale of a 1960s family who mistakenly live in a bomb shelter for thirty-five years is an upside-down version of *Pleasantville*. A young man who has grown up in the shelter finally comes out one day into the 1990s and meets and falls in love with a young girl. The *Ozzie and Harriet* family values of chivalry and virtue that are ridiculed by modern society are all this boy knows. And it is precisely those values that make him the individual with the most quality and character in the angst-ridden, cynical, lawless world around him. Innocence and purity are elevated as virtue rather than embarrassment.

ACTION OVER CONTEMPLATION

It follows that if there are no rules and we must create our own meaning through our choices, then to fail to do so would be to waste one's life. Any action or experience would be better than the pursuit of mere intellectual knowledge. Existentialism repudiates the abstract reasoning of traditional philosophy as a dead end, preferring instead the concrete realm of experience. The modernists thought that through science and reason we would discover the underlying essence of things. But we cannot find such order or meaning in a chance universe. Science and reason only lead to despair (angst) because science and reason cannot uncover meaning or value; we must *create* meaning through our individual choices and action.

This rejection of abstract reason as a means of discovering truth in favor of concrete "experience" is what Kierkegaard meant when he said that truth is subjectivity.[14] Truth is not something outside of us that we discover through cold, impersonal propositions, but rather it is something we experience subjectively, inwardly and personally. This subjectivity is why such stress is placed on individual choice, commitment and action. Our acts, not our thoughts or ideas, define us. We are the sum total of our choices and actions. For the existentialist, we *are* what we *do*.

The influence of an existential emphasis of action over contemplation can be seen in many movies. *Paycheck*, a movie about the ability to see the future, debates the issue of determinism and free will. In response to the claim that knowledge of the future would ruin our life in the present, a character argues, "All we are is the sum of our experiences." *Alexander*

---

[14]Søren Kierkegaard, *Concluding Unscientific Postscript,* trans. David F. Swenson and Walter Lowrie (Princeton, N.J.: Princeton University Press, 1941), p. 116.

tells the story of the ancient marauding Macedonian multiculturalist Alexander the Great in his pursuit of world conquest. The movie contrasts the contemplative life of men like the intellectual Ptolemy with the gusto of ancient Greek action lived out in Alexander. The film opens with a quote from Virgil, "Fortune favors the bold." In other words, the consideration of right or wrong in behavior is an impediment to worldly success. Action is what changes the world, not rational contemplation. In good existential fashion, Alexander proclaims: "Fear of death is the cause of all our misfortunes." "Conquer your fear, and I promise you, you will conquer death." "In the end, all that matters is what you've done." So we are the sum total of our choices or actions in an amoral universe.

Thumbsucker is a quirky comedy about a teen who struggles to overcome his insecurities around his family, friends and schoolmates. He has tried all means of stopping his thumbsucking habit, from hypnotism to drugs for ADD, and has not been able to stop. A doctor tells him that we really don't have the answers to the human condition; each of our attempts to find the solution are just our confused way of wandering through life. Actions may be stumbling, but they are better than theories.

Stranger Than Fiction's Harold Crick is advised to do nothing in order to thwart the will of his narrator, but he does anyway and is almost killed by a freak accident with a wrecking ball. The literature professor chides him with "Harold, you don't control your fate" but ultimately tells him that he might as well just go out and live his life, acknowledging that the narrator may indeed kill him. "You have to understand," Harold responds, "this isn't a philosophy or a literary theory or a story to me. It's my life." "Absolutely, so just go make it the one you've always wanted." Action over contemplation. Go out and live life and experience it rather than theorizing or worrying about it.

KIERKEGAARD IN THE MOVIES

One of the consequences of an emphasis on action over contemplation in a universe of self-created meaning is that commitment becomes elevated over contemplation. If there is no underlying meaning or purpose to reality, then it is inauthentic to seek for that purpose. We won't find it. Every minute we spend trying to discover such meaning is another wasted minute we should have spent creating our own meaning through our own choices. Authentic living is made by committing to a course of action. And in a meaningless universe, that means commitment is ultimately a leap of faith.

As mentioned earlier, one of the grandfathers of existentialism is Søren Kierkegaard. This melancholy nineteenth-century Danish philosopher is the famous source of the concept of the "leap of faith." The leap is necessary, according to Kierkegaard, because reason cannot be successful in finding the true meaning of life in the universe. Rationality goes only so far. You can't prove or disprove God and meaning in life, because such things are contradictory to the rational mind. They are beyond proof and can be understood only by an irrational commitment of faith *against* the evidence. Whereas the secular existentialist claims there is no underlying meaning to life, Kierkegaard, as a Christian, thought there was (namely, God), but we can't find that meaning through contemplation of the rational mind.

Kierkegaard believed that humanity has three stages of existence: the aesthetic, the ethical and the religious.[15] The aesthetic stage consists of a person in bondage to his passions. He is egocentric, living for the gratification of his pleasures. He seeks the fulfillment of his senses as a means of significance. But eventually he realizes that he can never get enough this way and is driven to despair (angst).

KIERKEGAARDIAN ETHICS
Joe Versus the Volcano
City Slickers
Groundhog Day
Unstrung Heroes
Box of Moonlight

At this point, he takes a leap to the next phase, the ethical. In the ethical phase the person seeks discipline and order as a means of salvation. He commits to rules, obeying duty because he thinks that by order and moral obligation he may attain the meaning he seeks. But the stress of this impossibility again leads to despair and to another leap into the final stage, the religious.

---

[15]These ideas are developed in his books *Either/Or* (1843) and *Fear and Trembling* (1843).

When a person makes the final religious leap, he realizes full maturity and dependence upon his Creator through absolute devotion. This "purity of heart to will one thing," as Kierkegaard put it,[16] is marked by the suspension of the ethical by behavior that is normally condemned by society or even the conscience as immoral. But only by ignoring the mind can a person achieve the salvation he seeks. Kierkegaard used the example of God asking Abraham to kill his own son Isaac as the ultimate situation of the religious man, a person suspending his personal morals and understanding in order to find God.

Several movies of recent years are almost textbook examples of Kierkegaard. In *City Slickers,* written by Lowell Ganz and Babaloo Mandell, three friends are trapped in the aesthetic stage by their yearly pursuit of adrenaline highs at bull runs, scuba diving, baseball fantasy camp and target parachute jumping. Phil (Daniel Stern) engages in adultery because of his frigid, domineering wife. The youth-and-sex-obsessed Ed (Bruno Kirby) is on a perpetual quest for younger women to bag. And Mitch (Billy Crystal) reaches a midlife crisis, wondering, "When is it ever going to be enough?" Phil and Ed are in the aesthetic stage, while Mitch is an ethical man, always doing the right thing, the moral thing (that is, not sleeping around), but still lacking meaning in life as death looms on his horizon.

Mitch decides to go on a cattle drive with the other two in order to "find his smile." When he does, he meets Curly (Jack Palance), a tough, mysterious cowboy possessing enigmatic wisdom. Mitch asks Curly what he thinks the secret to life is, and Curly raises his index finger and answers, "One thing." He says, "Stick to it, and the rest of life don't mean a thing." When Mitch asks what the one thing is, Curly says, "That's what you've got to figure out."

After the long cattle drive, it finally hits Mitch that they were seeking the wrong thing all along. By trying to find out what the "one thing" is, they had missed the understanding that it isn't a specific one thing that they need; it's commitment to *any* one thing. It is single-minded devotion that satisfies the heart, not some external thing. This is Kierke-

[16]Alasdair MacIntyre, "Kierkegaard, Søren Aabye," in *The Encyclopedia of Philosophy*, ed. Paul Edwards (New York: Macmillan, 1972), p. 336.

gaardian commitment of the will—but without God.

In Danny Rubin's *Groundhog Day*, Bill Murray plays a cynical weather reporter who gets stuck living the same incredibly boring day over and over again (literally) in the worst hick town with the worst hick people he can imagine. As Sartre said, "Hell is other people."[17] This is an analogy for many who feel as if every day of their life is the same boring experience in which nothing really matters (shades of Sisyphus). When he realizes this curse, he reacts by going through the three stages.

First, since the end of every day reverts to the day before, he decides to imbibe in selfish things, since he won't have to suffer consequences. He pigs out on unhealthy food, seduces as many women as he can, robs a Brinks car, same day after same day. This is the aesthetic stage of complete abandonment to the flesh. The world becomes his playground. But this also becomes boring for him, and he is led to despair (angst) and starts killing himself in different ways, only to wake up alive again, as he was the day before.

Then he enters the ethical stage by deciding to use his knowledge of events to do the moral thing, to help people. Every day he saves the same kid from falling out of a tree, the same man from choking on food in a restaurant. But this messiah complex also leads to despair.

It is not until he decides to personally and selflessly love a woman (played by Andie McDowell) that he finds redemption. At first he uses his cumulative knowledge of her interests to woo her into bed, but then he realizes that his existence is not for himself but for selfless devotion to another. Again, it's the religious stage, including the same kind of commitment, but without God.

NIETZSCHE IN THE MOVIES

Nihilism is a particular vein of existentialist antiphilosophy that has its origins in Friedrich Nietzsche's writings. It is noted for its emphasis on the meaninglessness of existence because of the inability to rationally

---

[17]Jean-Paul Sartre, *No Exit and Three Other Plays* (New York: Alfred A. Knopf, 1955), p. 47.

justify moral standards external to humanity.[18] Although despair is a common disposition of nihilists, Nietzsche used it as his steppingstone to propose that individuals should optimistically create their own morality in the vacuum that is left. As Kaufmann notes, the genetic influence of Nietzsche's thought on existentialism is profound,[19] and so is his influence on Woody Allen. Let's look at the themes that dominate this Nietzschean evangelist of nihilism.

Many of Allen's films are chock full of angst-filled searches for significance and "final experiences" resolved in characters either accepting their insignificant place in the universe or self-destructing. In *Hannah and Her Sisters*, Woody Allen plays a character whose brush with mortality inspires him to engage in an existential search to find the meaning of life by actively trying different religions like Catholicism, Buddhism and Hare Krishna. The movie displays title cards through the film that express existentialist ideas like the "big leap" of faith (Kierkegaard) and "the meaninglessness of life" (Dostoevsky). His quest to "be logical and put the world back into rational perspective" lands him in a movie theater where he concludes in classic existential resignation to enjoy the experience of life instead of the mental torment of contemplating unknowable spiritual truths:

> What if the worst is true? What if there is no God and you only go around once, and that's it? Well, don't you want to be part of the experience? I'm thinking to myself I should stop ruining my life searching for answers I'm never going to get, and just enjoy it while it lasts.

Zelig is a comedy about a little guy with a bizarre psychological dysfunction who takes on the physical traits of those he is around. He ends up meeting historical figures like Stalin, Hitler, Churchill and others, and we see him looking like each one of them. This is a fable about a guy who has to realize that he has a problem with being "others-directed" and that he can only find redemption when he becomes "inner-directed" or "self-directed"—another Nietzschean theme. Allen Bloom, the distin-

---

[18]Robert G. Olson, "Nihilism," *The Encyclopedia of Philosophy,* ed. Paul Edwards (New York: Macmillan, 1972), p. 517.

[19]Kaufmann, *Existentialism,* p. 100.

guished political philosopher, notes:

> Woody Allen's comedy is nothing but a set of variations on the theme of
> the man who does not have a real "self" or "identity," and feels superior to
> the inauthentically self-satisfied people because he is conscious of his sit-
> uation and at the same time inferior to them because they are "adjusted."
> This borrowed psychology turns into a textbook in *Zelig,* which is the
> story of an "other-directed" man, as opposed to an "inner-directed" man,
> terms popularized in the 1950s by David Riesman's *The Lonely Crowd,*
> borrowed by him from his analyst, Erich Fromm, who himself absorbed
> them (e.g., *innige Mensch*) from a really serious thinker, Nietzsche's heir,
> Martin Heidegger.[20]

Bloom concludes with astonishment at how doctrinaire Woody Allen's
"Americanized nihilism"—a nihilism based on a profound German philosophy—has become in the American entertainment market.

Crimes and Misdemeanors marks the penultimate high point of Allen's crusade of nihilism. Martin Landau plays an upstanding doctor
who struggles with guilt over his adultery and consequent hired murder
of his mistress. His rabbi, who counsels him in spiritual matters, is going
blind, symbolizing the blind faith and inadequacy of religion.

Allen himself plays a filmmaker doing a documentary on a Jewish
existentialist theologian wrestling with the evil in the world. Landau remembers his dinner-table family discussions as a child in which his religious and atheist relatives argued over the Holocaust. The conclusion of
Landau's atheist kin: there is no God; there is only the will to power. The
reason why Hitler lost was not because he was wrong but because the
Allies were stronger. Might makes right, the ghost of Nietzsche forever
haunting celluloid.

At the end of the film Landau relieves his conscience by recognizing
that "in the absence of a god, man assumes responsibility for his own
actions." By freeing himself from the external oppression of religious
guilt, in a "tragic" freedom he carves his own future and so the past guilt
fades away. Condemned to be free—because all guilt is, according to

---

[20]Allan Bloom, *The Closing of the American Mind: How Higher Education Has Failed Democracy and Impoverished the Souls of Today's Students* (New York: Simon & Schuster,
1987), p. 144.

this nihilism, the product of an artificial pressure by an external code of conduct that violates our ultimate autonomy—the character gets away with murder and purges his conscience in the process.

In true existential expression of the ultimate control over the self, the Jewish theologian commits suicide (shades of Jaspers and Hemingway). To conclude the film Allen gives a final statement about life fitting of Nietzsche himself:

> We are all faced throughout our lives with agonizing decisions—moral choices. Some are on a grand scale. Most of these choices are on lesser points. But we define ourselves by the choices we make. We are the sum total of our choices. Events unfold so unpredictably, so unfairly. Human happiness does not seem to be included in the design of creation. It is only we with our capacity to love that give meaning to the indifferent universe. Most human beings seem to have the ability to keep trying, and even to find joy from simple things, like their family, their work, and from the hope that future generations might understand more.

"We are the sum total of our choices"—that recurring theme in existential movies rears its head again. In other words, morality and conscience are not objective reflections of the underlying moral order created by God, but rather are a function of the human being who creates meaning in a meaningless, amoral universe. This struggle with the origin of conscience as rooted in society and the desire to rid oneself of guilt from immoral behavior is a common theme in Allen's movies and, not surprisingly, in his personal life as well. After all, ideas do have consequences.

Sixteen years later Allen made *Match Point*, a seemingly virtual remake of *Crimes and Misdemeanors*. It's the story of a middle-class Englishman, Chris (Jonathan Rhys Meyers), who falls in love and marries a woman from a wealthy family, but continues in a passionate adulterous affair with an American actress, Nola (Scarlett Johansson). Nola becomes more and more demanding of his attention, even to the extent of threatening to reveal herself to his wife. Chris realizes that if Nola reveals the adultery to his family, he will lose his entire life of wealth and comfort and live in poverty with his passionate mistress. So he takes the only way out for a pragmatic nihilist: kill the mistress and return to normal life. Chris is shown early on reading *Crime and Punishment* by Dostoevsky, which is about Raskolnikov, a student who kills someone as an expression of his belief in the Overman of Nietzsche, the man who is "above society's petty constructed moralities." Chris kills Nola and successfully makes it look like a drug killing, and he gets away with the crime.

What is so significant about this movie is that it illustrates how much further Allen has sunk into his Nietzschean worldview since he made *Crimes and Misdemeanors*. Both *Crimes* and *Match Point* are about adulterers who have their adulteresses killed to protect their money and status in life. In *Crimes*, the hero wrestles with his Jewish religious moral heritage and overcomes it. But in *Match Point*, there is only one reference in the movie to religion and that is scorned by aristocratic snobbery as the "despair of faith being the path of least resistance." In *Crimes*, Allen sought to prove God was dead. In *Match Point*, he assumes it.

In *Crimes*, the "hero" hires a killer to do the dirty work, in *Match Point*, the "hero" does the murder himself. This marks a logical step in Allen's Nietzschean philosophy of morality. If there is no morality that is truly binding on us, then we ourselves should not feel guilty in killing those who are in our way. In hiring a killer *(Crimes),* you are still admitting a measure of guilt by having someone else do the dirty work. But in *Match Point*, Allen is saying, if guilt is socially imposed, then we should be able to kill with our own hands and get over it. Chris muses to himself after the murder, "You learn to push the guilt under the rug. The innocent are sometimes slain to make way for a grander scheme." Exactly the language of Raskolnikov, exactly the language of Nietzschean nihilism.

Match Point is not a moral tale condemning nihilism; it is affirming it. Unlike its literary reference, *Crime and Punishment*, the hero gets away with not paying for the crime, and he does not suffer from guilt, both cornerstones of Dostoyevsky's moral Christian worldview. At the end, Chris concludes in a monologue, "It would be fitting if I were apprehended, and punished. At least there would be some small sign of justice. Some small measure of hope for the possibility of meaning." Our desire to see the criminal pay for his crime affirms in us the mythology that there is purpose in the universe and that evil will be punished. So, because Chris is not caught and not punished, Allen is thumbing his nose in the face of meaning, purpose and God.

One caveat to all this Allenesque chic nihilism is what Francis Schaeffer referred to about God's image in man. Despite the dark worldview consistently driving Allen's work, God's image nevertheless is not without presence. *Cassandra's Dream*, a more recent Allen movie, is a classic tragedy about two young brothers (Ewan McGregor and Colin Ferrell) hired to kill a man in order to overcome their financial problems. After killing the man, one of the brothers easily accepts what they have done, while the other brother is haunted by his religious scruples of "breaking God's Law." He still believes there is a God and a Judgment Day and wants to turn himself in. Their dilemma is ultimately ended when the two brothers get into a scruff and the morally bothered one accidentally kills the other, and finally kills himself. They reap what they have sown. This classic tragic view of internal moral conscience and consequences that keeps creeping back into Allen's films may, after all, reflect the autobiographical struggle of unresolved issues in the filmmaker himself—hopefully.

NIETZSCHEAN ETHICS

Annie Hall

Manhattan

Stardust Memories

Hannah and Her Sisters

Bullets over Broadway

Deconstructing Harry

K-PAX

Eternal Sunshine of the Spotless Mind

The Weather Man

Beowulf

Synecdoche New York

Friedrich Nietzsche's oddball idea of "eternal recurrence" or "eternal return" was another logical result of the "death of God" philosophy regurgitated from ancient Greek Stoicism. Nietzsche understood that linear history, with its beginning, middle and end, reflected a Christian worldview of origins and purpose, so he tried to replace that linearity with a cyclical view in order to avoid the inescapable logic of God's existence from a finite universe. This view of eternal recurrence posited that the universe, being eternal, had no beginning but was forever changing. Since the universe is infinite, it will ultimately keep changing through every possible change, recycling all possible states over and over throughout all eternity. There is no heaven, no eternal reward and punishment; there is simply the eternal return of everything.[21]

Eternal recurrence fits well with the scientific theory of an oscillating universe, which posits that the universe is not merely expanding from the Big Bang but is eventually going to stop and fall inward into a Big Crunch—over and over again, like a bouncing ball, from Big Bang to Big Crunch to Big Bang and back again.

A cinematic expression of eternal recurrence occurs in *Eternal Sunshine of the Spotless Mind*, written by Charlie Kaufman. The story is a romance between Joel (Jim Carrey), a nerdish boring nobody, and Clementine (Kate Winslet), a wacky impulsive girl. They fall in love and out of love because they end up getting on each other's nerves. In order to purge herself of all the memories of Joel, who made her miserable, Clementine goes to a special doctor who can erase memories.

When Joel discovers her betrayal, he goes to purge his memories of her as well. Unfortunately, in the middle of the erasing, we are in Joel's mind, and he decides he doesn't want to erase her because there was so much good that he experienced with her. So he seeks to try to save some of those memories by harboring them in secret recesses of his mind. One of the characters at the memory erasure office quotes Nietzsche, not once, but twice, just to make sure we get it: "Blessed are the forgetful: for they get the better even of their blunders."[22]

The two lovers end up together again, without knowing who each other is, and start a romance all over. In a plot twist, the two of them learn that they have been together in the past and erased their memories, which makes them consider breaking up to avoid the inevitable suffering. Clementine says they'll just end up in the same cycle as before, ending in breakup and grief because their nature doesn't change. They are the same people, and they will end up doing the same thing to each other.

---

[21]Friedrich Nietzsche, *Thus Spoke Zarathustra,* in *The Portable Nietzsche,* ed. and trans. Walter Kaufmann (New York: Penguin, 1982), pp. 332-33, 341; and *The Gay Science: With a Prelude in Rhymes and an Appendix of Songs,* ed. Walter Kaufmann (New York: Random House, 1974), pp. 273-74. A. J. Hoover, *Friedrich Nietzsche: His Life and Thought* (Westport, Conn.: Praeger, 1994), pp. 174-83.

[22]Friedrich Nietzsche, *Beyond Good and Evil,* sec. 217.

But Joel tells Clementine, Okay. So what if that happens. He's willing to pay that price. There is so much fun along the way before they get there. They decide to just go for it anyway. And we see the skipping replay of their dance in the snow, a visual version of DJ remix techniques.

In this Nietzschean "morality" fable, the characters are doomed to the eternal return of their failures because we all remain eternally the same and never change. We are "redeemed" by stoically accepting the cycle and going along for the ride.

In *The Weather Man*, written by Steve Conrad, Nicolas Cage plays David Spritz, a ladder-climbing weatherman on the local channel who is struggling to get his big break. His kids are losers, his dad is dying of cancer, and he can't stop fighting with his wife. The central metaphor of the film is the unpredictable weather (read: chance). As one weather pro tells us, "It's just wind. It blows all over the place. I don't predict it." David echoes this realization in his life: "Things didn't work out the way I predicted." His life has become vanity, striving after wind. "I'm fast food," he concludes. "Every year, the possibilities of who I could be get reduced to one, who I am." Rather than changing and reconciling with his family, he believes people don't change, so he chooses his career in the big city. Pop nihilism, pop Nietzsche.

Beowulf, adapted by Neil Gaiman and Roger Avery from the Old English epic poem, is a pagan tale about the heroic exploits of the legendary Anglo-Saxon monster-slayer in ancient Scandinavia. In this modern adaptation, the warrior Beowulf is a mighty hero who battles the monster Grendel and, ultimately, a dragon to defend his hard earned kingdom, a kingdom expressed in feasting, "merriment, joy and fornication." One of Beowulf's advisors is a sleazy Christian convert of dubious character who tells another warrior he can go to heaven if he "accepts the one and only God." When the monster Grendel comes a munching, the Christian says, "Maybe we should pray to the new Roman God Christ Jesus. Maybe he can relieve our affliction." Beowulf responds in pagan pride, "No. We need a hero," and destroys the monster himself.

But an interesting turn occurs near the end of the film. After Beowulf falls into sexual temptation, he hides the dirty deed from his villagers. And that character flaw haunts him for years. When a dragon terrorizes his kingdom (and the cross of Christ is useless against it), he realizes it is the direct result of his past fleshly deeds and admits it is the "sins of the fathers" (a biblical term) that haunts him and causes the destruction upon his people. He is not the hero everyone thinks, for he is just a fallible man. Yet, now that he is old and no longer fighting dragons but wars with men, he complains, "The time of heroes is dead. The Christ God killed it. There is nothing left but martyrs, weakness and shame. We men are the monsters now." In other words, Christianity, in overthrowing pagan mythology, brought with it a turn from clans conquering monsters of the unknown to men conquering other men and nations. In this way, *Beowulf* subverts Christianity, which had originally subverted paganism by deconstructing trolls, dragons and other superstitions as false explanations for man's plight. But to the filmmakers it appears that this new Christianity is an imperialistic fun spoiler, removing the magic of the ancient heroic period and its revelry of "merriment, joy and fornication" and replacing it with shame culture.

Though the thematic emphasis on pride and the temptation of the flesh in the film could be construed as Christian, they are more germanely an expression of the classical tragedic notion of *hubris*. Hubris was the pride that led to the fall of many a Greek pagan hero, from the epic tales of Herodotus and Homer to the Athenian tragedies of Aeschylus and Sophocles. As Oedipus comes to rescue the city of Thebes from its plague and a riddling Sphinx monster in Sophocles' classic, *Oedipus the King*, so Beowulf comes to rescue the Danish mead hall from its plague of the monster Grendel. The parallels with Greek pagan heroism abound in this Old English poem.

Shades of Nietzsche abound in this modern retelling. Nietzsche's contempt for Christianity lay in what he considered contempt for the body, and life itself, in its search for spiritual abstraction and the afterlife. He praised paganism not because he believed in pagan gods but because he saw in it a more "earthy" and glorious will to power. Like the movie *Beowulf*, he considered pagan mythological deities superior to Christianity because they were "honest" anthropomorphic renderings of humanity's weaknesses and strengths (Beowulf's fleshly indulgence), while Christianity was a "corruption of souls by the concept of guilt, punishment and immortality"[23] (as played out in Beowulf's Christian advisor). "Christianity has cheated us out of the harvest of ancient culture,"[24] Nietzsche complained. He considered the Dionysian celebration of the senses to be embedded in the blood and soil virtues of pride, courage and freedom (the virtues in *Beowulf* as well). The Christian in the movie, however, embodied the antithesis of these "virtues": "Christian, finally, is the hatred of the spirit, of pride, courage, freedom, liberty of the spirit; Christian is the hatred of the senses, of joy in the senses, of joy itself."[25] *Beowulf* reflects the effect of Nietzschean resentment of Christianity over its pagan rivals.

QOHELETH SPEAKS

Existentialism is the foundation of many modern movies. The reason it is so powerful an influence is precisely because it is partially true. It arrives at the inescapable conclusion of life's absurdity from the modern premise that there is no God and that we live in a chance universe. If there is no God, then there is no ultimate meaning to the universe. If there is no ultimate meaning, then we are truly alone, condemned to our freedom, forced to create our own meaning. God and all forms of external rules, like morality, are oppressive forms of control.

The book of Ecclesiastes addresses this condition of facing the angst of a world without meaning. The Preacher, Qoheleth, agrees with the existentialist, saying, "Behold, all is vanity and striving after wind" (Eccles 1:14). He tries to seek wisdom, but this leads to despair. "For there is no lasting remembrance of the wise man as with the fool, inasmuch as in the coming days all will be forgotten" (Eccles 2:16). He experiments with the hedonistic pleasure-seeking of the aesthetic but concludes

EXISTENTIALIST REDEMPTION
Forrest Gump
Zelig
Crimes and Misdemeanors
City Slickers
Groundhog Day
Legends of the Fall
Babe
Match Point
Stranger Than Fiction

---

[23]Friedrich Nietzsche, *The Antichrist,* sec. 58, in *The Portable Nietzsche,* ed. and trans. Walter Kaufmann (New York: Penguin, 1992), p. 649.

[24]Nietzsche, *The Antichrist,* sec. 60, in *The Portable Nietzsche,* p. 652.

[25]Nietzsche, *The Antichrist,* sec. 21, in *The Portable Nietzsche,* p. 589.

again that "all was vanity and striving after wind and there was no profit under the sun" (Eccles 2:11). He even embraces absurdity, madness and folly, but yet again a crisis encounter with death fills him with angst, for "the wise man's eyes are in his head, but the fool walks in darkness. And yet I know that one fate befalls them both" (Eccles 2:14).

Yet the difference between the Preacher and the existentialist is the difference between redemption and resignation, heaven and hell. The existentialist concludes that in a godless universe all of our dreams and words are empty. Since there is no underlying meaning or creator, we create our own (in essence, we become our own "gods"). The Preacher, on the contrary, concludes that we must return to the God we have ignored, for only then can the experience of life be made meaningful again. "For who can eat and who can have enjoyment without Him?" (Eccles 2:25). "For in many dreams and in many words there is emptiness. Rather, fear God" (Eccles 5:7). This is not a leap into the dark of an irrational void; it is a reasonable return to the God we knowingly rejected (Rom 1:18-23).

It is also instructive that this man of experience would conclude, after "all has been heard," that truly authentic existence is not found in freedom from rules but in following the warning to "fear God and keep His commandments, because this applies to every person. For God will bring every act to judgment, everything which is hidden, whether good or evil" (Eccles 12:13-14).

WATCH AND LEARN

1. Have your small group read Ecclesiastes, and then get together to watch *Groundhog Day*. What experiences do Bill Murray's character and the writer of Ecclesiastes share? In what ways does the movie differ in viewpoint from Ecclesiastes? Try to illustrate your answers with actual texts from Ecclesiastes. Discuss how Ecclesiastes balances the extremes of despair and hope.

2. Watch any one of the movies mentioned in this chapter, and discuss how it deals with chance over destiny, freedom over rules and experience over reason. In what ways do you agree with the filmmakers, and in what ways do you disagree?

5

POSTMODERNISM

Many cultural analysts point out that we are currently in a "postmodern" society.[1] In its more complex form postmodernism conjures up such complex technical terms as *deconstructionism, semiotics, metanarratives* and *totalizing discourses.* But in a more generic sense it refers to the questioning of all claims to certain, objective and universal knowledge about reality.[2] It is a rejection of the exalted autonomous reason and scientific reductionism of modernism.

As previously stated, the premodern view of reality founded on the supernatural and discovered through faith was replaced by the modern view of reality founded on the natural and discovered through rationality and scientific observation. Even though these two stages of history could be considered hostile to one another, they still shared the belief in an objective and certain universal reality. The premodern and the mod-

---

[1]Gene Edward Veith Jr. claims that the term *postmodern* was originally coined in the 1940s by famous historian Arnold Toynbee but that it became officially acknowledged by some in the early 1970s with the destruction of the Pruitt-Igoe housing development in St. Louis. See Gene Edward Veith Jr., *Postmodern Times: A Christian Guide to Contemporary Thought and Culture* (Wheaton, Ill.: Crossway, 1994), pp. 39, 44-45.

[2]Stanley J. Grenz and John R. Franke, *Beyond Foundationalism: Shaping Theology in a Postmodern Context* (Louisville, Ky.: Westminster John Knox Press, 2001), p. 21; Veith, *Postmodern Times*, pp. 39, 44-45.

ern may have disagreed about the *nature* of reality, but they both believed that there *was* a knowably certain reality and that it was incumbent upon people to discover that reality and align themselves with it. But with the coming of romanticism and existentialism came the lack of concern for objective reality, replaced with a subjective interest in the human experience.

It is easy to see why the next step in philosophy would naturally be the questioning or denial of certainty and objective reality itself: the postmodern project. But like existentialism, postmodernism also has both a Christian version and a secular or atheist version. In its Christian incarnation postmodernism is a "soft postmodernism" that questions our dogmatic certainty and interpretation while maintaining the Bible as the ultimate source of truth about God, faith and practice. It is not that the Bible is questionable; it is our *interpretation* of the Bible that is *always* questionable. Because all reading of the Bible is ultimately interpretation, we must maintain a hermeneutic of finitude and "sinitude." Our finiteness and our sinfulness severely inhibit our ability to know objectively and for certain whether our interpretation of reality through the Scriptures is "the right interpretation." We can never escape our human sinfulness and therefore can never know truth "objectively" outside of our fallen ability to interpret. Christian postmodernism is not the rejection of reality or rationality, but a recognition of the lack of certainty in our knowledge claims because of a "chastened rationality," as postmodern Christian authors Stanley Grenz and John Franke explain.[3]

The secular version of postmodernism is atheistic and could be considered "hard postmodernism" because it denies not merely our knowledge of reality but in some cases reality itself. It ultimately rejects all absolute claims, and considers the Christian God to be the ultimate dictator of such absolute claims and in need of a revolutionary overthrow. The death of God in secular existentialism became the death of reality in secular postmodernism. Both these philosophies consider the claims of a biblical God to be inherently tyrannical because they impose an outside will upon humanity, which is considered to be autonomous and self-creating in its val-

---

[3]Grenz and Franke, *Beyond Foundationalism*, p. 23.

ues and knowledge. To be sure, there are significant differences between the two philosophies, such as the individualism of existentialism versus the collectivism of postmodernism, but as James W. Sire explains, "Existentialism is the philosophical basis for postmodernism."[4]

The two worldviews agree that since there is no underlying objective reality, then there is no absolute reference point to judge true and false, right and wrong, real and unreal. There is no ultimate order in the universe, no foundational reality, no absolutes that require our obedience. But whereas the existentialist idolized the individual as supreme, the postmodernist posits the loss of identity for the individual in favor of collective groups of people (cultures) constructing reality through their own interpretations and imposing them on others. We are not individuals with a capacity for objective rationality; we are products of cultures or "interpretive communities" that contain certain prejudices and biases inherent in our thoughts and language.

PRISON HOUSES OF LANGUAGE

Language can be a powerful tool to oppress people. One example is the use of euphemisms to justify evil deeds. A euphemism is an indirect word that is used in the place of a direct one in order to soften impact and shape attitudes. In the antebellum South, for example, proslavery individuals described blacks as "chattel" property in order to deny the humanity of those whom they were enslaving. In World War II the Nazis described their murdering of Jews as "the final solution to the Jewish problem" in order to deny the humanity of those whom they were murdering. In a very real sense, the language of a culture shapes the thoughts and actions of that culture.

These cases illustrate the ways in which language can be a powerful tool for oppressing particular groups of people by reshaping the thoughts of a society and justifying evil deeds. Traditionally understood, language seeks to describe or refer to reality with a more accurate use of language. We correct bad language and beliefs with more objectively true language. So we call "the final solution" what it really is: a Holo-

---

[4]James W. Sire, *The Universe Next Door: A Basic Worldview Catalog* (Downers Grove, Ill.: InterVarsity Press, 1997), p. 38.

caust of murder. And we call racism what it really is: damnable hatred. But the secular postmodern believes there is *no* objective reality, so any alteration of language is simply changing from one oppression to a different oppression. What we think is reality is actually a social construct of our language. We "see" through the filter of our language. People are therefore trapped in "prison houses of language."[5]

Another commonality between the two secular versions of existentialism and postmodernism is the negation of reason as a means of discovering truth. But rather than merely rejecting the ability of reason to discover truth, as the existentialist did, the postmodern now rejects reason altogether as a "mask of power" that is used by one culture to enslave another. Reason is not an objective criteria to discover transcendent truth, but a social construction of Western imperialism. The belief in objectivity actually objectifies people into tools for power. "Binary thinking"—like right and wrong, true and false—is an exclusionary expression that must be overturned for a pluralistic decentralization of society into segments of constituent people groups.[6]

Postmodernists focus on "deconstructing" a belief by uncovering the various hidden or unconscious cultural prejudices that shaped it, rather than determining the verity of a truth claim. After all, if there is no transcendent truth or objective reality, then no belief or worldview *about* reality can be verified. Propositions about reality are reducible to personal agendas or biases, so all debate or inquiry reduces to the uncovering of these biases. Postmoderns will even go so far as to say that personal identity is also an illusion, because we are constructed by our society. This is what is meant by the "death of the author." The individual identity of authors disappears when we uncover the social and cultural biases behind their texts.

This "hermeneutics of suspicion" is used by the postmodern to question all "metanarratives." Veith says, "'Metanarratives' are big stories

---

[5]Of course, the negation of objective reality and referential language is itself an objective claim using referential language. For the proposition to be true, it would necessarily be false.

[6]This warring tribalism is why so much of postmodernism is "rage-oriented," because it is founded in the elevation of personal subjective emotions over objective rational truth. If there is no objective standard, then the one who speaks loudest wins.

that give meaning to our little stories. They are 'large scale theoretical interpretations purportedly of universal application'; that is to say, *worldviews*. Postmodernism is a worldview that denies all worldviews."[7] In other words, worldviews, religions or even philosophies are simply extensive "stories" that we tell ourselves to create the world the way we want it to be. They are absolutes, and absolutes must be rejected.

And the postmodern emphasis is on story *as fiction*. Gone is the idea that any story is actually true. If there is no objective reality outside of ourselves, then all of our ideas of reality can only be fiction, rationalizations of our own prejudices. There is ultimately no such thing as nonfiction. All stories are fiction, even "true stories."

THE INVASION

An example of the deliberate attempt to communicate a postmodern worldview is the most recent remake of *Invasion of the Body Snatchers*, called simply *The Invasion*. Written by David Kajganich, this incarnation of the classic is about alien spores that come to earth via a space shuttle and infect people, turning them into a soulless, emotionless herd with the burning desire to infect everyone else with their bird-flu-like DNA. The DNA does not take over the body until the host is asleep, so the goal of this paranoid chase thriller is for the heroine, a psychiatrist name Carol (Nicole Kidman), to stay awake and rescue herself and her child from the infected herd.

The Invasion is a blatant parable of postmodernism. At a fancy dinner party, Carol debates with a Russian diplomat who claims that "what makes us human" is our animal nature "driven by primal instincts" and hidden behind a "thin veneer" of civilization, which is an illusion. Iraq, Darfur and other political unrest prove that we could have peace only at the expense of losing our humanity. The diplomat offers a nihilistic will to power as "the truth." Carol then appeals to the postmodern notion of truth as a social construct. She tells him, "When someone starts talking to me about the truth, what I hear is what they're telling me about themselves, more than what they're saying about the world" (deconstruction). She then proudly proclaims herself a "postmodern feminist."

---

[7]Veith, *Postmodern Times,* p. 49.

The central metaphor of the movie is the postmodern notions of the loss of identity and oppression of "the other." To the postmodern, our problems arise because of cultural imperialism; we see those who are not like us ("the other") as being a threat, so we oppress them. Modernism argues that the way we overcome our subjective prejudices and "otherness" is to unite under the allegedly transcultural objective authority of reason and science. We must suppress our emotions and use our reason to unite and solving humankind's problems, which arise from the irrational passions and tribal instinct.

In *The Invasion*, the infected people who are without emotions are the embodiment of modernity. They incarnate the suppression of human passion and individuality in emotionless affect. At one point, Carol's best friend, Ben (Daniel Craig), is infected and appeals to her to join them because the problems of the world are from our "otherness." He concludes in modern utopian fashion that they are "building a world without war, without poverty, without murder, without rape. A world without suffering. Because in our world, no one can hurt each other or exploit each other or try to destroy each other, because in our world, there is no 'other.'" They are like a grove of aspen trees that are all "completely connected in harmony with each other—as one." The infected body snatchers are a symbol of the modernists who claim that the suppression of our passion with reason will bring world peace (unity).

The only problem is, in order to accomplish this unity, we must lose our personal identity by dissolving into the collective group and suppressing our humanity, which is our passion and emotions. In a moment of self-revelation for the heroine, Carol muses that her scientific use of drugs such as antidepressants is really not all that different from what the virus accomplishes in suppressing the symptoms of our problems. In a way she has been guilty of aiding and abetting the modern enterprise of reducing our humanity to scientific and rational categories. Once the infection is overcome and people return to their normal selves, the movie concludes that wars and violence may continue in the world because of our distinct diversity, but we maintain the higher value of our humanity with such diversity.

What is ironic about the movie is that while proclaiming postmodernism as the solution to modernism, it actually makes an unwitting argument *against* postmodernism. In postmodern theory, there is no individual identity; we are the products of the prejudices and biases of our social-cultural community. This multicultural diversity may appear to be pluralistic or tolerant, but the result is really the opposite. The broader imperialism of a one-world unified modernism is simply replaced by a localized tribal imperialism, but it is still imperialism: people losing their individual identities, being defined by external systems of order, or metanarratives. The postmodern "self" has no more of an existence of individual identity than that claimed against modernity. The postmodern self is submerged into the culture and language it is a part of. Postmodernism is as much a suppression of the individual as is modernity, just on a local scale rather than a global one. But the result is the same.[8]

THE DARK KNIGHT

As mentioned earlier, *The Dark Knight* presents a postmodern morally ambiguous universe in its storytelling. The Batman seeks to maintain a moral code while fighting the ultimate agent of chaos, the Joker. This is a villain who cares nothing for money, sex or power. He is not crazy, he is just evil, something modern humanistic man cannot comprehend. As Alfred says, he "just likes to watch the world burn." The Joker even mocks our humanistic attempt to explain all evils in terms of past psychological victimization. He tells entirely different cliché stories about the origin of his mouth scars. The Joker is quite literally the ultimate postmodern *übermensch,* the next stage in the evolution of man who denies moral absolutes. If life has no transcendent meaning, then chaos has as much value as order. This is the meaning behind his claim that "I'm not a monster, I'm just ahead of the curve." He quotes Nietzsche with a comic twist, "Whatever doesn't kill me, makes me stranger." He

---

[8]In a way, this confusion of messages illustrates the postmodern nature of the production of the movie, which includes a pastiche of multiple viewpoints from the multiple producers and directors hired to make changes on the movie after it had already been shot and edited.

says, "The only morality in a cruel world is chance," and proves it by helping to transform Harvey Dent into a criminal through the chance of a tossed coin.

This movie asks the question, how far can one go to seek justice? Should we break the law in order to enforce it? Is everyone in this world morally compromised? Are moral absolutes livable? The one good cop, Lieutenant Gordon, is illegally allied with a wanted criminal (the Batman); good old Alfred talks of being on a peacekeeping mission that burned down an entire forest to catch a single criminal; the Batman stops Harvey Dent from torturing a terrorist for information, but then he ends up torturing the Joker for the same reason. Normal good cops seek to kill an innocent citizen in order to save unknown hospitals from being blown up; the Batman illegally wiretaps the entire city's cell phones in order track down the Joker.

Is there really a difference between the good guys and bad guys or is it all relative? Is there really goodness in society, or are we all capable of becoming the enemy? At first there certainly appears to be little difference between good and evil. Dent muses that we either die a hero or live long enough to become a villain. Harvey Dent is the most upright prosecutor of criminals in the city, yet fulfills his aphorism by becoming a villain himself through a tragedy. As the Joker claims, "When the chips are down, these civilized people will eat each other." The Batman has to fight SWAT officers in order to save innocent citizens at one point. Yet, it seems there is ultimately goodness in Nolan's Gotham universe. In a dramatic incarnation of the classic ethical "prisoner's dilemma," two ships of people, one filled with citizens, the other filled with prisoners, are given the choice to either blow up the other ship or be blown up themselves. But in the end, even the prisoners choose life and throw the detonator away.

Yet in spite of this apparent moral impulse, the movie ends with the Batman taking the fall for the crimes done by Harvey Dent in order to save all the good he had accomplished from being undone. As the Dark Knight concludes in quintessential postmodern fiction, "Sometimes, the truth isn't good enough. They need more. They need their faith rewarded." What matters is a story of goodness to inspire people to do right, not actual goodness, because *that* is a bit too impossible. It doesn't matter whether something is true, but whether you believe in it. We tell ourselves fictions in order to get by in a relative universe. *The Dark Knight* is not your average comic book movie; it is a postmodern philosophical treatise on ethics that equals the metaphysical inquiry of *The Matrix*.

PULP FICTION

Pulp Fiction, Quentin Tarantino's pièce de résistance, marked the breaking and entering of postmodern filmmaking into the mainstream culture from its more independent, art-house and foreign film environment. It was the movie that started it all, and it did so with style.

Before *Pulp Fiction*, many movies had used the flashback as a technique to break up linear storytelling into a more interesting variety. But *Pulp Fiction* told a story mixed up out of sequence, showing the middle at the beginning, bouncing back and forth in time, and even ending with a character's earlier life *after* showing his death. This subversion of linear narrative created a whole new postmodern, nonlinear context for viewing story.

And the style of the film also embodies the eclecticism of postmodern fashion. In his book *Introducing Postmodernism*, author Richard Appignanesi points out the legacy of postmodern architecture on the broader art world as returning to ornament, "with references to the historic past and its symbolism, but in the ironic manner of parody, pastiche and quotation."[9] Postmodern art is an eclectic mix of styles, borrowing from all movements, all systems, maintaining no style of its own except for the hodgepodge of disparate elements amalgamated into a diverse whole.

There is no better description of *Pulp Fiction* than pastiche. It revels in bad pop culture. The story takes place in an undisclosed time period that looks like the 1970s, with black Afros and long hair. The soundtrack is an eclectic mix of everything from Chuck Berry to the Tornados. We see *Clutch Cargo* cartoons (kitsch) and motorcycle exploitation films on the television, references to the Fonz from *Happy Days,* and—the apex of it all—an entire sequence at a retro diner where waiters dress up like fa-

---

[9]Richard Appignanesi, Ziauddin Sarder and Patrick Curry, *Introducing Postmodernism* (New York: Totem, 1998), p. 116.

mous people in entertainment history, like Ed Sullivan and Marilyn Monroe.

And *Pulp Fiction* is a world without absolutes, without the finer distinction of good guys and bad guys. In fact, there really are no good guys at all. There are only differing levels of comparative badness. Butch, the two-timing, fight-fixing boxer, is not as bad as the small-time lovey-dovey restaurant robbers. But they're not as bad as Vincent, the hit man with a heart of gold (and cultural sensitivity) who kills people. But Vincent is not as bad as Marsellus, the brutal gangland boss who kills people for giving his wife a foot rub. And none of them are as bad as the two kidnapping, torturing sadomasochistic hicks.

In many ways *Pulp Fiction* was one of the first self-consciously postmodern mainstream films, heralding a new way of looking at reality in storytelling. It would soon be followed by a plethora of movies playing with and questioning the difference between reality and fantasy, truth and illusion, fiction and nonfiction, authentic and artificial. This questioning of reality in the movies can be categorized into two ways, both of which we will look at: (1) the *fusion* of reality with fantasy and (2) the *confusion* of reality with fantasy.[10]

THE FUSION OF REALITY WITH FANTASY

Literature and film have often provided a portal between the two worlds of fantasy and reality, from rabbit holes to wardrobes to time machines. But the modernist approach to storytelling uses fantasy or illusion as a means of expressing the true underlying reality of existence. The action in *Star Wars* may have taken place in a galaxy far, far away, but this movie really tells a tale about good and evil right here in our own world. It took itself seriously as a world unto itself in order to capture and express *our* reality in the metaphorical terms of another world.

The postmodern sensibility questions the very idea of an objective "reality," so it concludes that story cannot be about reality; it can only be about *story*. It contains a self-awareness of its own narrative conventions

---

[10]I use the term *fantasy* here not in the specific sense of fantasy genre, with its mystical creatures and such, but in the more general sense of creative imagination as opposed to factual events.

and structure. Witness such live action/animation hybrids as *Who Framed Roger Rabbit? Cool World* and *Monkeybone*, in which the protagonists self-consciously interact with cartoon fantasy worlds that they know and understand to be cartoon fantasy worlds. *Enchanted* has a princess in an animated Disney-like world of fairy tales cursed to enter the live-action real world of modern day New York, where her notions of fairy-book romance are confronted with "reality." In the end, different characters exchange their places in the real world and the fairy-tale world based on their own preferences for the kind of story they want to live within.

Others use live-action fantasy, but the context is still the same: the intersection and fusion of reality with fantasy. In *Jumanji* and *Zathura* a board game opens a doorway for a world of fantasy creatures to invade children's real lives. *Finding Neverland* and *Bridge to Terabithia* use the idea of fantasy worlds coming alive in the minds of people awakening from their dreary lives. *Bedtime Stories* and *Inkheart* have protagonists with the magical ability to bring to life characters they find in books. *Pan's Labyrinth* embodies Bruno Bettelheim's theory of fairy tales, spoken of earlier, in a young girl coping with mortality and real-world evil by retreating into her own fantasy world of imaginary creatures. *Miss Potter*, the story of Beatrix Potter, author of the children's book *The Tale of Peter Rabbit*, shows her drawings come to life in her mind's eye.

Self-conscious storytelling is also the basis of the horror franchise *Scream* and its sequels. Here you have horror movies deliberately describing the conventions of horror movies *within* the movies themselves and then overthrowing some of those conventions or even mocking them. The equally successful horror-spoof franchise *Scary Movie* and its sequel takes it one step further and spoofs the *Scream* franchise—a spoof of a spoof. These are movies that are about movies that are about movies.

In *Scream,* writer Kevin Williamson has his characters talk about what happens in classic horror films, like *Nightmare on Elm Street, Halloween* and *Friday the 13th*, throughout the entire film, while the same things happen to them. The "rules" of horror films are laid out explicitly:

(1) You can never have sex. The minute you get a little nookie, you're as good as gone. Sex always equals death. (2) Never drink or do drugs. The sin factor. It's an extension of number one. And (3) never, ever, ever, under any circumstances, say, "I'll be right back."

Of course someone just then says, "I'll be right back"—and he is killed. The characters even speak of their own world in terms of it being a horror movie. The heroine, Sidney Prescott, doesn't watch horror films "because they're all the same. It's always some stupid killer stalking some big-breasted girl—who can't act—who always runs up the stairs when she should be going out the front door. They're ridiculous." When the killer attacks Sidney in her house, she tries to go out the front door, but it's too well locked, so she is forced to run up the stairs, just like the convention that it is. Later on Sidney's boyfriend describes life as "one great big movie. Only you can't pick your genre."

The idea of a story within a story is not novel. From the Bible to Shakespeare and other sources, plays within plays have been a helpful dramatic tool to ancients and modernists alike. The difference lies in the postmodernist's intent to focus on the story as a story, and *only* as a story, not as a means for communicating reality. Remember, for the postmodern there is no objective reality for art to communicate, so art is about art, not about something else. An obsession with the shallowness of genre for its own sake is the postmodern hallmark of identity.

Shrek, written by Ted Elliot, Terry Rossio, Joe Stillman and Roger S. H. Schulman, is another example of a self-referential genre movie, in particular, a fairy tale deconstructing fairy tales. It's the story of an ogre named Shrek whose life of angry solitude in the swamp is violated by homeless fairy-tale characters who have been dispossessed by the evil Lord Farquaad. In order to get his swamp back, Shrek must go and rescue Princess Fiona from a dark tower guarded by a dragon and bequeath her to Farquaad. He's interested in saving the princess only to save his swamp.

On the journey back, the princess openly complains about how this very story is not following the necessary structure of a fairy tale. She is supposed to be rescued by a handsome knight who loves her, not by an ugly ogre who couldn't care less about her. She's also supposed to be a fair, helpless maiden, not the impolite and obnoxious kung fu expert that she is. This kind of banter abounds throughout this anti–fairy tale, as does crude humor and other mocking of traditional fairy tales. In one scene, parodying a famous scene from a Disney movie, Fiona sings a song with a songbird, but she hits a pitch so high and loud that the bird explodes, and so Fiona cooks the bird's three eggs for breakfast.

The final moral of *Shrek* is also an upending of a traditional fairy-tale plot. Fiona is cursed by a spell that during the night hours changes her beautiful Barbie-doll looks into those of an ogre. But the spell will be broken and she will remain as "true love's beauty" permanently when she engages in "love's first kiss." By the end, she and Shrek have fallen for each other and they kiss. But rather than true love's beauty being the Barbie doll, she becomes the ogre permanently—which suits Shrek perfectly!

For all of *Shrek*'s anti–fairy tale veneer, it actually communicates some very traditional fairy-tale morals: one should marry for true love, not position or power; beauty is in the eye of the beholder; true beauty is the inner person; or as Shrek himself says, "You shouldn't judge people before you know them." This apparent anti–fairy tale turns out to be a traditional fairy tale after all—but with an attitude.

Lady in the Water, written and directed by M. Night Shyamalan, is a self-referential story about the mythical story structure of life. Cleveland (played by Paul Giamatti) is a manager at an apartment complex who discovers a nymph-like woman named Story in the building's pool. Story is supposedly there because of the fulfillment of some prophecy. She is to affect someone who will write a book that will change the country. In other words, the world is changed through Story.

As Cleveland seeks to figure out who is her target, he is told he must find several "allies." He asks a resident who is a film critic to help him, since he knows the conventions of storytelling. The critic then helps Cleveland figure out who in the apartment complex fits the bill for each element of mythic story: the Guardian, the Healer, the Circle of Sisters, the Interpreter and others. In ironic humor, the film critic is a cynic who can't appreciate stories and hates most movies precisely because they all have these same patterns and genre formulas. He is later caught in the hallway with a wolf monster and talks to himself about how this is just like a horror movie where the jerk gets cornered but gets away just in time. He gets chomped by the monster.

Atonement, adapted by Christopher Hampton from Ian McEwan's novel, is an epic romance of two lovers, Cecilia (Keira Knightly) and Robbie (James McAvoy) separated by the jealousy of a young girl, Briony. Briony notices the two lovers in secret, and because she has a crush on Robbie, she gets angry and accuses him of a sexual crime he did not commit. He is sent off to World War II to avoid jail, and the entire story is about his attempt to get back with his lover, Cecilia. They manage to do so in the end and to try to rebuild their lives together. But then, the film ends with Briony as an old woman, and we discover that the happy ending we witnessed was, in fact, not the truth but a fiction that she wrote in her new novel about her past. In fact, the lovers never got together but died apart in the war, unatoned tragedy. But, Briony concludes, reality is not redemptive, and we tell ourselves happy fictions so we can find meaning and feel better about life. This is a claim that there is ultimately no true atonement in life, so we make up happy endings in our stories to make us feel better. In a sense, our "happy fictions" are our self-concocted atonement: a truly despairing view of ultimate reality—and postmodern to the core.

OTHER FUSIONS

The fusion of reality and fantasy is given a more literal twist in Woody Allen's *The Purple Rose of Cairo*. In this story, the heroine's pathetic, miserable life with an abusive husband is improved when a dashing, romantic movie hero literally walks out of a movie screen and into her life. The movie explores the differences of the fantasy life we envision in movies and the hard realities we actually experience as the movie character has difficulty getting along in a real world that does not comport with his movie existence.

Another result of the fusion of reality and fantasy is the melding of real-life characters into fictional stories. After all, if the two worlds are blurred, then why not blur historical characters with other fictions? *I.Q.* is a "what if?" story about Albert Einstein matchmaking for his niece. Academy Award–winner *Shakespeare in Love*, by Marc Norman and Tom Stoppard, is a fictitious love story about how Shakespeare came up with

Romeo and Juliet, written and acted in the style of a Shakespearean romantic comedy. It is a story about a storyteller telling stories. *Girl with a Pearl Earring* is a fictional rendering of the origins behind Vermeer's famous haunting painting of the same name. *Anchorman: The Legend of Ron Burgundy* is a deliberate fictional farce about a true reporter. *The Brothers Grimm* is another fun fantasy about the real-life authors of fairy tales. *Becoming Jane* is an unashamedly speculative literary theory of how Jane Austen came up with the characters in her novels from her own life. *300*, the story of the Spartan warriors who held off the Persian army at Thermopylae, is a proudly deliberate legendary exaggeration of the story, which is ironically true to the mythical grandiosity of how the Greeks might have made it if they had movies.

The dark side of this storytelling genre is *The Player,* Michael Tolkin's black comedy of the insanity of Hollywood. It's a crime drama of a producer killing a screenwriter and taking the credit for his screenplay—and he gets away with it, defying the justice-oriented endings of most Hollywood films. Many movie stars appear in cameos throughout the film as themselves in this blending of fiction and reality. In fact, making a movie about the moviemaking business, with all its sense of shallow unreality, has become a genre in and of itself, hearkening back to the classics *Sunset Boulevard* and *Day of the Locust.*

HOLLYWOOD SELF-REFERENCE
The Big Picture
Swimming with the Sharks
Get Shorty
Burn
Hollywood
Bowfinger
Notting Hill
State and Main
The Majestic
Full Frontal
Hollywood Ending
The Last Shot
Team America: World Police
For Your Consideration

The mockumentary, a genre almost singlehandedly made popular by Christopher Guest, is a prime example of the postmodern twist on reality. It is a fictional farce masquerading as a documentary to give it a more "realistic" sense. Its central conceit is precisely our own self-conceit, how we see ourselves as more important than we are. Mockumentaries question our view of reality as being self-serving; we are prisoners of our own interpretation. Guest's first mockumentary hit was *This Is Spinal Tap*, which was a mockery of the self-importance of a British rock band in the early 1980s. *Best in Show* poked fun at the obsession of dog show handlers, *A Mighty Wind* chuckled at the exalted self-image of 1960s folk musicians in the modern 1990s, and *For Your Consideration* lampooned the search for significance in Hollywood actors who deceive themselves into thinking they might be nominated for an Oscar, based on Internet rumors—the ultimate fiction.

A Knight's Tale is Brian Helgeland's fictional medieval story about jousting, with the historical English poet Geoffrey Chaucer as one of the characters. In this movie, medieval jousting tournaments are staged like modern sports contests, complete with the crowd clapping to the song "We Will Rock You" by the modern band Queen, as well as a royal dance breaking out into modern choreography to a David Bowie song. Here is self-conscious storytelling about stories with no pretense to reality.

Perhaps the epitome of the fusion of fantasy and reality, of the past with the present, of a movie within a movie, is *Moulin Rouge* by Baz Luhrmann. This musical fantasy reinvents the myth of Orpheus as a turn-of-the-century Bohemian cabaret in Paris. Yet most of its songs are from the likes of Elton John, Madonna, the Police, David Bowie, the Beatles and other late twentieth-century pop artists.

TRUE LIES

Gossip

The Tailor of Panama

The Game

Under Suspicion

Mulholland Drive

Historical characters like Henri de Toulouse-Lautrec show up in this fictional paean to indulgence and style, an environment where the aristocracy (fantasy) commingles with the bourgeoisie (reality). It is hyperpaced and fragmented and even has a "play within the play" that recapitulates the same story that is happening to the characters themselves. In the movie an impoverished poet falls for a courtesan in a cabaret whom a jealous duke is trying to own for himself. The play that the poet has written and the courtesan is acting in, with the financial support of the duke, is about a Turkish harem woman who falls for a poor writer instead of her rich sultan. And the title of the cabaret play is "Spectacular, Spectacular"—

another reflection of the postmodern obsession with spectacle over depth, style over substance, story over reality.

THE CONFUSION OF REALITY WITH FANTASY

The fusion of fantasy with reality can be taken a step further into a blurring or confusing of the two to the point where we are not sure which is which or whether there is a difference at all. If *Pulp Fiction* opened the doorway to the use of nonlinear reality in popular movies, then two movies, *The Sixth Sense* and *The Matrix,* both released in 1999, marked the next step into the *confusion* of reality with fantasy.

In M. Night Shyamalan's *The Sixth Sense,* the main character, Malcolm (a child psychologist played by Bruce Willis), discovers that his own sense of reality is the exact opposite of reality. And there is no greater confusion than to think you are alive when in fact you are dead.

The Matrix and other sci-fi movies take this same reality blindness to a technological extreme. The genre of science fiction seems well suited for the postmodern fusion/confusion of reality. Steven Connor writes in *Postmodern Culture,* "Science fiction is a particularly intriguing case for postmodernist theory, precisely because the genre of science fiction belongs, chronologically at least, to the period of modernism's emergence. . . . Modernism experimented with ways of seeing and saying the real; science fiction experimented realistically with forms of reality themselves."[11]

Blade Runner was the cult classic that first gave us a postmodern questioning of the real and the artificial. Its hero, Deckard, is a bounty hunter tracing renegade androids who are virtually indistinguishable from real humans, only to discover in the end that he himself might be an android. This revelation remains deliberately ambiguous by the storytellers (less so in the director's cut) in order to leave us wondering and debating about it for years to come. Most books discussing postmodernism have used *Blade Runner* as their example of postmodern filmmaking in all its detail, so we will move on to more recent films.

---

[11]Steven Connor, *Postmodernist Culture: An Introduction to Theories of the Contemporary* (Cambridge, Mass.: Blackwell, 1997), p. 134.

The Matrix, The Thirteenth Floor and *eXistenZ* have all extended the *Blade Runner* real/artificial motif into a new horizon: virtual reality. The dawning of a new millennium of virtual reality in computers has brought a new vision of humanity and its future. And that new vision is a postmodern one through and through. What these movies do is establish a virtual reality made through computers that is so real that the characters do not know the difference between the virtual world and their real world—one of the philosophical corollaries to the postmodern notion that there is no "text," no ultimate underlying reality. If all we have are our own cultural prejudices, by which we construct the world around us, then in fact we exist in a continuum of infinite "realities," all relative to the individual and his or her interpretation.

The Matrix has reshaped the sci-fi genre for the new millennium and established the postmodern paradigm in storytelling. In *The Matrix* Neo keeps a computer disk hidden in the pages of an actual, well-known postmodern book, *Simulacra and Simulation* (in the chapter "On Nihilism"). The word *simulacrum* is defined by David Harvey as "a state of such near perfect replication that the difference between the original and the copy becomes almost impossible to spot."[12] In like manner Neo soon discovers that what we all think is the real world is actually a virtual world created by computers that have conquered the human race and turned people into energy sources to run the computers. We are literally having the life sucked out of us and have been given the illusion of the matrix so that we do not wake up to our slavery.

This syncretistic film mixes the Christian idea of spiritual rebirth with the Neo-Platonic notion that enlightenment is found in our "waking up" from our ignorance. What we think is reality is actually a dream state that blinds us to the true state of humanity. Morpheus, the person appointed to find "the One" who will free us from the illusion of the matrix, echoes the essence of this theme of questioning reality when he asks the as-yet-unenlightened Neo:

Have you ever had a dream, Neo, that you were so sure was real? What if

---

[12]David Harvey, *The Condition of Postmodernity: An Enquiry into the Origins of Cultural Change* (Cambridge, Mass.: Blackwell, 1995), p. 289.

you were unable to wake from that dream? How would you know the difference between the dream world and the real world?

Ironically, though the film plays with Eastern concepts of physical reality being a projection of mind ("there is no spoon"), the story still necessitates a real world that opposes the illusion. And this real world, which is not a creation of the mind, is bound by harsh reality, laws of nature, right and wrong. This real world is not even as enjoyable as the illusory world. The "enlightened" guys eat goop for food, dress in rags and fly around in a ravished, postapocalyptic environment without any sunlight. But it's clear that this dark reality is preferable to a fantasy illusion that makes us happy. Why? Because it's the truth—it's *reality*. And reality is ultimately preferable to dreams or illusions, even if it is harsh and depressing.[13]

Not all movies that deal with the illusion/reality game are sci-fi. It has become a creative technique explored successfully in such films as *The Usual Suspects*, in which the narrator telling the story of a criminal heist turns out to have fooled the police and audience about his own innocence. The narrator turns out to be the true criminal, and by the time he gets away, we learn that the entire movie we've just seen has been his deceptive storytelling—and we bought it. This film thus offers a postmodern challenge to how easily we are deceived about what we think is reality.

The technique of filming characters' lies as if they were truth has been used in many films. In *Under Suspicion* an effective police detective (played by Morgan Freeman) is so immersed in psychological analysis that through sheer verbal coercion he brings a wealthy man (played by Gene Hackman) to a tearful confession of a child murder. We even see the murder replayed through Hackman's viewpoint. The only problem is that Hackman is ultimately proven innocent of the crime, thereby illustrating the power of suggestion upon our memories and understanding of facts and reality.

Other movies tell a more traditional story about the vulnerability of our culture to the confusion of illusion and reality, and the descent into

---

[13]The independent film *Waking Life* (2001) by Richard Linklater is a postmodern polemic of a character who wakes up from dreams into other dreams and can never seem to find his way to "reality," all the while listening to a litany of individuals espouse their personal existential, postmodern and evolutionary philosophies.

self-deception that occurs when individuals play to that weakness. *Shattered Glass* tells the story of Washington, D.C., journalist Stephen Glass, who rose to fame as a staff writer for the *New Republic*, until it was uncovered that most of his stories and sources were either partially made up or entirely fabricated. *The Hoax* is the story of Clifford Irving's gutsy fabrication of an "authorized autobiography" of Howard Hughes in the 1970s. At moments in the movie, Irving begins to believe his own lies as he manufactures memories of facts in order to sound more convincing. The taglines of the movie play with the postmodern emphasis of story over truth—"Never let the truth get in the way of a good story"—and even call into question the trustworthiness of the movie itself, "Based on the true story. Would we lie to you?"

Another film that uses the inability to distinguish between illusion and reality is *Fight Club*, starring Brad Pitt and Edward Norton. In this deeply disturbing film adapted by Jim Uhls from the novel by Chuck Palahniuk, the main character, a nameless "Jack," struggles through an angst-ridden, white-collar, consumer lifestyle. He sees the emptiness of this experience and falls into faking terminal diseases so he can go to support groups and connect with those who are facing death and sloughing off the façades of life. For him, encountering death is a means of finding life.

But these vicarious encounters with mortality soon prove ineffective, and Jack meets Tyler Durden, a wild and crazy anarchist who starts a "fight club" with Jack where men can break through their meaningless existence via the shock of pain experienced in their fights. This is a creed of existentialism: authentic existence is discovered through encounters with pain and death that emphasize the urgency of living.[14] Or as the philosopher Heidegger would have it, "My own personal history is authentically meaningful when I accept responsibility for my own existence, seize my own future possibilities and live in enduring awareness of my own future death."[15]

It is here that Jack finally has a divine epiphany, or more accurately, a

---

[14]Peter Koestenbaum, "Jaspers, Karl," in *The Encyclopedia of Philosophy*, ed. Paul Edwards (New York: Macmillan, 1972), p. 256.

[15]Quoted in Terry Eagleton, *Literary Theory: An Introduction* (Minneapolis: University of Minnesota Press, 1983), p. 65.

diabolical bombshell, when he comes face to face with the fact that Tyler is his own suppressed alter ego that is leading him to self-destruction. Tyler was a creation of Jack's own mind. Now Jack must liberate himself from his unregenerate dark side if he is to find redemption. This theme of self-delusion and the depraved side of humanity is reminiscent of the classic Robert Louis Stevenson tale *Dr. Jekyll and Mr. Hyde.*

A movie that questions our epistemic search for truth and our inimitable propensity to self-deception is the low-budget independent sleeper hit *Memento*, written and directed by Christopher Nolan. This mystery thriller's central premise is about an insurance claims investigator named Leonard (Guy Pearce) who is seeking the man who raped and killed his wife. When he finds him, he will kill him. His problem is that he was himself cranially wounded in the attack and has lost his short-term memory in the process. He forgets everyone he now meets as well as everything that occurs in his life after the attack. Consequently, he can trust no one and must constantly rediscover what he is doing and who he meets every few hours or so. He ends up tattooing the most important things he must remember onto his body and takes Polaroid photographs of people, places and things in order to jot down important notes to himself.

The gimmick of this film is that it uses postmodern nonlinear storytelling. It tells the story in reverse! So we begin with Leonard shooting the alleged killer and then discover with the hero his past as we progress backward toward the beginning. This technique of reversing the entire story helps us experience the hero's lack of memory of his own experiences.

All along the way, we don't really know who he can trust and who is deceiving him. And as we get to the end of the story, which is actually the beginning, we learn that he killed the wrong man, because in the midst of a heated dispute with the very guy who was helping him he intentionally jotted down notes against him that weren't true. He vents his anger in a fit of rage, and because he trusts only what he has written (but can never remember that he deliberately wrote it wrong), he ends up killing the wrong man.

But that's only half of it. *Everyone* in the movie ends up using our hero in one way or another. And his own self-deception is highlighted by the fact that because of his memory loss, he ends up forgetting that he was the one who accidentally killed his wife! She was not killed in the attack; she was a diabetic, and he killed her by accidentally giving her an overdose of insulin. He "remembers" this story as someone else's story in order to alleviate his guilt.

Memento carries the astute insight that we are self-deceiving creatures by nature who are easily deceived by our own whims and are therefore unworthy of the faith we place in ourselves. If our epistemic starting point, our standard of truth and knowledge, is itself flawed, then our beliefs about the world are flawed and will lead to false conclusions and bad decisions. In other words, the starting point in which we place our faith had better be correct to begin with or we're in trouble. And it had better not be ourselves, because we are the source of our own problems. As Leonard repeats to himself in the movie, "We lie to ourselves to make us happy."

At the end of *Memento* Leonard tells himself, "I have to believe in a world outside my own mind. I have to believe that my actions still have meaning . . . even if I can't remember them. I have to believe that when my eyes are closed, the world's still there." Leonard here makes an irrational leap of faith in an objective world he cannot prove (due to his lack of memory) in order to live with meaning rather than absurdity.

A movie that downplays the truth of memories in favor of feel-good fictions and legends is *Secondhand Lions*, written by Tim McCanlies. It is the story of a young introverted kid (Haley Joel Osment) left one summer on the porch of his eccentric great-uncles (Michael Caine and Robert Duvall). The uncles don't like being around people, and there is speculation that they have a secret fortune stolen from Al Capone hidden somewhere.

The kid reignites their lives, and they bring fascinating fantasy to his. The uncle played by Caine ends up entertaining the kid with stories about the uncles' adventures during the war. The tales are depicted like an Indiana Jones story, very romantic, with the love of a princess and fighting Arabs in the desert. The moral of the story comes from Duvall when he tells the kid, "It don't matter if it's true or not. Sometimes, you just gotta believe in some things like courage and honor cause that's what it's all about." In an ironic twist at the ending, it appears that the stories may be real after all, when a son of one of the legendary Arabs flies in on a helicopter to visit the old geezers.

In *Big Fish* Will, played by Billy Crudup, tries to establish a relationship with his dying father, Ed, played by Albert Finney. Ed has been a teller of tall tales his entire life; a catfish the size of a man, a giant, a circus with a werewolf ringleader, a mysterious happy town called Spectre and many other tales fill his biography with magical imagery. Will figures his father lived in a fantasy world as an escape from the boredom of his real life. Ed yells back that he has been nothing but truly himself. When Will tells his own son the story of his dad's death, however, he believes his son is not ready to understand, so he embraces his father's fantasy tales and even recounts them to his son. Will says at the end, "A man tells his stories so many times, he becomes his stories. In that way, he becomes immortal." The movie suggests that fictions can capture the truth in a deeper way than mere historical recounting of events.

OTHER CONFUSIONS

The Blair Witch Project, an extremely low-budget box office hit written and directed by Daniel Myrick and Eduardo Sánchez, is another example of the postmodern illusion/reality confusion. It's a story of some young adults who go off into the woods of Burkittesville, Maryland, to make a documentary of the legend of the Blair witch—a tradition that seems to surround multiple murders throughout the local history. The moral of this parable of our fascination with evil is that without a moral compass to guide us, we will be overcome by the very evil that we seek to understand.

The kids get lost in the woods without a compass and are eventually overtaken by the killer behind the legend. The groundbreaking uniqueness of this story is its fabrication as a true documentary using the film footage discovered in the woods several years after the students went missing. This pseudo-documentary, "real TV" approach brought a new depth to the scariness of horror movies because of its pretended realism, and it spawned a genre that is being repeated in movies like *Cloverfield* and *Quarantine*.

Even the *Blair Witch* website, which was hugely successful, was designed to appear like a true reporter's presentation of historical facts and evidence surrounding the event and its history. And most disturbing of all, this blurring of fantasy and reality was so successful that many young people actually believed it *was* a true story—a rather macabre revelation of the gullibility of the postmodern generation, children who will believe falsehoods simply because they saw it in the media.

Sliding Doors is an example of the many-worlds idea as well as the "butterfly effect" of chaos theory, which states that the smallest changes in a system can result in dramatic ramifications on other interacting systems (e.g., small differences in weather patterns create widely divergent results). Gwyneth Paltrow stars as a woman whose life we see split into two lives that run parallel, with the mere difference of catching a train or not. In the one life, she *doesn't* catch the train and is therefore not home in time to catch her boyfriend in bed with another woman, keeping her life the same in its self-deception. In the other life, she catches the train on time and catches her boyfriend, and so her life takes a completely different turn. The movie intercuts between these "lives" of one person as they each head toward widely different conclusions. This butterfly-effect notion of many worlds is also apparent in *The One*, where characters interact with 124 different parallel universes, and in *The Butterfly Effect* and *A Sound of Thunder*, where time travelers muck up the past over and over creating multiple different endings in their present.

Some of the most recent cinematic expressions of the postmodern illusion/reality confusion is *Final Fantasy: The Spirits Within* and *Beowulf*. Based respectively on a video game and an ancient story of a warrior battling a monster, these two films use the most lifelike animation yet created. Every attempt was made with state-of-the-art software to create human characters that did not look like animated cartoons but like real flesh-and-blood actors. The stated goal of many computer animation studios is to ultimately achieve a style of animation that is so real that the audience will not know the difference. They will create virtual human characters that appear to exist but are actually manufactured illusions.

A Beautiful Mind is an exploration of the confusion of fantasy and reality. Genius mathematician John Nash suffers from schizophrenia and imagines several people into his life—people who lead him into paranoid delusionary behaviors. He doesn't believe that these people are hallucinations until he realizes that they haven't aged after many years. The drugs prescribed to fight his schizophrenia impede his mathematical abilities, so he decides to face his delusions without medication. With the help of his wife, he gains victory over his mental dysfunctions; the hallucinations don't go away but recede into the background.

The Jacket is a thriller about a Gulf War veteran, Jack (Adrien Brody), who is falsely charged with murder and is placed into an asylum where a doctor (Kris Kristofferson) uses experimental therapy on him. The vet is tied in a straitjacket and placed in a morgue shelf where sensory deprivation creates an altered state of consciousness that somehow projects him into the future. He is confused because the experience seems so real. But a doctor explains to him, "Your mind doesn't have the ability to distinguish between reality and delusion." While on one of his future time travels, he falls in love with a woman, and on another he discovers he has been killed (not long after entering the asylum) and tries to figure out how he can stop it. But he is unable to stop his demise so he decides to be in his alternate world at the very moment he dies, in order to transfer forever into that world.

Vantage Point is a story about the president of the United States being assassinated, as retold through the vantage point of eight different eyewitnesses or participants at the event. Rather than containing multiple worlds, this approach illustrates the multiperspectival nature of reality. Different people see the same facts differently and interpret them differently because of their own stories, coming to different conclusions about what actually happened. By illustrating the subjective nature of all observation and experience, indeed of all history, this is perhaps the most realistic application of the postmodern questioning of reality.

CONCLUDING NONSCIENTIFIC POSTSCRIPT

The claim that reality is not objective but subjective and relative leaves the postmodernist on the horns of a dilemma. If this relativism is not absolutely or objectively true for everyone, then there is no obligation to believe it. If relativism *is* absolutely and universally true, it would be false because relativism denies absolute truth by definition. So in order for relativism to be true, it would have to be false: reductio ad absurdum (reduction to absurdity).

Furthermore, we could not know that our perceptions of reality were in fact illusions unless we could point to an objective absolute standard of real versus illusory perceptions. The claim of illusion presupposes a knowledge of reality against which illusion is shown to be illusion; otherwise, you simply cannot know it is illusion. Rather than concluding that all is illusion and that we have no knowledge of reality, the honest skeptic will ask, how do I know which ultimate standard of reality is true?

And yet, in concert with postmodernism, it is entirely within the parameters of the Christian worldview to question our *views* of reality because the Scriptures affirm fallen humanity's reasoning and imagination as so infected by sin that our view of reality is "futile," "corrupted" and "darkened" (Eph 4:17-18, 22). In effect, the Bible declares that sinful humanity is in the matrix. In similar language to Morpheus, the Scriptures declare that unbelievers are born as slaves (Rom 5:12; Jn 8:34), blind to the real world (2 Cor 4:3-6), unable to even see reality unless one takes the red pill and awakens in his "afterbirth" (Jn 3:3).

Remember Paul's Damascus encounter with Jesus (Acts 26)? He was fighting the very one he thought he was serving. Reality was the opposite of what Paul thought it was. And the plot twist here is that even with God at the foundation of our worldview, our finitude and inability to understand reality knows no bounds (Job 38—41). Thus, even Christians should have a humbled hermeneutic or a chastened rationality in their own interpretations of the Bible and reality. It is good to question our views of reality because we have so often been wrong.

Postmodern analysis exposes many of the false assumptions inherent to our modern Enlightenment way of thinking. And many of the movies we have examined in this chapter do just that. While questioning our notions of reality, many of them do not deny reality altogether, and this makes them postmodern in a "soft" sense, not necessarily in a "hard" sense. There is a difference between *soft* postmodernism, which legitimately questions our notions of authority, certainty, knowledge and reality, without relativizing all truth claims, and *hard* postmodernism, which denies the possibility of all absolutes or of knowing reality at all, which is self-refuting.

In light of this balanced understanding, it would be inappropriate for Christians to disparage and condemn all postmodern techniques of filmmaking as inherently negative or antibiblical. The Bible itself uses such techniques as nonlinear storytelling (the Prophets), matrix-like delusions of reality (2 Kings 6; Jn 3), multiple perspectives (the Gospels), fictional stories about reality (parables) and an emphasis on story over rational dialectic (Genesis to Revelation). And the Scriptures use these techniques in the service of a metanarrative of objective reality that we can only see through a glass darkly (1 Cor 13:12). Much of how society conceives reality *is* wrong, and people are in need of an awakening from the dream of their own illusion—or more accurately, *delusion* (Rom 1:18-22). The postmodern illusion/reality dilemma within a biblically based context is a great storytelling tool to challenge our assumptions about reality and truth.

WATCH AND LEARN

1. Watch *The Last Action Hero* or *The Purple Rose of Cairo*. What is being professed about the nature of reality and fantasy, and how they affect each other? Refer to specific scenes and dialogue in the movie that reinforce your point. What claims are made about indulging in fantasy? What is the movie arguing about the proper place for fantasy entertainment in our lives? In what ways do you agree and disagree?

2. Watch *The Matrix*. Which world is better: the real one or the computer-generated one? Why? Examine the argument made by Cypher, the character who betrays Neo. In what ways does his attitude reflect those of actual people in our contemporary world? How does the movie reflect your own worldview on how people are deceived about reality?

6

OTHER WORLDVIEWS

Although existentialism and postmodernism are influential viewpoints in many movies today, they are not the only ones. In this chapter I would like to offer a brief survey of some other worldviews that have played at a theater near you: romanticism, monism, evolution, humanism and Neopaganism in the movies.

ROMANTICISM

A worldview that shares some overlap of ideas with existentialism is romanticism. In fact, romanticism in some ways predated and led to existentialism. Beginning roughly around the late eighteenth century, romanticism was not so much a defined philosophy as a diverse movement away from the results of the Enlightenment.

Romantics considered the calm, orderly, rational harmony stressed in classical science and arts to be deadly to the human spirit. Aristocratic norms were suffocating to the soul. The scientific analysis of nature was antithetical to meaning and value, which resided in the imagination. As Wordsworth wrote, "We murder to dissect." William Blake added, "Art is the tree of life. Science is the tree of death." Enlightenment reason and science attempted to tame nature, which resulted in the exploitation and dehumanization of the industrial revolution. So the romantics revolted.

The Encyclopedia Britannica explains some of the characteristic traits of the romantic revolt:

> A deepened appreciation of the beauties of nature; a general exaltation of emotion over reason and of the senses over intellect; a turning in upon the self and a heightened examination of human personality and its moods and mental potentialities; a preoccupation with the genius, the hero, and the exceptional figure in general, and a focus on his passions and inner struggles; a new view of the artist as a supremely individual creator, whose creative spirit is more important than strict adherence to formal rules and traditional procedures; an emphasis upon imagination as a gateway to transcendent experience and spiritual truth.[1]

Romanticism was a literary, artistic as well as philosophical movement. Some of its more visible advocates were the poets Wordsworth, Blake, Shelley, Byron and Keats as well as musicians Beethoven and Mozart, painters Goya, Delacroix and Turner, and the novelist Victor Hugo.

Because of the romantics' exaltation of emotion and denigration of reason and rules, one could say that the current theme, found in many movies, of following your heart instead of your head (or doing your duty) is a reflection of a romantic worldview in film.[2] The worldwide megablockbuster to end all blockbusters, *Titanic,* is a gigantic expression of this rejection of social norms in favor of personal intuition, or the heart-over-head view of the romantic. James Cameron uses the post-Victorian setting of the early twentieth century, with all its traditional propriety and alleged repression, to express a defiant romanticism.

---

[1]"Romanticism," Encyclopedia Britannica 2003 Ultimate Reference Suite DVD.
[2]Michael Medved is the one to thank for this concept of "follow your heart over doing your duty" in the movies. I first heard him point this out on his radio talk show and took a shine to it because, of course, it's true. He expounded how movies of yesteryear tended to emphasize doing one's duty over following the heart. I have added the interpretation that this springs from our existentialism-infected culture.

The heroine, Rose, is oppressed by a controlling and violent fiancé, Cal, who epitomizes the worst of a patriarchal aristocratic society. To the modern mindset, male headship leads *only* to oppression and violence, and so Cal is a male oppressor. Rose's redemption is found in rejecting her obligations to these social norms and choosing her own future by following her heart.

To be sure, the violent Cal is an undesirable mate for Rose. But the alternative in this story is not the rational choice to submit oneself to another *trustworthy* person. Rather it is the irrational resignation to one's intuitive feelings. Jack has Rose stand at the front of the ship and then close her eyes and release her grip to "feel" the freedom of letting go. When they dance, he tells her, "Just move with me. Don't think." When Rose disagrees with Cal over a Picasso painting (a postmodern artist), she tells him, "There's truth without logic." And that truth is in the heart.

ROMANTICISM

A Time to Kill

Jefferson in Paris

Meet Joe Black

The Mask of Zorro

Mulan

Star Wars: The Phantom Menace

Crazy in Alabama

Bicentennial Man

Hercules

Beyond Borders

Cold Mountain

Sideways

Finding Neverland

Take the Lead

When Rose first talks with Jack about her dreams, she wishes she could just "chuck it all and become an artist, poor but free," or maybe "a dancer like Isadora Duncan, a wild, pagan spirit." Here is a romantic, feminist longing. She envies "wandering Jack" because he lives the free-spirited life of a romantic artiste—he is poor but having fun, living a moment-by-moment, experience-by-experience existence. Jack's buddies fret over his impossible desire for the aristocratic Rose. "He's not being logical," says one. "Amoré is'a not logical," replies the other. Indeed Jack is not logical, because he is a romantic who lives by his heart. And when he is implicated in stealing Cal's huge diamond, Rose chooses to believe Jack against all evidence. *She listens to her heart.* At the end of the story she says that Jack saved her "in every way that a person can be saved" because he not only saved her physically but also freed her from the oppression of her social norms.

To be fair, Jack did save Rose from an oppressive marriage and from the nightmare of living a false life determined by others. As the pictures on her bedside at the end illustrate, because of Jack she would go on to experience the things she longed for: horseback riding like a man (not side-saddle) at the Santa Monica pier, flying a plane like a man (traditionally, a male adventure) and even living a romantic life (as the glamour portrait indicates). And in the final shot we see Rose die and find her way to "heaven" in the arms of her ultimate savior and redeemer: Jack—as she remembered him. To find such love of another human is the highest aspiration in this film, the chief end of man.

The literary genius of *Titanic* lies in Cameron's ability not merely to tell an interesting love story but also to incarnate the change of an era into the characters and even the ship itself. The story is used as a metaphor for the death of traditional order (patriarchy) and the rise of egalitarianism, with a new romantic ethos of personal autonomy. Cal and his stuffy, aristocratic, old-order bunch are controllers of women and proud of their intellec-

RECONSTRUCTING TRADITIONAL GENDER ROLES

The Color Purple

Thelma and Louise

Fried Green Tomatoes

The Piano

G.I. Jane

Girl, Interrupted

Titanic

Dr. T. and the Women

Mona Lisa Smile

North Country

Revolutionary Road

The Women

tual power, which is dying under the weight of its own pride. It is not without irony that this romantic tale of liberation should take place on the "unsinkable" *Titanic*, the highest achievement of humankind's "unsinkable" rationality and order, the fruit of the Enlightenment and resultant industrial revolution.

Following one's heart instead of one's head is a common idea in most romance movies. It often involves the pairing of a rigid, rules-oriented person with an unpredictable, free-spirited partner, thus making room for dramatic conflict and/or humor, as well as the romantic notion of redemption through passion. A variation of this romantic obsession with following the heart is found in most romantic movies depicting the love of two humans as the ultimate meaningfulness in life, transcending everything. The Beatles musical *Across the Universe* is a story about a self-interested artist and a social activist who fall in love. It argues that no matter what higher causes or purposes separate two people's lives, "all you need is love" between two people to overcome those problems. This is the exact opposite theme of the classic *The Way We Were* where political or social causes are shown to be of much higher value to who we are than love. *Feast of Love*, an ensemble drama of love stories, concludes, "[Human] love is the only meaning there is to this crazy dream" of life.

Some recent movies go against the grain of the follow-your-heart mentality. They affirm the need for redemption found in doing what is morally right over following your heart, or pursuing discipline over instant gratification. A movie that presents a remedy to the romantic obsession with the heart is *Sense and Sensibility* (1995), adapted by Emma Thompson from the Jane Austen novel. In the 1800s the word *sense* was a reference to the mannerly restraint of the mind, while *sensibility* referred to the passions. This dichotomy is played out in the two lead characters: Elinor (played by Emma Thompson) and Marianne (played by Kate Winslet).

Elinor, the mature, restrained one (representing sense), does not reveal her feelings readily. She is thoughtful and slow to speak but quick to listen. Her love for respectable young Edward is repressed because of his engagement to another woman and the potential for scandal. She refuses to let her passions interfere and break someone else's heart. So she patiently waits for another good man to come along.

Meanwhile, young and vivacious Marianne is a romantic (representing sensibility). She chides Elinor for her propriety: "Always prudence, honor, and duty. Elinor, where is your heart?" Marianne is in love with the idea of love, imbibing the passionate, romantic fury of young Willoughby, who is handsome, exciting, adventurous—and a fraud. Because of her slavery to her passions, Marianne fails to see this deception in Willoughby's treasure-seeking manipulation until it is too late and he dumps her, leaving her heartbroken and lost. She fails to see the steady and true love of the dedicated yet unflattering Colonel Brandon until she realizes that true love is commitment based on endurance and character, not feelings.

And Elinor receives her love in Edward after a long, painful loneliness when it turns out that Edward's engagement is broken. Their love for one another is finally expressed, and Elinor breaks out into the most powerful display of weeping in the film. Hers is a heart properly held in check by the head. In both cases, that of Elinor and of Marianne, the highest goal of true and abiding love is found in the restraint and subjugation of the emotions by the mind.

Another tenet of romanticism is the idea that we are saved by beauty. If our intellect is a form of slavery to science and reason, then our imagination is the means of spiritual freedom. William Blake spoke of "arts redeeming power."[3] Percy Bysshe Shelley wrote, "The great instrument of moral good is the imagination."

Finding Neverland, written by David McGee, is a quintessential romantic fairy tale. It's the story of the man who created Peter Pan, Sir James Matthew Barrie (played by Johnny Depp). He meets a widow (played by Kate Winslet) with three boys and befriends them all. One of the boys, Peter, has lost his innocence to cynicism because of his father's death. And now his mother, the widow, is dying of a sickness. Peter doesn't see the fun in life. He cannot play imaginatively with his brothers, because it's all just foolishness. He has a keen awareness of death. Barrie is more the child and tries to get little Peter to explore his imagination. So we have a man-child teaching a child-man how to rediscover imagination, to regain his lost innocence.

RATIONALITY AS OPPOSED TO THE IMAGINATION

FairyTale: A True Story
Finding Neverland
The Brothers Grimm
King Kong
The Legend of 1900

In true romantic passion, the already married Barrie misdirects his love toward the fun-loving widow who becomes his muse, rather than on his own boring aristocratic wife.

---

[3]Hans Rookmaaker, "The Artist as Prophet?" vol. 5, pt. 2 of *The Complete Works of Hans Rookmaaker* (Carlisle, U.K.: Piquant, 2003), pp. 172-73.

While they never consummate their emotional adultery, they embrace each other as soul mates. The only sin to the romantic is to restrain the heart. "Follow your heart" is his mantra. Doing the right thing becomes oppressive.

Neverland becomes the symbol for imagination, indeed salvation, and Barrie's wife wants him to take her there (in his heart), but instead he takes the widow. And we see this metaphor depicted when the widow dies. With all the religious fervor of a born-again Christian, a character proselytizes her to "believe in fairies, and it will make her well again." In her mind's eye we see an imaginative representation of her entering Neverland (read: heaven substitute). Eternal life is not resurrection in an afterlife but eternal youth in the imagination. Barrie tells her mourning sons, "Mom is still here on every page of your imagination. She'll be with you always."

This secular romanticism seeks to ignore God but maintain transcendence by hijacking the language and concepts of religious faith and substituting creativity and imagination for the deity. It worships creation in place of the Creator.

Art then becomes the means of redemptive activity and the artist its prophet. As Hans Rookmaaker put it in his article "The Artist as Prophet?": "The artist was seen as prophet, high priest, and in any case as spiritual mentor of humanity. This role was assigned to the genius, the genius as the creative force in human life. In a certain sense the idea of the genius was a secularization of the old concept of the divinely inspired prophet."[4]

Rookmaaker defines this understanding of the artist as prophet as "the idea that artists express their time, interpret it and are prophets, in that they with their artist's soul sense sooner than others what is essential and can therefore indicate what direction the future will take. In this they are ahead of us who are not artists, and this is why we often do not understand the newest art."[5]

So the artist-as-prophet myth goes like this: Prophets are ahead of their times, which explains why they don't fit in with "normal" society

---

[4]Ibid., p. 171.
[5]Ibid., p. 176.

and justifies their often selfish, juvenile and tyrannical behavior. Thus, they are misunderstood by the masses, accompanied by personal torment and decline into drugs, immorality or madness. It is their genius that is stultified by a mediocre world of "normality." In other words, it's everybody else's fault that they're such jerks. *Shine,* a biopic about pianist David Helfgott, is one example of this approach.

To be fair, romanticism is not confined to secular or pagan interpretations. Like existentialism, there have been many Christians who could be considered romantics in a limited sense. For instance, C. S. Lewis and J. R. R. Tolkien considered themselves romantics to the extent that they eschewed the excesses of modernism in dehumanizing man and devaluing the imagination. Sauron's minions of evil raping the environment to build a war machine was an illustration of how the industrial revolution killed the magic of life. Lewis wrote an apologetic for the recovery of mystery and emotion in the Christian faith with *The Pilgrim's Regress: An Allegorical Apology for Christianity, Reason and Romanticism.*

Just because romanticism is ultimately unbiblical does not mean that all of its claims are unbiblical or that God does not value imagination or creativity. There is some truth to every

ARTIST AS PROPHET OR ÜBERMENSCH

Gothic
Wolf at the Door
Sid and Nancy
Vincent and Theo
Impromptu
Shakespeare in Love
Naked Lunch
I Shot Andy Warhol
Basquiat
Surviving Picasso
Shine
Pollock
Quills
Frida
Girl with a Pearl Earring
Modigliani
Walk the Line
Immortal Beloved
Copying Beethoven
Goya's Ghosts

philosophy man conjures up. There has to be, or they wouldn't have the power to captivate souls. In my book *Word Pictures: Knowing God Through Story and Imagination,* I provide extensive documentation for the fact that God may use reason and propositional truth, but he uses imagination as the dominant means of conveying his Word in the Bible. In fact, one could argue that God values the images, symbols, poetry, emotion and stories of imagination far more than the logic, science, propositions and debate of rational discourse. God said, "I will be your God, and you will be My people" (Jer 7:23) (a "romantic" relationship), not "I will be your proposition and you will be my systematizers" (an intellectual abstract concept).[6] So the extremes of romanticism do not condemn a proper embrace of emotion, nature, beauty, art and imagination. A biblical approach to worldviews requires discerning the truth from the error through applying the lordship of Jesus Christ to every thought and idea (2 Cor 10:5; Col 2:8).

Imagination, when properly rooted in the ultimate Creator has true value and meaning in reflecting God's image. Imagination as *imago populi* (the image of man) is idolatry and spiritual death. Imagination as *imago Dei* (the image of God) is truth and redemption. One might say we all could use a little romanticism, couched within a Christian context, to overcome the dearth of humanness that modernity brings to our lives.

MONISM IN THE MOVIES

As indicated earlier, monism is an Eastern worldview that is becoming more fashionable in the West. Monism is the belief that all of reality is ultimately one and that distinctions among things are mere illusion *(maya)*. When I look at a tree or at you, the fact that I see the "other" as separate from me is an illusion because ultimately I am one with the tree and with thee.

Humanity's problem is therefore ignorance. The reason we act wickedly is that we do not know that we are one with all things. If people could only experience oneness with that which they see as separate, they would find peace. This is why monists say that all the different religions are merely masks for the same God. This pantheistic enlightenment is the redemption that is boldly evangelized in mainstream movies with similar premises like *Powder* and *Phenomenon*.

Powder, written and directed by Victor Salva, is the story of an *E.T.*-like rejected messiah. Nicknamed "Powder" for his albino skin, he is a young

---

[6]Thanks to Steve Schlissel for this aphorism.

man who is discovered to have the "greatest intellect in the history of mankind" and who is rejected by everyone for his "differentness." A lightning accident before his birth is the cause of his electromagnetic power and his ability to use a higher percentage of his brain than the rest of us.

In a similar spirit, *Phenomenon,* written by Gerald Di Pego, is the story of a simple, small-town mechanic, George Malley (played by John Travolta), who also is struck by a mystical bolt of light from the sky. After he picks himself up off the ground, his mind starts to expand and accelerate in intelligence, which results in alienation from his neighbors.

The redemption communicated by these films is twofold. First, their themes contain the postulate of the Enlightenment: salvation comes through reason. Both George and Powder are portrayed as thoroughly evolved men, superior in intelligence and highly sensitive to the human condition.

After George is hit by his mystical lightning, he is able to master overnight the Spanish he had been having a difficult time learning. He then goes on to learn Portuguese in twenty minutes. He reads three books a night, every night, comprehending the mysteries of photovoltaics and quantum physics. He starts to invent things that will solve people's technological problems, like more efficient solar-panel technology and a car that can get ninety miles to a gallon of manure. His mind is so energized that he cannot sleep, and he even develops telekinetic abilities, moving small objects with the power of his mind. Powder also retains everything he reads and blows away the IQ tests. And yet he is quintessentially a Christlike lover of all life, be it a deer in the woods or a rebellious, hateful reform school kid.

George is also a Christ figure. Because people cannot understand his newly acquired powers, they become afraid of him, thinking he was touched by aliens. But not the woman he has fallen in love with—or her children. George soon discovers the real reason for his increased brain power: a tumor has buried its roots deep into his brain, and in a strange twist of fate, instead of attacking his brain, it has energized it to its height of genius.

But the tumor finally runs its course and begins to kill George. The kids are sad to see him dying and think they will miss him, but he gives them a humanist "last supper" by telling them to bite into an apple because, when we eat an apple, "it becomes part of us, and we can take it with us forever." Meanwhile, the song "Have a Little Faith in Me" plays over the visuals of the kids taking bites in remembrance of George.

The movie ends with a "resurrection" scene of a huge, once-unfruitful field, now ripe with a harvest of corn because of George's advice. We are witnesses to a secular miracle of rebirth, the dying and rising of a corn god. And we see, one year later, the whole town joyfully celebrating George's birthday with newfound community and happiness—a secularized version of church fellowship.

Powder and *Phenomenon* both conclude that if we only used more of our minds, then we would see our interconnectedness with all things and act more wisely. Knowledge and education breed virtue. George and Powder are examples of the human potential, the possibility of what everyone can be, if we only used our heads more.

Second, both movies offer a Westernized, bastardized version of monism. At one point in the movie, when Powder is at the carnival with his love interest, he explains to her that the reason why people are so messed up is because they see themselves as separate from each other and separate from everything. They think in terms of "distinctions" instead of "oneness." He explains that if we could only see that underneath there is no distinction and we are all one, then we would live in harmony and love. In this viewpoint, redemption is achieved through eliminating all distinction in our thinking.

In *Phenomenon* George sees more and more clearly as he gains his freakish knowledge and tries to reach out to the community by answering their questions. He tells them that the largest living organism in the world was discovered to be a grove of aspen trees in Colorado. Investigators found out that all the trees were "one giant organism with the same root system." It would be hard to find a film that makes a stronger pitch for the supposed underlying oneness of all things.

One film that does is *I Heart Huckabees*, written by David O. Russell. It's a movie that incarnates the philosophical battle that monism has with its diametric opposition, *atomism*. If monism is the belief that all reality is ultimately connected and one, atomism is the belief that all of reality is ultimately separated particles of matter (from which we get the word, "atom"). Monism is about ultimate unity, atomism is about ultimate diversity—connection versus alienation. The clever twist about *Huckabees* is that rather than having philosophy be the underlying structure of the film, it is explicitly part of the plot itself. This movie could be called a philosophical farce.

Albert Markovski (played by Jason Schwartzman) is a tree-hugging lefty protesting against the huge corporation Huckabees to keep it from plowing over a small marshland and putting up another one of its chain malls. But he's losing control of his enviro-wacko coalition to his friend, Brad (played by Jude Law). He's facing his own personal angst. A series of coincidences (chance) guide him to hire a husband-wife team played by Dustin Hoffman and Lily Tomlin, "existential detectives" who seek out meaning and purpose in the lives of people who can't find any in the universe. They have a "coincidence file" on each subject they investigate.

Hoffman and Tomlin are "monists" who specialize in "crisis investigation and resolution," as their business cards say. They seek to convince our hero Albert that his alienation is an illusion and that "there is not an atom in our bodies not forged in the furnace of the sun," and therefore "there's no such thing as you and me," "everything is the same, even if it's different," because "the whole truth is, everything is connected."

Ultimately, Albert's redemption will be his discovery that "everything you could want or be is everything you already are." This is Eastern style monistic self-enlightenment. But the problem is that the villain, in the form of French nihilist writer Catarine Vauban, as well as her disciple, Tommy (played by Mark Wahlberg), is also after our hero, to try to free him from the monists to realize that "it's all random and cruel," "nothing is connected, there is no meaning," and "the world is temporary, identity is an illusion, and everything is meaningless."

The witty repartee and philosophical bantering back and forth about ontology, metaphysics, "desire, suffering and pure being" is all rather clever and enjoyable for those interested in philosophy, but *I Heart Huckabees* is able to take what would otherwise be considered high-brow intellectual philosophizing and incarnate it into a comedy for the average viewer.

EVOLUTION IN THE MOVIES

Since evolution is an assumed paradigm of interpretation in modern society, it is no surprise that it shows up in not a few movies. As pointed out earlier in the chapter on storytelling, some films like *Planet of the Apes* and *A.I.: Artificial Intelligence* seek to demythologize religion by showing it as a social construct created to give meaning to what is ignorantly misunderstood about the "science" of evolution. But there are many others that use the evolutionary worldview as a foundation for their storytelling.

Bicentennial Man, adapted by Nicholas Kazan from Isaac Asimov's *The Positronic Man*, is the tale of a robot's two-hundred-year journey to become a human being. Robin Williams plays Andrew Martin, an android servant who by a strange anomaly (read: "evolutionary mutation") develops the capacity for emotions. Through sheer accumulation of data he develops sentience and transplants lifelike internal organs into his body, an obvious mirror of evolutionism. True to the materialist presupposition that intelligence is reducible to mere organized complexity, Andrew is said to be "every bit as complex" as (and therefore no different from) humans. By the end of the film, Andrew argues for legal acceptance as a human from the judicial powers that be and "dies" a "human being."

The computer-animated *Dinosaur*, written by John Harrison and Robert Nelson Jacobs, is a clever expression of the newer neo-Darwinian notion of evolution through cooperation rather than the old Darwinian paradigm of competition. After a meteor hits the earth and destroys the prehistoric Edenic environment, the dinosaurs must seek out a new "promised land" in which to live. But as they go on their journey, they are hunted down by the big, bad carnivores.

They begin their journey, squabbling with self-interest and allowing the weaker animals to be overrun and consumed by the "competitive" predators, those terrible lizards. But after a Moses-like herbivore encourages them to cooperate, they learn that they will survive through helping one another rather than competing for survival. *Dinosaur* thus embodies the theory of evolutionary psychology that cooperation rather than competition is a trait of survival of the fittest.

The older Darwinian notion of survival of the fittest still holds up though in other movies espousing an evolutionary worldview. Some movies embody the evolutionary ethic of survival of the fittest simply by portraying a story of a violence-filled animalistic world that focuses on "kill or be killed" with little or no reference to human value or morality. Movies like *Alien vs. Predator, Assault on Precinct 13* (2005), *Sin City* and *Hostel* are examples of this evolutionary metaphysic embedded in the ethos of the story, rather than explicit reference to science.

On the other hand, *Collateral*, written by Stuart Beattie, is a movie that argues against this evolutionary ethos by contrasting the survival of the fittest ethic with an ethic of self-sacrifice more akin to Christianity. Tom Cruise is Vincent, a hitman that hijacks cabbie Max (Jamie Fox) to take him around LA so he can pull off five hits for the evening. Max is a man who has sought to live safe and protect himself, while taking no risks in life or love. Max is all about self-preservation, while Vincent is all about predation.

Vincent's "gusto living" of killing is justified by an appeal to evolution and to the fact that life is meaningless and absurd, which means no behavior is morally right or wrong, we're just survival machines. Vincent tells Max, "We gotta make the best of it. Improvise, adapt to the environment. Darwin, sh-- happens, I Ching, whatever man, we gotta roll with it." "Our fate's intertwined, cosmic coincidence. That's the why. There's no reason. There's no good reason, there's no bad reason. We live or die." Max asks, "Then what are you?" Vincent concludes, sounding like Carl Sagan and Stephen J. Gould expounding on human insignificance in an evolving universe, "Indifferent. Get with it. Millions of galaxies of hundreds of millions of stars, we're a speck on one. We're a blink. That's us, lost in space."

MORAL DISCIPLINE OVER SELF-GRATIFICATION

White Squall

Unfaithful

Spanglish

13 Going on 30

Jersey Girl

Shall We Dance?

Just Friends

Coach Carter

Junebug

The Break-Up

You, Me and Dupree

Black Snake Moan

Bella

Vincent is the incarnation of evolutionary theory, man as animal without transcendent morality. And he is philosophically correct. If there is no transcendent meaning or morality, then no behavior can be morally condemned as evil. There are simply predators and prey, molecules in collision. Max has a revelation about his own fear and self-preservation and makes a decision to crash the car in order to kill the assassin along with himself. Max gives up his desire for survival and sacrifices himself to stop the evil. *Collateral* is a movie that deconstructs the evolutionary ethic of survival of the fittest as logically leading to the justification of evil, and counters it with the Christian ethic of self-sacrifice.

Another movie that communicates this logical conclusion of evolutionary theory is *The Downfall*, adapted by Bernd Eichinger from several books, which tells the story of the last days of Hitler in his bunker. As Hitler and his top henchmen use the language of Darwin, "evolution," "survival of the fittest," "natural selection of the weak," we see the logical fruit of the evolutionary worldview in the evil and self-destruction of National Socialism. The Nazis were simply following the logical dictates of evolutionary theory in weeding out the weak and unfit members of society.

Two horror movies that affirm the evolutionary worldview are *The Cave* and *The Descent*. Both movies are about deep cave spelunkers who get trapped down in the bowels of the earth, only to be hunted down by some carnivorous blind creatures of the dark. These creatures turn out to be humans, who were trapped below many years ago, and evolved into predators through tooth-and-claw survival and adaptation to their environment.

The Cave adds a jab at religion by showing a church with paintings of these creatures as demons. In other words, the belief in demons originated in an ignorant, prescientific misinterpretation of evolution. *A Sound of Thunder* takes this impossible evolutionary premise to an extreme by showing how a time-machine traveler changes all of history by interacting with the past, thus creating mutated monsters of evolution in the present.

Master and Commander, adapted by John Collee from several Patrick O'Brian novels, is a period action piece that attempts to portray evolutionary science as a moral corrective to man's violent war-like nature.

The central dramatic premise is the hunt by the British naval commander Captain Jack Aubrey (Russell Crowe) for a French warship. But the meat of the story is Jack's leadership of his men and his friendship with the ship's doctor and naturalist, Stephen Maturin (Paul Bettany).

The naturalist is a man of science, and Jack is a man of war. In the film, science always seems to take a back seat or supporting role to war rather than the pursuit of knowledge itself being primary. There is a sequence where they pass by the Galapagos Islands, the famous site of Darwin's finches, but about fifty years before Darwin would go there and write his world-changing book, *On the Origin of the Species*. The doctor wants to stop for some research, but Jack pushes on because the imperatives of war outweigh the "useless" examination of species—an obvious irony in light of the impact of evolutionary theory to come. This is intended to show the blind-sided nature of military hegemony. The centrality of war may win battles but may also keep us from "great scientific achievements" that will change the world far more than war.

But when the doctor is injured and needs to get to dry land for surgery, Jack puts his conquering aside and takes him back to the Galapagos Islands to heal, which allows some scientific exploration to be done as well. It is a powerful moral choice of humanness and shows the effect that the naturalist has on bringing balance to Jack's military leadership. In other words, for the overarching power of the military, science becomes the balancing power of compassion and reason. This naive religious view of the salvation of science fails to recall the weapons of mass destruction created by the men of twentieth-century science who applied the evolutionary ethic of natural selection through the technology of pogroms, gulags, gas chambers and firing squads.

Another attempt to moralize evolution is made in *Kinsey*, written by Bill Condon. It's the story of Alfred Kinsey (played by Liam Neeson), whose infamous pseudo-scientific studies on male and female sexuality, beginning in the 1930s, have been recently discredited by such authors as Judith A. Reisman, Susan Brinkman and others.[7] The scandal of it all

---

[7]Judith A. Reisman, Edward W. Eichel, J. Gordon Muir and J. H. Court, *Kinsey, Sex, and Fraud* (Lafayette, La.: Huntington House Publishers, 1990); Judith A. Reisman, *Kinsey: Crimes and Consequences: The Red Queen and the Grand Scheme* (Arlington, Va.: Insti-

is that Kinsey explored and frankly communicated details of sexuality in an American culture that had "suppressed" talking about such things. He sought to legitimize pornography and sexual perversion by wrapping it in an academic veneer of scientific analysis.

Kinsey's science was evolutionary materialism, the belief that all of reality is reducible to matter evolving through physical and chemical processes. A logical consequence of this belief is that there is therefore no such thing as absolute morality. Also, there is no moral difference between man and animals, because man is just another evolving animal, creating a diversity of values without ultimate right and wrong. As Kinsey says in the movie, "The only way to study sex is to strip away everything but physiology" (as if morality has nothing to do with human behavior); "Human beings are just larger, slightly more complicated gall wasps"; "Every living thing is different from every other living thing"; and "Diversity becomes life's one irreducible fact." The obvious agenda of this stress on diversity without unity is the moral equivalency of all sexual practices—the attempt to legitimize sexual perversion.

While the movie shows that some people's lives are ruined by sexual experimentation, its conclusion is that it *is* morally acceptable for others whose lives are satisfied with it. Perhaps the most telling scene of the whole movie is when Kinsey and a fellow researcher meet with a man so perverse in his sexual behavior that he has had sex (including rape) with thousands of people, dozens of species of animals, and molested hundreds of preadolescents, all the while keeping detailed journal entries on it all. This depraved monster is the ultimate scientist. The young researcher actually gets morally indignant and leaves, but not Kinsey. No, he says the kid just gets a little judgmental sometimes.

The criminal pervert reminds Kinsey of his own words, "Everyone should do what they want." But Kinsey replies, "I've never said that. Nobody should hurt anyone." But Kinsey *did* say it—when he said earlier in the film that if everyone is having all this socially unacceptable sex, then "everybody's sin is nobody's sin. Everybody's crime is nobody's crime." This is in fact another way of saying everyone should do what they want

tute for Media Education, 1998); Susan Brinkman, *The Kinsey Corruption* (Westchester, Penn.: Ascension Press, 2004).

and no one should be able to condemn them.[8]

What Kinsey and the filmmaker do not seem to realize is that the condemnation of pedophilia and other perversions unacceptable to them are also morally suppressive impositions upon nature. Adding a stipulation that "nobody should hurt anyone" is in fact a subjective moral judgment that suppresses certain kinds of sexuality. So, the question then becomes, who says nobody should hurt anyone in sex? Kinsey? So, Kinsey's sexual orientation is now the absolute? And whose definition of "hurt" is the absolute definition anyway? If there are no absolute sexual morals, then one man's hurt is another man's pleasure. One can easily see how this moral relativism is created to try to justify one's personal sexual preferences, but it ends up unable to condemn any sexuality without denying its own claims. And all of this in the name of evolution and nature creating "diversity" without moral judgment.

HUMANISM IN THE MOVIES

Another worldview of important consequence in many movies is humanism. The "Humanist Manifesto 2000" states as its "call for a new planetary humanism" that humanism is "a renewed confidence in the power of human beings to solve their own problems and conquer uncharted frontiers." The document is vague and generic in its claims to seek human rights and advancements through "scientific naturalism" and technology as opposed to "world views accepted today [that] are spiritual, mystical, or theological in character."[9]

As David Noebel reveals in his *Understanding the Times*, previous Humanist Manifestos and other humanist authors convey the humanist worldview more concretely as atheistic, "'rejecting supernaturalism' and 'seeking man's fulfillment in the here and now of this world.'" Humanism dogmatically asserts "the belief that humanity is the highest of all beings; and truth and knowledge rest in science and human reason."

---

[8]What the filmmaker does not go on to tell us is that the real person this criminal was based on actually continued in correspondence with Kinsey, who used his journal entries for his research. So Kinsey was a criminal—an accomplice to pedophilia and other crimes—and the filmmaker considers him a hero for it.

[9]Paul Kurtz, "Humanist Manifesto 2000: A Call for a New Planetary Humanism" <http://www.secularhumanism.org/index.php?section=main&page=manifesto>.

"The Humanist Manifesto II" proclaims its creed that "no deity will save us; we must save ourselves." Some of the more well known humanists have been famous skeptic Bertrand Russell, science fiction writer Isaac Asimov, the editor of *Free Inquiry* magazine, Paul Kurtz, and American educational philosopher John Dewey.[10]

Humanism includes some of the various elements of worldviews we have already discussed in relation to other movies. So in a sense, humanism is the broadest worldview that can be attributed to a movie that rejects the supernatural and considers redemption to be found in our own humanity through science and human reason. Let's take a closer look at a couple other movies that communicate a humanistic worldview but ironically subvert epic religious stories to communicate that humanism.

Troy (2004), adapted by David Benioff from Homer's epic poem *The Iliad,* is the famous classic Greek tale of the siege and fall of the city of Troy at the hands of united Greek forces around 1250 B.C. One of the distinctives of Homer's original poem is the place given in the plot to the pantheon of Greek gods. They laugh, they scorn, they fight and seduce their way into affecting the history of nations and lives of individuals. But this supernatural element is entirely deleted in this movie. In fact, it is turned on its head. One of the main themes in the movie is about the overthrow of religious beliefs by a belief in the power of man and his reason (humanism). Both Greek and Trojan cultures are depicted as superstitiously religious, but the "heroes" of the battle, the main warriors on each side, Achilles for the Greeks (Brad Pitt) and Hector for the Trojans (Eric Bana), are clearly humanists.

When told by his father, Priam, the King of Troy, that they can win the war because Apollo watches over them and Agamemnon (the leader of the Greeks) is no match for the gods, Hector replies skeptically, "And how many battalions does the sun god command?"

Achilles captures the Trojan temple of Apollo, and when his own soldier suggests it is not wise to offend Apollo, Achilles chops the head off the statue of Apollo in blasphemous defiance because he doesn't believe in the gods.

---

[10]David Noebel, *Understanding the Times: The Collision of Today's Competing Worldviews* (Manitou Springs, Colo.: Summit Press, 2006), pp. 59-63.

At a Trojan war counsel, Hector mocks the religious use of bird signs, and when challenged about his sacrilege, he explains his humanistic conversion, "I've always honored the gods. But today I fought a Greek who desecrated the statue of Apollo. Apollo didn't strike the man down. The gods won't fight this war for us." In other words, the gods are irrelevant superstitions; humans must save themselves.

A captured vestal virgin priestess of Apollo challenges Achilles, "Why did you choose this life [as a warrior]?" He responds in humanistic fashion, "I chose nothing. I was born and this is what I am." He returns the challenge, "And you, why did you choose to love a god. I think you'll find the romance one-sided [atheism]. The gods envy us. They envy us because we're mortal. Because any moment may be our last. Everything is more beautiful because we are doomed. We will never be here again [no afterlife]." In this humanistic subversion of the Greek religion, Achilles does not believe in the supernatural or in the afterlife. He believes that because this life is all there is, that makes this life more precious.

Throughout the film, the famous Greek concept of "glory and honor" is thrown around. But since these characters don't believe in an afterlife, their glory would not come from eternal life in an afterlife, but rather from being remembered in stories for "thousands of years"—a sort of literary afterlife if you will.

ODD COUPLINGS (REDEMPTION THROUGH PASSION)

What About Bob?

Legends of the Fall

Don Juan DeMarco

Bridges of Madison County

Tin Cup

Box of Moonlight

Forces of Nature

Chocolat

Bridget Jones's Diary

Along Came Polly

Finding Neverland

Meet the Fockers

The Notebook

In Her Shoes

The Matador

Stranger Than Fiction

Across the Universe

No Reservations

The emotional power of epics lies in their transcendence. Historical battle epics like *Braveheart, The Patriot, Last of the Mohicans* and *Rob Roy* linger in our souls because of the transcendence of the worldview in the story. The characters are fighting for things like freedom, love and honor because there is a transcendent reality beyond this life. In contrast, transcendence is denied in the very essence of *Troy*'s story, replaced by an immanent theory that meaning can be found only in this life.

In a way, *Troy* is an anti-epic, and for that reason it does not move the soul like the examples above do. Instead, it leaves one with a sense of emptiness. If a story denies transcendence, it denies the very foundation of any true meaning to our experiences on earth. Without a foundation in a transcendent (supernatural) love, courage and purpose are in reality mere physical spasms, foolishness and self-delusion. Without transcendent meaning, our self-created meanings in this life are simply fairy tales of delusion that only serve to make us feel good about our ultimately meaningless nonexistence.

Of course, the Christian worldview would agree with the criticism of pagan religion in the movie *Troy*, but the filmmakers should have taken a lesson from King Solomon regarding its humanistic emptiness:

> For there is no lasting remembrance of the wise man as with the fool, inasmuch as in the coming days all will be forgotten. And how the wise man and the fool alike die! . . . The conclusion, when all has been heard, is: fear God and keep His commandments, because this applies to every person. For God will bring every act to judgment, everything which is hidden, whether it is good or evil. (Eccles 2:16; 12:13-14)

Another humanistic war epic is *300*, adapted by Zack Snyder from Frank Miller's graphic novel about the Battle of Thermopylae in 480 B.C. between the Persian hordes and three hundred Spartan warriors. These three hundred Spartans held off hundreds of thousands of Persians at a narrow pass called the Hot Gates. *300* embodies a humanistic worldview, contrasting the nefarious religion of Persia and its despotic "god-king" Xerxes against the democratic rationality of Sparta. "Reason," a recurring word and concept throughout the movie, is linked with democracy and freedom, while religion is linked with tyranny and slavery.

The narrator of the story inspires his soldiers, likening the Persian army that is encamped against them to a "beast ready to snuff out the world's one hope for reason and justice." The Spartan king, Leonidas (Gerard Butler), is forced to consult the ephors for approval of going to war. The ephors are the religious leaders in Sparta, who are depicted as leprous lecherous sleazebags. They tell Leonidas to "trust the gods," to which he responds, "I prefer you trusted your reason." The narrator heaps ridicule and scorn on them as "diseased old mystics, worthless remnants of a past darkness," "remnants of a senseless tradition," "old wretches," "lecherous old men, souls as black as hell" and "worthless, diseased, rotten, corrupt." And all of that in one scene, no less. It would be an understatement to say that the storytellers here do not like religion.

Leonidas's wife asks the senate at Sparta to send an army to help out the Spartans at Thermopylae: "Send the army for the preservation of liberty, send it for justice, send it for law and order, send it for reason," she proclaims. At the end of the movie, the narrator continues to inspire the Greek armies to fight against Persia to "rescue the world against mysticism and tyranny. And usher in a future brighter than anything we can imagine," no doubt referring to the bright future of modernity.

Of course, the Christian would readily agree with the Spartan condemnation of the pagan idol worship of Persia. One is reminded of how God turned the Babylonian "god-king" Nebuchadnezzar into a stark raving madman to show him who was God. But *300* seems to consider all religion as "mysticism" at war with reason and freedom, which would ultimately include Judeo-Christianity. When the Persian pagan "god-king," Xerxes, confronts the Spartan king, Leonidas, he says to him, "Come, let us reason together," which happens to be a well-known quotation from the Judeo-Christian God in the Bible (Is 1:18). This subtle linking of diverse faiths reveals a humanistic worldview in *300* that believes reason can save humankind from the "ignorance" and "superstitious slavery" of *all* religion.

NEO-PAGANISM IN THE MOVIES

Neo-Paganism is a worldview steeped in the occult sciences. Traditionally, occultism is known for its spiritual emphasis and supernatural power orientation, along with a "secret knowledge" approach to redemption. Those who are initiated into a secret knowledge of the truth are enlightened and find a personal harmony with nature and the ability to wield nature magically for their own purposes. Since Nature is a feminine deity in this view, New Age goddess religion is a large part of many occult rites.

Rather than mere gender equality before the law, Neo-Paganism seeks the overthrow of Judeo-Christianity, in which men are the leaders in the home and public roles.[11] The Wiccan religion is simply modern witchcraft and embodies the Neo-Pagan worldview. Wicca rejects the monotheistic religion of Christianity as male and therefore oppressive. Wicca is pantheistic, worshiping many little gods that are all subordinate to the ultimate goddess, sometimes referred to as "Sophia" (the Greek term for wisdom).

A New Age twist to the goddess cult is the belief that the earth itself is a living organism with a feminine spirit or consciousness. This spirit is called "Gaia" (the name of the earth goddess in Greek and Roman mythology). *Final Fantasy: The Spirits Within,* the photorealistic animated movie, is a sci-fi interpretation of this Gaia hypothesis. The Gaia spirit of the earth fights back against environmentally destructive humanity by creating deadly phantom spirits to kill humans. M. Night Shyamalan's *The Happening* is another movie that embodies this idea of an earth with consciousness. Although it doesn't claim the Gaia hypothesis, it reflects a similar idea of an earth that "fights back" against the "polluting" humans, its plants deliberately releasing toxins in the air to kill humans. And doing so with a calculated intelligence.

The key to Wiccan or Neo-Pagan redemption is the casting off of Christianity with all its patriarchy, rationality and control, in favor of a free-spirited, feminine chaos of nature. According to Neo-Pagans, the Christian God is a "sky god," so Wiccans in contrast worship nature and the earth (Gaia). This is why Wiccans are often environmentalists and New Agers.

Witchcraft is ritualistic and therefore a symbol-oriented sacramental system. Wiccans engage in "drawing down the moon" ceremonies (an-

---

[11]Along with more traditional forms of feminism, Neo-Paganism shares a disdain for patriarchy. Of course, what is often portrayed as patriarchy (abusive, lecherous, traitorous men) is actually *the abuse* of patriarchy rather than the true form of it. In feminist movies most men are portrayed as weaklings, scoundrels, brutes or hypocrites, and the women are usually the only ones capable of quality human relationships.

other antithesis to the Christian "sun God," as they call him), indulge in ceremonial "Sabbat" celebrations of the changing of the seasons and engage in rituals of "magick" to harness the power of nature for their own benefit (as opposed to "magic," which is tricks of illusion).

Wicca is popping up in mainstream movies like *The Craft, Practical Magic, Chocolat, The Cell* and *Bewitched*. Anticult author Tal Brooke points out that some acceptable forms of "good" witchcraft are already adopted on television with *Charmed* and *Sabrina, the Teenage Witch*. He quotes Carol LeMasters, a witch author, about feminist origins and elements of Wicca:

> Alienated from Judaism and Christianity for their male biases, feminists of the late 1960s and early 1970s were searching for an alternative. They drew from a variety of sources, the most influential of which was Wicca. Women took from the Craft not only its worship of a goddess but its respect for nature, magical practices and ritual structure. Celebrations of moons and Sabbaths, casting circles, raising energy, chants and dances, candles and incense—all came from neopagan and Wiccan groups flourishing at the time.[12]

The Cell, written by Mark Protosevich, is a Wiccan Neo-Pagan story of occult redemption, or in other words, liberation from the "evil," patriarchal religion of Christianity. Jennifer Lopez is Catherine, a psychoanalyst who must enter the mind of a comatose killer in order to discover the whereabouts of his last victim, still alive, hidden in a building somewhere.

When Catherine enters the killer's mind, she is accosted by bizarre, dreamlike images that represent his patriarchal upbringing. And this patriarchy is the ultimate cause for the suppression of the killer's "inner child," represented quite literally as an innocent little boy flitting around painfully confused in the dark recesses of his mind.

We see suns and moons rise and fall in time-lapse synchronicity—an expression of the cyclical birth-and-death veneration of nature worship. She encounters images of the killer's abusive father baptizing him cruelly

---

[12]Tal Brooke, "Spellbinding a Culture: The Emergence of Modern Witchcraft," *SCP Journal* 24, no. 4 (2000): 8.

as a child (more anti-Christian symbols), leading him to an epileptic seizure. She sees a horse dissected and sliced up into coldly rational Cartesian slices. She encounters medieval Inquisitional tortures and the like. All of these are hideous expressions of masculine religion.

In order to defeat the killer, she lures him into her own mind and overpowers him with her goddess power, expressed in Wiccan symbols. She is all decked out as the goddess and engages in an abbreviated ceremony of drawing down the moon. With the Neo-Pagan god Pan in the background, she crucifies the killer, who is portrayed as a hunter-like "horned god," thus expressing the triumph of the free-spirited feminist goddess over the old patriarchal Christian God of violence and domination.

Read this quote from famous witch Starhawk to catch the Wiccan occult allusions also contained in *The Cell*:

> The horned God, the most male in the conventional sense, of the Goddess' projections, is the eternal Hunter, and also the animal who is hunted. He is the beast who is sacrificed that human life may go on, as well as the sacrificer, the one who sheds blood. He is also seen as the sun, eternally hunting the moon across the sky. The waxing and waning of the sun throughout the seasons manifest the cycle of birth and death, creation and dissolution, separation and return.[13]

All this Neo-Pagan symbolism is certainly not a magical incantation that will seize the soul of the viewer by merely watching it. But it is important to recognize what symbols are being absorbed by our culture because symbols carry powerful underlying effects on our collective culture. The acceptance of Neo-Pagan symbols in a society marks the emerging acceptance of new ideas, new philosophies, new religions.

Neo-Paganism can be seen as the driving force behind the Oscar-nominated *Chocolat*, adapted by Robert Nelson Jacobs from Joanne Harris's novel. In this clever version of Neo-Pagan redemption, an entire French town is oppressed by the moral scruples of a patriarchal Roman Catholic mayor. The town is then scandalized by the arrival of a mysterious single mother, who rejects the mayor's "conventional" re-

---

[13]Quoted in ibid., p. 12.

ligion in favor of her Mayan mother's pagan origins. She arrives in the middle of Lent, no less, and opens a chocolate shop.

Chocolate is a metaphor in the film for forbidden passions, and soon the chocolate seller turns the town upside down with her free-spiritedness. She helps a physically abused wife to leave her husband and empower herself in feminist fashion. The mayor opposes her and attempts to reform the wife beater along traditional religious lines, also known as Christian repentance.[14] His attempts fail, showing the inadequacy of Christianity to solve the problem. But the mayor continues on in his obsessive campaign against her and the "immoral" gypsies she keeps company with until he can no longer hold back his own passions for the chocolate she wields. He finally gives in and consumes the brown stuff with Dionysian abandon, learning that so-called intolerance and old-time Christian religion are no match for the alleged "freedom" of feminist Neo-Pagan liberation.

An interesting antidote to Wiccan Neo-Pagan earth worship is the movie *The Wicker Man* (2006), a remake written by Neil LaBute. The story is about a police officer named Edward Malus (Nicolas Cage) who investigates the disappearance of a child he fathered out of wedlock with a woman years ago. The woman is on an island off Puget Sound. When Edward gets there, he discovers the island is a matriarchal paradise of women. Little girls are taught in school that the essence of the male is the phallic symbol (mere procreation tools, call it: "reverse objectification"). Men's tongues appear to be cut out, and they are reduced to breeders and physical laborers who are forcefully uneducated. The island engages in harvest festivals of offerings to "the great mother goddess."

When Edward tries to figure out what is going on with these women, the head matriarch of the island explains to him the history of their Celtic ancestors who "rebelled against the suppression of the feminine," and were subsequently victimized by "persecution" such as the Salem witch trials. Edward responds, "Men are what, second-class citizens?" She responds, "No. Not at all. We love our men. We're just not subservient to them. They're a very important part of our little colony. Breeding,

---

[14]Christians who reject occult witchcraft as demonic are often demonized themselves in such movies as *The Scarlet Letter* (1995) and *The Crucible* (1996).

you know. . . . We procreate because that's the desire of the goddess. To assure ourselves a worthy offspring. The strongest, finest, the most sturdy of our kind." Edward surmises, "I see. Female."

The Wicker Man ends with a major twist, revealing that the missing child was merely a ruse to draw Edward to the island in order to capture him and offer him as a human sacrifice to the goddess at the harvest festival. This horror film reverses the usual Hollywood claims of the oppression of patriarchal "sky God" religion (read: Christianity or Mormonism, LaBute's original faith) and shows that matriarchal goddess-earth religion results in just as violent oppression. Put into postmodern lingo: this story is a subversive narrative that delegitimizes radical feminism and its Neo-Pagan counterpart as gynophilic male-hating imperialism.

THE WORLD IN DRAMATIC VIEW

If this exploration of different worldviews presented in movies proves anything, it is that the storytellers of cinema are engaging in their craft with an intent to communicate their view of the world and how we ought or ought not to live in it. They have discovered the power of a well-told story combined with a well-thought-out philosophy that is creatively embodied in a story through character, plot and image. In the same way that worldviews involve a network of individual ideas that are interconnected to serve a greater philosophical interpretation of our experience, so movies are a network of events, images and themes that serve a unified story by interpreting our experience through the effective means of drama.

WATCH AND LEARN

1. Watch *Serendipity* with some women and men together. Discuss the ways in which the fate language mirrors Christian language about God. In what ways does the fate language differ? What is the movie saying about passion and spontaneity in relationships versus commitment and loyalty? In what ways do you agree or disagree with this conclusion? How did you feel about the fiancés of the main characters and how serendipity affected them?

2. Watch *Chocolat* with men and women together. Discuss the ways in which the movie portrays moral and immoral people. In what ways is it inaccurate or stereotypical? Stereotypes usually arise from an imbalanced portrayal of exclusively negative or exclusively positive character traits. Choose one of the characters in the story (the mayor, the French woman, the young priest) or the groups of people (the gypsies, the townspeople) and discuss whether you think they are stereotypical or not. If they are stereotypical, how would you make their portrayal more realistic? What do you think is the correct biblical response to the French woman and her temptations entering the town? What do you think is the correct biblical response to the gypsies? What do you think is the correct biblical response to the wife-beating husband?

SPIRITUALITY IN THE MOVIES

JESUS

"Who do you say that I am?" That's the question posed by Jesus to Peter in the Gospel of Matthew. Peter's response: "Thou art the Christ. The Son of the living God." So goes the foundational confession of the Christian church.

But just what does the concept of "Christ" entail? What exactly does it mean to be the "Son of God"? So goes the history of New Testament interpretation, and with it a plethora of varying opinions, from the literal generational seed of the early church fathers to the mythical avatar office of modern New Agers, from orthodoxy to heterodoxy, from confused human to gnostic deity. Just about any and every conception of Jesus is available to the modern palette investigating the scholarship on this extraordinary man.

And for those interested in film history, the options are equally varied. A survey of the portrayal of Jesus in the movies yields an interesting mixture of both historical and mythical, human and divine, sinner and saint. In fact, one might say that the history of Jesus in the movies is precisely a history of the theological struggle between Christ's identity as

God and his identity as man. In this chapter, I will explore this identity as it works its way out in the movies through three different ways: Jesus as God, Jesus as man and Jesus as myth.

JESUS AS GOD

Among the earliest portrayals of Christ is Cecile B. DeMille's silent epic *The King of Kings* (1927). This extravaganza of special effects depicted the supernatural in all its glory, including a crucifixion scene of immense devastation that rivals the Holy Grail finale of *Indiana Jones and the Last Crusade*. Miracles are unabashed in this one.

In the movie, Jesus is depicted sanctimoniously unemotional and donning a subtle glowing halo at times. Scenes are blocked out to visually match over 270 different beloved religious paintings of the past. DeMille allayed concerns over sacrilege and blasphemy by concealing Christ's portrayer, H. B. Warner, as much as possible between takes and off the set.

Later in 1959, with the advent of sound, director William Wyler would maintain Christ's supernatural deity in *Ben Hur* by keeping him silent and off-screen in his various encounters with Judah Ben-Hur. Charlton Heston's mystically hypnotized gaze at the Christ, coupled with the ethereal music at each encounter, enhanced the effect.

Although *King of Kings* (1961) and *The Greatest Story Ever Told* (1965) both employed similarly unearthly music, they were already beginning to downplay the miracles and upgrade the humanity. We see a couple miracles of healing in both of them but are now hearing more "stories" about walking on water and other miracles than seeing them—whispering the possibility of exaggeration. The Last Supper scene of *Greatest Story* resembles Leonardo Da Vinci's humanistic Renaissance painting more than it does a Hebrew Passover.

Jeffrey Hunter played the youthful-blue-eyed-Aryan-WASP-movie-star Jesus in *King of Kings,* while Max von Sydow *(Greatest Story),* imported for his exotic foreign mystery, played a short-haired-long-faced-Sad-Sack-Byzantine Jesus. While *King of Kings* placed the gospel narrative in the midst of the broader epic-picture context of the political struggle of imperial Rome against the spiritual rebellion of its subjects, *Greatest*

Story emphasized the more pietistic spiritual transformation of individuals through the preaching of Jesus.

The solemn teacherly Jesus of *The Greatest Story* just doesn't hold a dramatic candle to the revolutionary Jesus of *King of Kings*, but both capture different sides of the same historical Messiah, an unassuming peaceful man whose radical message of personal repentance and transformation would scandalize society and bring down an empire.

Ironically, one of the earliest Jesuses in film is already a more humanistic one. D. W. Griffith's four-story epic *Intolerance* (1916) interweaves the fall of Jerusalem with the St. Bartholomew's Day Massacre of Protestant Huguenots by Catholic rulers, the fall of pagan Babylon to religious rivalry and the social destruction that moralistic reformers bring upon then-modern America. His Jesus is contrasted with the religious hypocrisy of the Pharisees.

Robert Powell's hypnotic-eyed Jesus-who-never-blinks that appeared in Franco Zefferelli's miniseries *Jesus of Nazareth* (1977) seems to have somewhat of a balance of humanity and deity. But miracles are at a minimum, necessitating an almost grunting effort by Jesus to accomplish them, and his most effective influence is his success as a storytelling rabbi.

JESUS AS MAN

Nineteenth-century German liberal scholarship had a profound effect on civilization through the efforts of such theological dark-hole, twentieth-century disciples as Martin Dibelius and Rudolph Bultmann, and more recently, the Jesus Seminar. Following the legacy of David Hume's empirical skepticism of the miraculous, these theologians operated upon an antisupernatural presupposition: they ruled out miracles by definition and reinterpreted them as having natural explanations, mistaken or misconstrued by believers as divine.

Jesus now became a human revolutionary who was *misunderstood* as God through the fanatical devotion of his followers. The Christ story changed from the New Testament concept of an individual God-man fulfilling prophecy to redeem his people into a modern Freudian messiah, a product of the psychology of the masses creating and establishing a messiah where none existed.

By the 1970s this antisupernatural theology was fashionable in the common culture, and it became acceptable to portray Jesus as a mere man without deity altogether. The rock operas *Jesus Christ Superstar* (1972) and *Godspell* (1973) capitalized on this humanistic castration of deity. Both movies ended with Christ's death, omitting the resurrection altogether. Andrew Lloyd Webber was quoted as saying that he deliberately portrayed Jesus as a mere man in *Superstar*, which explains the conspicuous absence of miracles in the story. In this story, Ted Neely's rock-n-roll messiah glides through the story not even sure what it's all about, ending in confused resignation to the inevitability of fate. Actual words of Jesus are used throughout *Superstar* but they are changed to mean the opposite of their original context. When asked by Caiaphas if he is the Christ, Jesus answers, "That's what you say. You say that I am" (Mt 26:64). What was in the first century Hebrew culture a legal formal declaration of identity has now become an Americanized statement of blame shifting. According to this view, it is *the people* who make a messiah out of a man. Jesus is now a seventies-nonviolent-peace-demonstrator scapegoat for the military industrial complex.

The reluctant messiah mythology is taken to the nth degree in Monty Python's *The Life of Brian* (1979)—a comedy of a blubbering-idiot-Jesus stand-in, a case of messianic mistaken identity. The masses operate on herd instinct and out of their desperate psychological vacuum create a messiah to meet their needs. And they do it whether the "messiah" wants it or not. We see crowds misinterpret mistakes as miracles and goofy prattling as the fount of wisdom. This mass hypnotism is the essence of all messianism to the filmmakers. We the people make gods of men, and we make them in our own image. As Voltaire once quipped, "God made man in his image, man is now returning the favor."

So step one in the humanization of Jesus was to tell the story with fewer and fewer miracles. Step two was to play out Jesus as just a man misunderstood for deity. Step three would involve making him a sinner like everyone else. In the infamous *Last Temptation of Christ* (1988), Willem Dafoe plays a confused-epileptic-temper-tantrum Jesus. Unfortunately, the brouhaha surrounding the film focused on the sex scene between Jesus and Mary Magdalene. Technically, this scene was arguably appropriate if taken as it was meant to be: a dream sequence of temptation from Satan, not unlike the vision of temptation the Son of God endured in the wilderness (Mt 4).

What was more problematic in terms of New Testament Christianity was the fact that Jesus was portrayed as a sinner who didn't know his own identity as Christ and didn't want to have anything to do with God. He is not only a reluctant messiah, but hates God for his cruelty in "choosing" him. God gets back at Jesus by giving him brain seizures till he submits. Jesus talks of his burning lusts for sex and calls himself Satan. And the flip-flop is made complete by making Judas a hero who is commanded by Jesus to betray him against Judas's better judgment. How's that for complete role reversal? This portrayal of Christ as sinner and dissident was the true blasphemy of the movie.

This miserable Jesus, a figment of the mystical occult thinking of Nikos Kazanzakis, is more a part of a surrealistic Dali painting than of New Testament literature. While some of the miracle scenes are incredibly moving experiences, Scorsese had no real problem showing them because the whole movie is one big surreal dream anyway.

The apostle Paul is portrayed as irreverently unconcerned with the historical reality (or unreality in this case) of Christ's resurrection in favor of an imagined one more powerful with which to comfort the masses. Religious events did not actually occur; they are only mythological and occur in our minds and hearts, expressing our faith rather than history.

If the cinematic Jesus has been progressively stripped of his deity, one can only imagine the shell of a man that will result if exploitation director Paul Verhoeven (*Showgirls, Basic Instinct, Total Recall*) gets his hands on the Master. Fueled by the postmodern Jesus Seminar that decides all New Testament evidence of Messianic godhood to be illegitimate by majority vote, Verhoeven has announced his intentions to make a film of this "demythologized" Jesus. Fortunately, he has been trying for many years without success.[1]

---

[1]Considering Verhoeven's worldview, it is probably not too presumptuous to forecast a Jesus who is the guilty man with "the woman caught in adultery." His miracles will be reduced to magic tricks he learned in Egypt. And Verhoeven's most difficult dramatic decision will likely be over what weapon Jesus should brandish when overturning the moneylenders in the temple, an Uzi or a 9mm Glock semi-automatic?

A LITTLE BIT OF BOTH

To be fair, there are some celluloid Jesuses that deserve some praise. In 1979 the Genesis Project gave us the Jesus-with-a-bad-haircut in the simply titled *Jesus* or *The Jesus Film*. This film is faithful to the Gospel of Luke in its story as well as dialogue. It was picked up by the evangelical organization Campus Crusade for Christ, and has been translated into more than one thousand languages and growing.

This somewhat dated Jesus may not reach many sophisticated American moviegoers, but it has been shown to millions of others around the rest of the world with great effect—seen by more people than any other film in history. Perhaps this Jesus is the most true to the Gospel texts in that he is literally preaching the gospel to all the ends of the earth.

A literal word-for-word translation of the life of Jesus was created in Visual Entertainment's *The Gospel According to Matthew* (1995). This miniseries portrays Bruce Marchiano as a smiley-faced-California-surfer Jesus. Though his deity is clearly presented through Saint Matthew's Hebraic mindset, his smiling laughter and warm-heartedness make him one of the most human Jesuses without negating his divinity.

But the balance of humanity and divinity would soon be rivaled with *Jesus: The Epic Mini-Series* (2000), starring Jeremy Sisto as the politically-correct-lovey-dovey-pacifist-television Jesus. This series gives us a "culturally sensitive" multicultural cast for the man for all nations, just to make sure no one is intolerantly left out. Joseph is a grumbling German-accented father. A Scottish John the Baptist yells "Freedom" like some kind of Braveheart and bows, hands clasped like the Buddhist Dali Lama, when he talks about doing good. An English Pilate and English Romans (always a popular accent for bad guys trying to rule the world), and a French Satan speaking in that seductively villainous revolutionary accent.

Though the movie strikes the best balance of a Jesus who laughs and cries (even laughs with hecklers at the Sermon on the Mount), plays and whips, and avoids publicity but performs miracles, it nevertheless has its own gestures of the cultural context of its creators. There is a focus on "love" and "tolerance" over other principles of exclusivity and holiness. There is less emphasis on his teaching and more on the political tribalism and intolerance of the time period. It even gives a nod to an apocryphal story from one of the Gnostic gospels (now in vogue) where Jesus as a child in Egypt made some clay pigeons turn to life. In the movie, he actually heals a killed bird, to emphasize his love.

Of course, most of this variety of Jesus' human reactions is based on actual events from the Gospels, but the choice to focus on certain aspects of teaching to the exclusion of others is itself a biased agenda that must be acknowledged. That said, there are some very moving and true moments in this presentation because the storytellers created a personal context for all the miracles and relationships that Jesus had with the people.

True to the upside-down insanity of modern times, the next TV Jesus is hermeneutically deconstructed and historically revisioned in *Judas* (2004). In this story, Judas, not the Master, is the protagonist. No mention is made of the fact that he used to pilfer from the disciples' treasury (Jn 12:6), and his handing Jesus over to judgment is sanitized; Judas expects that Jesus will be treated fairly by the high priest. What a nice guy, this Judas. The storytellers paint Judas as sympathetic to the Zealot cause and driven by his desire to see the Romans overthrown, his hearty zealousness for Israel frustrated by Jesus' spiritual kingdom.

The Jesus in *Judas* is a Dr.-Phil-Scooby-Doo-Shaggy-Malibu Jesus. He gives Judas the money purse because, as he says, "I'm terrible with money. I seem to lose it." Jesus *apologizes* for turning over the tables of the moneychangers in the temple, saying, "I lost my temper." When Jesus is frustrated about spreading his ministry, Judas gives him the idea of multiplying his impact by giving the disciples his power, as if Jesus couldn't think beyond his own tribal ignorance.

Poor Judas, this production would have us believe, is just a victim of his own low self-esteem. Jesus wants better for him: "I wish you could love yourself the way I do."

THE RESURRECTION

One of the most important doctrines of New Testament Christianity is the physical resurrection of Jesus. While the resurrection is the post-climactic dénouement in each of the four Gospels, it remains the central tenet that separates orthodox Christianity from other religions. While all other religious, social and political leaders teach dogma that is abstract and unrooted in history, Jesus claims to authenticate his teaching by his ability to raise from the dead (Jn 2:18-22), something no one else has either claimed or achieved. It is one thing to preach a philosophy or theology, it is quite another to back it up with authority.

And the resurrection is necessarily physical. Physical death is the great equalizer of all humanity, so mastery over death is the exclusive prerogative of divinity. Everyone knows the story of doubting Thomas who wouldn't believe the risen Savior even when he saw him. Jesus then replies by having Thomas put his hand in the wound in Christ's side. Thomas responds, "My Lord and my God" (Jn 20:26-29). In the Gospel of Luke, the disciples think they are seeing Jesus' ghost when he replies, "See My hands and My feet, that it is I Myself; touch Me and see, for a spirit does not have flesh and bones as you see that I have" (Lk 24:36-40).

This spirit and flesh distinction, while prominent in the Bible, is not quite as willingly portrayed in the cinema. The spiritualized metaphor of "living on in the memory" is often preferred to outright death-defying resurrection. *Intolerance* merely shows the glowing light from a heavenly vision stopping wars and hatred. Is this the second coming or just a cinematic symbolic portrayal of the power of love? *The Greatest Story* has a last shot of another visionary image of Christ projected spiritually in the clouds overlooking the disciples, no nail wounds on his hands (just a vision?).

Jesus of Nazareth has a last scene of Jesus teaching his disciples but we're not sure if this is actual or just a memory of Peter's past experience with Jesus. The lack of any wounds on Christ's body again indicates the latter. Even in *King of Kings*, the final scene is of the disciples before a metaphorical shadow of Jesus forming a symbolic cross on the sand.

While *Jesus, The Gospel According to Matthew* and *Jesus: The Mini-Series* all have post-resurrection appearances with a wounded Jesus, *The Mini-Series* localizes it to only one appearance privately to the apostles rather than the many other public appearances the New Testament records.

And of course let us not forget the total and deliberate negation of resurrection altogether in the demythologized Christ stories of *Last Temptation, Superstar* and *Godspell*. We simply end with his death. The tendency is clearly toward an inability to "take it all so literally" as they say. And literality is exactly what the last image of Jesus in the movies is not about.

JESUS AS MYTH

The final approach to Jesus is perhaps the most relevant to a postmodern mind that has sloughed off all pretension of factual history in favor of the radical relativism and subjectivist metaphysic of deconstructionism: that fashionable ideology that dismantles every text into an arbitrary vessel ready for manipulation by any subject for any cause.

There is ultimately no "text" to any manuscript such as the New Testament; there is only "Christ mythology" expressed through the subjective minds of first-century patriarchal Jews. The important point in the end is not that there was a Jesus, but that we *believe* in a "savior" that enlightens our way. What was desacralized in *Last Temptation* and mocked in *Life of Brian* has become a concept actually embraced by some postmodern filmmakers. The use of Christlike symbolism embodies a powerful means of persuasion to the postmodern mind.

The late mythologist Joseph Campbell has become a sort of Christ himself in Hollywood. As pointed out earlier, Campbell posited an underlying mythic structure to all storytelling that follows a character arc of redemption for the hero. The hero starts out in his ordinary world receiving "the call" to adventure but is reluctant. A traumatic experience occurs that propels him into the story against his will, and he soon embraces his fate. He gathers his allies against the villain and overcomes various obstacles until he faces death in some manner (his own or another's). After his dark night of the soul he "seizes the sword" and in a supreme ordeal fights the final battle. He then takes the road back after a resurrection (real or symbolic) and returns to his ordinary world with an elixir that brings new life to his ordinary world.[2]

---

[2]Joseph Campbell, *The Hero with a Thousand Faces* (Princeton, N.J.: Princeton, 1949, 1973). See also: Christopher Vogler, *The Writer's Journey: Mythic Structure for Storytell-*

Sound familiar? According to Campbell it's the foundational myth of all hero stories in all cultures, including Christ's. As discussed in earlier chapters, "myth" in this context is not a negative falsehood, but a positive expression of a universal truth. All cultures have mythologies or underlying beliefs that guide their living. And Christ mythology is one of those.

In a real sense *Jesus Christ Superstar* and *Godspell* already initiated this mythic theme by portraying their stories as literal theatrical presentations within the films, postmodern "stories about stories." In *Superstar* we see the bus of thespians arrive, put on their costumes of ancient and modern fusion, and setup stage for their rock opera. The important point of these theatrical Christs is the myth of the story, not the factuality of it.

POSTMODERN CHRIST MYTHS

One of the largest grossing movies of all time, *E.T.* (1982), was a deliberate retelling of the Christ story with a little alien Christ as the hope of humankind. He comes from "another world," gathers his disciples, is rejected by the status quo, has healing powers, is killed by the state, is resurrected and ascends back to the heavens. The writer, Melissa Matheson, commented on her intense demands to maintain certain story elements because of their affinity to the New Testament Gospels.

Another positive Christ myth is resurrected in *The Green Mile*, adapted by Frank Darabont from the novel by Stephen King. This movie rewraps the Christ story into a racial context by incarnating the Christ figure in a huge, wrongly accused black man, condemned to die in the electric chair for murdering two small girls in the rural South of the 1930s.

The prison guards soon learn that the prisoner John Coffey (whose initials are the same as Jesus Christ's) is able to heal people's infirmities by touching the affected parts of their bodies. At first Coffey resurrects a dead mouse, then he heals the head guard (played by Tom Hanks) of a urinary tract infection, and finally he heals the warden's wife of a death-bed tumor. During the healings, we see Coffey take the infirmity onto himself and then spit it out in the form of a swarm of flies. In the Bible, Satan is given the name Beelzebub, which means "Lord of the Flies," so

---

ers and Screenwriters (Studio City, Calif.: Michael Wiese Productions, 1992).

healing represents a redemption from his power.

John Coffey ends up dying for the crimes of the real killer, the innocent in place of the guilty. He is led like a lamb to the slaughter at his execution, and death is swallowed up in victory as the electric chair is never used again—and the resurrected mouse lives on forever. *The Green Mile* retells the story of Christ as a "pure soul" who is punished by the world.

Other movies, like *Powder, Phenomenon, Forrest Gump* and *Being There,* also prefer to use the Christ myth as a paradigm for their lead characters—unlikely, hesitant heroes who are rejected by their society but are in the end embraced as saviors. Screenwriter Randall Wallace has expressed his intent behind *Braveheart* as its being a reflection of the gospel. In the same way that William Wallace's martyrdom became the loss that won Scotland's freedom, so our own spiritual freedom is wrought from the self-sacrifice of Jesus Christ.

Hannibal, written by David Mamet and Steven Zaillian and sequel to the Academy Award–winning *Silence of the Lambs,* is an ironic postmodern recasting of the Christ story—in a way, a fitting expression of our social decay and cultural depravity. This anti-Christian myth gives the Christ role to the villain, the infamous Hannibal Lecter. Pazzi, the Italian cop who tracks down Hannibal in Florence, is a clear Judas rewrite. Not only does he betray Hannibal for $3 million (a multiple of the thirty pieces of Judas's silver), but he is also killed in exactly the same way as Judas, by hanging and having his bowels spill out, after a history lesson about the biblical Judas Iscariot given by Hannibal himself.

> **MOVIES EMPLOYING THE CHRIST MYTH**
>
> *Being There*
>
> *E.T.*
>
> *Jesus of Montreal*
>
> *Powder*
>
> *Phenomenon*
>
> *Spitfire Grill*
>
> *Sling Blade*
>
> *The Mask of Zorro*
>
> *Les Misérables*
>
> *The Matrix*
>
> *Gran Torino*
>
> *I Am Legend*

Hannibal has a gruesome "last supper" with Clarice (his nemesis *and* love interest) that is quite literally the eating of a body. When he discovers Clarice's self-loathing thoughts, he jabs that she would like the apostle

Paul because he hated women too—a reference to Paul's instructions to women to be subject to their husbands as their husbands are subject to Christ (Eph 5:22-24). Hannibal ultimately "ascends to heaven" in a jumbo jet.

The Mask of Zorro (1998), written by John Eskow, Ted Elliot and Terry Rossio, is a clever New Age deconstruction of the Christ myth. The story is about the transfer of the Zorro mantle from the older current Zorro (played by Anthony Hopkins) to the younger future Zorro (played by Antonio Banderas). That the concept of the *mask* of Zorro is used as the title is no coincidence. Harkening back to Joseph Campbell's *The Masks of God*, this story is about the *office* of messiah ("anointed one" to save the people) being fulfilled in different times by different men, but all wearing the same "mask" of savior. There is one Zorro mask worn by many "Zorros," just as Campbell would say there are many saviors in history, Buddha, Muhammad, Jesus, etc., all wearing the mantle of deliverer or savior.

But all is not dread for the faithful. The very power of Christ symbolism that is being reinterpreted within the secular context is surely an expression of the innate hunger within humanity for a messiah. The idea of a "super" hero who becomes an example for us through his own suffering and enlightenment is not intrinsically wrong; in fact, it is intrinsically a part of the New Testament message of Jesus (see Heb 2). The difference is in the content of the salvation offered. Where the New Testament Jesus knows exactly who he is and accepts his role "from the foundations of the earth" as the God-man, the modern cinematic Christ figure tends to be confused, reluctant and spurning of idolization by the masses. Where the New Testament Jesus says deny yourself, pick up your cross and follow me as God, modern cinematic messiahs tend to confirm the rejection of higher powers in favor of self-actualization.

The Matrix (1999), the sci-fi phenomenon written and directed by the Wachowski brothers, is a mixing of Greek and Christian mythology similar to the Neo-Platonism of earlier centuries. The parallels are obvious: Neo ("new man," "new Adam," played by Keanu Reeves) is "the chosen one" (Christ) who is prophesied to come and free the people from the deadly, controlling matrix that has enslaved all humans from birth, similar to the blind slavery of sin that everyone born into Adam has inherited (Romans 5). When people are awakened (enlightened) from their bondage, they appear like newborn babies from their life support pods, seeing the universal bondage all around them with new eyes, much like spiritual rebirth for the Christian (Jn 3).

Neo delivers an illegal computer disk to a fellow hacker, who jokingly says of Neo, "Hallelujah. You're my savior. My own personal Jesus Christ." When people are freed from the delusion of the matrix, they go

The Matrix	Christianity	Greek Religion
Morpheus: Declares "the one"	John the Baptist: Proclaims the Christ	Morpheus: god of dreams
Morpheus: A father to them	Father	
Neo	Son ("New Adam")	Greek for "new man"/ anagram of "one"
Trinity	Holy Spirit	Goddess
Slaves to A.I.	Slaves to sin	Plato's cave
Wake up in pod	Spiritual rebirth	Enlightenment
Cypher	Judas	
Oracle	Prophet	Oracle of Delphi ("Know thyself")
The one	Christ	Plato's philosopher king
Neo resurrected	Jesus resurrected	
Neo flies away	Jesus ascended into heaven	
Return of the one	The second coming	
Zion: The last human city	Zion: Promised Land/ body of Christ	
Nebuchadnezzar: Hovercraft	Nebuchadnezzar: King of Babylon (had dreams)	

Figure 5. Christian and Greek parallels in *The Matrix*

to a city called Zion—the same name as the biblical city of the Promised Land that is fulfilled in the church as the body of Christ.

Laurence Fishburne plays Morpheus (the name of the Greek god of dreams), who doubles as John the Baptist heralding the coming of the

Chosen One, a voice crying in the wilderness. And Morpheus is captain of the hovercraft Nebuchadnezzar, named after the Babylonian king in the Bible whose dreams only Daniel could interpret. Trinity is the name of Carrie-Anne Moss's character.

Neo is betrayed by Cypher, a Judas of the good-guy disciples. The messianic implications are crystallized when Neo gives his life to save Morpheus. He dies but comes back to life, resurrected by the kiss (breath) of Trinity, only to miraculously defeat the enemy. In the last shot of the movie Neo ascends into heaven in the clouds as he heralds his followers on a new quest to preach their gospel to all creation, that is, to all those in bondage to the matrix.

All the looking to the skies for alien saviors of evolution or looking within for humanistic self-exaltation, all the proclamations of movie messiahs for us to reject higher beings and look within ourselves for the answers, simply do not quench the overriding need in the human spirit for reconciliation with our Creator.

And then came Mel Gibson.

THE PASSION OF THE CHRIST

In 2004, Mel Gibson directed the newest film about Jesus called *The Passion of the Christ*. Every studio passed on the project so he funded it with his own money and made box office history.

The genesis of the film arose in Gibson's own spiritual journey.[3] He describes:

> I had to make this film; I couldn't not make it. About 13 years ago I came to a difficult point in my life, and meditating on Christ's sufferings, on his Passion, got me through it. Life is hard, and we all get wounded by it; I was no exception. I went to the wounds of Christ in order to cure my wounds. And when I did that, through reading, and studying, and meditating, and praying, I began to see in my own mind what he really went through. I began to understand it as I never had before, even though I had heard the story so many times.[4]

---

[3]A special thanks to my friend Goran Dragolovic for some of the insights in this chapter.
[4]"Is Mel Gibson Brave Heart? An Interview with the Director and Star" <www.usanext
.org/newsletter/viewarticle.asp?id=46>

From beginning to end, *The Passion* is a gut-wrenching experience that few walk away from unchanged. But it is not without controversy. In addition to claims of anti-Semitism, there are several other concerns that media-wise Protestants had with *The Passion*. Among them are its graphic depiction of violence, the second commandment prohibition of images, its scarcity of doctrinal teaching and the Roman Catholic viewpoints of its filmmaker.

Anti-Semitism. In light of Gibson's drunken outbursts of anti-Semitic slurs in 2006, some have felt that their accusations of *The Passion* as anti-Semitic are now vindicated. Some were originally concerned that the Jews in the movie were depicted as "Christ-killers." One proof of this accusation was the Jews handing Christ over and screaming, "His blood be on our heads." Even though this event was historically recorded in the New Testament (Mt 27:25) *by Jews*, Gibson went out of his way to avoid offense by cutting it out. This did not satisfy the more politically obsessed. They feared a new crusade against Jews in the twenty-first century fueled by *The Passion*.

In point of fact, the movie brings nothing to the mix of Jewish bloodguilt that is not in the New Testament itself. The New Testament, *written by Jewish men*, portrays Jewish leaders as conspiring to put Jesus to death (Mt 27:1), Jewish crowds screaming for Christ's blood (Mt 27:25), a *Jewish* Jesus preaching first-century Jewish guilt for rejecting the Messiah (Mt 21:33-43) and judgment by God for that rejection (Mt 23:29-34), and the *Jewish* apostles proclaiming the guilt of those first-century Jews in crucifying Christ (Acts 2:22-23; 7:51-52).

The real accusation is not that *The Passion* is anti-Semitic, but that the New Testament is anti-Semitic, indeed that all the Old Testament prophets are also anti-Semitic, since they made condemnations of Jewish apostasy and bloodguilt just as extreme as the New Testament apostles (Is 1:4; Is 5; Jer 25; Ezek 16). This is self-evidently ludicrous. These Jewish biblical prophets, in both Old and New Testaments, pronouncing judgment on the Jews are not anti-Semitic; they are God's mouthpieces of corrective moral truth. The Jewish prophets and apostles were not anti-Semitic, and neither is *the Passion*.

The gospel—rated R. The movie of *The Passion* begins in the garden of Gethsemane with Christ's betrayal at the lips of Judas and follows the last twelve hours of his earthly life and crucifixion, ending with a brief scene of his resurrection. But this is in no way merely another telling of the greatest story ever rehashed. It is an experiential exploration of the meaning of sacrificial substitutionary atonement like no other Jesus movie has ever depicted. Most movies about Christ have covered the injustice, beatings and crucifixion of our Lord and Savior—some of them better than others—but never like this. All other Jesus movies are revisionist candy-coated schmaltz compared to this one.

Gibson based the gruesome details of his film upon a famous clinical investigation of Roman crucifixion and punishment, "On the Physical Death of Jesus Christ," published in *The Journal of the American Medical Association* in 1986. The film translates this historical research onto the screen with a brutal vengeance: scourging whips of leather and bone ripping off flesh, pools of blood, an unidentifiable Christ with his face bashed in. And all of it true to the Scriptures:

> He was despised and forsaken of men,
> A man of sorrows and acquainted with grief;
> And like one from whom men hide their face
> He was despised, and we did not esteem Him.
> Surely our griefs He Himself bore,
> And our sorrows He carried;
> Yet we ourselves esteemed Him stricken,
> Smitten of God, and afflicted.
> But He was pierced through for our transgressions,
> He was crushed for our iniquities;
> The chastening for our well-being fell upon Him,
> And by His scourging we are healed.
> All of us like sheep have gone astray,
> Each of us has turned to his own way;
> But the LORD has caused the iniquity of us all
> To fall on Him.
> He was oppressed and He was afflicted,
> Yet He did not open His mouth;
> Like a lamb that is led to slaughter,

And like a sheep that is silent before its shearers,
So He did not open His mouth. (Is 53:3-7)

So His appearance was marred more than any man,
And His form more than the sons of men. (Is 52:14)

Part of the messianic prophecy of Isaiah 53 is shown at the beginning of the movie to provide a biblical context for understanding all the
violence that follows. And there is a lot of violence. The film is rated R
because of the graphic depiction of Christ's sufferings at the hands of
his accusers. But rather than "adding to the Scriptures," this historical
detail merely translates for contemporary culture what first-century
Jewish believers, to whom the Gospels were originally written, knew
all too intimately, having lost loved ones themselves to the barbarism
of Rome.

It is important to understand that the effectiveness of redemption portrayed in any story is exactly equal to the accuracy of the depiction of the
depravity from which we are redeemed. The brutal realism of Christ's
suffering points to the depth and costliness of atonement which was
achieved for God's people through his once-for-all sacrifice. To show
anything less is to diminish the gospel. Watching this movie, with its in-
your-face grisly realism, provides a much-needed corrective to our modern pseudo-gospels with their bloodless Jesuses who exist to fill one's
heart and life with peace, happiness and fulfillment, rather than to die in
place of sinners, saving them from God's wrath.[5]

Perhaps the most important aspect of the scandalous violence in *The
Passion* is its fidelity to the scandal of the cross presented in the New
Testament. This violence seemed to elicit a polarizing response be-

---

[5]It is important to note here that the emphasis on the literal blood of Christ is also a Roman Catholic aspect. Some Protestants accuse Catholicism of being a blood cult, but
that accusation is reversible to Protestants in that they can be accused of being a mental
cult. That is, Roman Catholicism is imbalanced in its immanent focus on the physical,
but Protestantism is imbalanced in its transcendent focus on the spiritual. Christianity
is both immanent and transcendent, physical and spiritual; Christ is both human and
God; truth is both incarnational and propositional. It could be argued that this immanent emphasis in *The Passion of the Christ* is an imbalance. However, since its Catholic
viewpoint is trinitarian, it is not a negation of Christ's divinity like a movie such as *The
Last Temptation of Christ*.

tween believers and unbelievers. Consider the scandalized reactions of some film critics:

> "One of the cruelest movies in the history of cinema. . . . The movie Gibson has made from his personal obsessions is a sickening death trip, a grimly unilluminating procession of treachery, beatings, blood and agony. . . . He falls in danger of altering Jesus's message of love into one of hate." —David Denby, *The New Yorker*

> "Near pornographic violence." —Kirk Honeycutt, *The Hollywood Reporter*

> " 'The Passion of the Christ' is violent, bloody, and sadistic. . . . [It] has to be the most graphic and brutal death ever portrayed on film. . . . I found it stomach-turning and deeply troubling." —Jeff Jacoby, *Boston Globe*[6]

It appears the Jewish *and* secular reactions to this film were already anticipated by the apostle Paul:

> For indeed Jews ask for signs and Greeks search for wisdom; but we preach Christ crucified, to Jews a stumbling block and to Gentiles foolishness, but to those who are the called, both Jews and Greeks, Christ the power of God and the wisdom of God. (1 Cor 1:22-24)

The cross of Christ, if communicated accurately, should scandalize the godless. As scholar N. T. Wright suggests, "The real scandal is not simply the death of the Messiah but the shameful and penal mode of that death."[7] A story of Jesus that does not scandalize the godless is a domesticated idol that the world can safely ignore with a dismissive, "Well that's all well and good for you, but not for me." A story of Jesus and his crucifixion portrayed inoffensively is simply not biblical. As Paul reiterates, "The word of the cross is foolishness to those who are perishing, but to us who are being saved it is the power of God" (1 Cor 1:18). The shocking violence of *The Passion* is perhaps Gibson's attempt to translate that scandal to our postmodern sensibilities. One thing is for sure, some Jews stumbled over it, and many Gentiles thought it foolish—just as the apostle Paul said they should.

---

[6]Special thanks to my illustrious friend Goran Dragolovic for these quotes as well as for the notion of the scandal of the cross.

[7]N. T. Wright, *The Climax of the Covenant: Christ and the Law in Pauline Theology* (Minneapolis: Fortress Press, 1993), p. 61.

Postmodern Christ narrative. As this chapter has argued, most Jesus movies tend to reflect the prevailing Zeitgeist of their era, and *The
Passion* is no exception. As pointed out earlier, the first Jesus movies,
produced in an era of belief, tended to emphasize his deity at the expense of his humanity *(Intolerance, King of Kings)*. Later movies, produced in an era of skepticism, tended to emphasize his humanity at the
expense of his deity *(Jesus Christ Superstar, Godspell),* or worse, made
him out to be sinful *(The Last Temptation of Christ)*. But all these movies were, to a degree, modernist renditions focusing on Christ's didactic teaching culminating in the cross as the ultimate embodiment of
that theology.

In *The Passion,* Gibson has chosen to dramatize a portion of Scripture
where our Lord has comparatively little to say ("He did not open His
mouth," Is 53:7) and very much to do. Thus it is not surprising that there
is relatively little overt doctrine in the film. The doctrinal perspective
that is set forth, however, spare though it may be, has a more postmodern visually-oriented focus. But it is consistent with the biblical narratives from which Gibson is working, and all of it serves to contextualize
the suffering, giving it meaning and purpose.

In the Middle Ages, Passion plays originated to dramatize the gospel
for the illiterate masses without access to holy writ. In a similar way,
many people today are largely *un*literate and image-oriented, with entertainment and media functionally operating as their canonical texts. People are bored with sermonizing and preachiness, especially in the arts.
They just won't listen to reason. They want to *experience* your metanarrative, not mentally process it with the questionable faculties of "logo-
centric" rationality.

Make no mistake, this postmodern prejudice can be imbalanced
and spiritually dangerous. But like Paul identifying to a degree with
pagan philosophers on Mars Hill (Acts 17), so *The Passion* meets the
postmodern challenge with a spiritually moving experience of Christ
that will no doubt elicit similar reactions from the masses. Some sneer
and others want to know more (Acts 17:32). The story is presented
through strong images and minimal dialogue that transcends culture
and denomination alike. That's the positive power of image. It may be

the *only* movie about Jesus that most postmodern young people will ever consider watching.

Traditional Protestant thinking has often emphasized a word-oriented theology to the near exclusion of image, and sometimes to the *total* exclusion of image, thus suffering under an imbalance opposite that of the postmodern. The truth is "the Word became flesh, and dwelt among us" (Jn 1:14), a perfect unity of word *and* image.

Roman Catholicism. Much has been made of Gibson's reliance upon the nineteenth-century Roman Catholic mystic Sister Anne Emmerich and her visions recorded in *The Dolorous Passions of Our Lord Jesus Christ*, as well as Mary of Agreda. But the overarching story structure is taken from the fourteen "stations of the cross," a tradition from before the seventeenth century that focused on specific moments in the narrative of Christ's passion, not all biblical, some apocryphal. These stations had evolved out of the need for the faithful to contemplate the passion of Christ without having to visit the Via Dolorosa in the Holy Land, something pilgrims had been doing since the days of Constantine. Too many of the poor could not afford a pilgrimage to the historic site of their Savior's passion, so the passion was brought to them.

Through the depiction of these fourteen events in paintings and carvings, the believer could move from station to station, praying through and contemplating the events leading up to the crucifixion and resurrection of Christ. The stations of the cross narrate the event through visual dramatic renditions, a primitive movie of sorts. Gibson's *The Passion of the Christ* is a cinematic incarnation of those fourteen stations of the cross, of which only one is explicitly extrabiblical. It is a scene of Veronica, a woman who, according to Roman relic tradition, wiped Jesus' face with a cloth and had his facial imprint in blood on the cloth.

Christ's actual teachings in the film are minimal and told in flashback, so truth is delivered more through context than proposition. For instance, the Lord's Supper is remembered at one point in Christ's bloody punishment. Yet this symbolic connection is entirely in accord with John's Gospel narrative, where eating Christ's "flesh" and drinking his "blood" is a sacramental connection with his death and suffering (Jn 6:52-59).

The sensitive and loving emphasis on Mary in the movie illustrates a definite Roman Catholic viewpoint, but if anything, Mary's part in the story is a welcomed corrective to the Protestant pendulum swing of downplaying the mother of Jesus. She is shown as a loving mother with a young adult Jesus who teases her affectionately. No "Queen of Heaven" there, just a good mom. She is shown racked with spiritual anguish— pierced in her own soul (Lk 2:35)—at every beating of Jesus. And whose mother would not vicariously experience the punishment of her son? There is a beautiful scene where Mary watches Christ fall on the Via Dolorosa and cannot help him, but in her mind she remembers him as a little child falling, herself running to his aid. Very moving, very real and very much like my own mom.

A stronger Roman Catholic emphasis is found in Mary's juxtaposition with the Satan character. In the Roman view, Mary and Satan are the two sides of the struggle over Christ's soul and suffering. This is why Satan and Mary are shown on opposite sides of the crowd following Christ and leering at each other. It is also the explanation of the "demon baby" image that forms an inverted evil image of the "Madonna and Child" so prevalent in Roman Catholicism.

After Christ's crucifixion, Mary holds his body after being taken down from the cross in what has come to be a symbolic Pietá pose. While it may be the case that the Pietá in Roman Catholic theology became a symbolic reference to Mary's co-redemptive unity with Christ, it was first of all an altogether believable expression of a mother's love of her dead son.

The problem with criticism of any and all extrabiblical details in this film about Christ is the inescapable speculation on *anyone's* part, Protestant, Catholic or other, in filming any story about Jesus. What Jesus wore, how he looked at people, where he was at any given moment, anything that is not exactly recorded in Scripture is speculation. The Bible does not record every single scientific detail of every event in Christ's life. The desire for such exhaustive detail is in fact modernist unbiblical prejudice. And even movies that are word-for-word adaptations necessarily contain all kinds of speculative details not spoken of in Scripture. So when retelling the story, speculation is unavoidable and not always a legitimate critique unless the retelling violates the intent of the text.

Mel Gibson's Roman Catholicism definitely affects the depiction in

The Passion of the Christ, but it brings accent and flavor to the film's orthodox presentation without slipping into heresy. Much of the Roman distinction is found in symbolic references that lend themselves to a diversity of interpretation. And if such symbolic references are so easily reinterpreted depending on the viewer's theological perspective, then those symbols need not compel us to specific didactic conclusions. Yes, *The Passion* bears a distinctly Roman Catholic influence, but it remains to be proven that that influence is detrimental to a Protestant appreciation or interpretation of the film.

Death versus resurrection. Lastly, it appears that the origin of Passion plays in the Middle Ages, another Roman source of Gibson's interpretation, was in part theologically motivated. Although there were Easter, Mystery and Miracle plays as well, the Passion play did tend to emphasize the death of Christ at the expense of his resurrection. True, the early church did not create art that focused on Christ's death. There were no crosses in the catacombs. Also true that the Protestant Reformation rightfully stressed the resurrection victory of Christ with his death as a means to that end. So, yes, there is the danger of imbalance in Passion plays.

But the focal point of Christ's death in Romanism was also practically motivated, rooted in the interest of the peasant class that was largely illiterate or without access to the written Scriptures. Drama could incarnate the gospel narrative for those without privileged status. The purpose of focusing on suffering was to evoke pity. The priests mistakenly believed that pitying Christ could be equivalent to faith. While this is a real danger for a non-Christian to fall into while watching *The Passion*, it is also a danger for *any* truth claim in today's world.

Our society often worships emotion over cognition or action. It mistakes feeling for participation. Many wrongly suppose that watching a celebrity charity rock concert is the same as actually helping the poor; they believe that weeping over the plight of starving children on TV is equivalent to feeding the hungry. So also many people mistakenly conclude that "believing in God" saves them from hell, being perilously unaware that even demons do so (Jas 2:19). So this problem of erroneous participation in truth is more a function of the social milieu than the fault of artistic image. We must be sure to communicate with those who watch *The Passion* that feeling sorry for Jesus as the ultimate victim is not the same as being his disciple.

Shortly after *The Passion*, *The Da Vinci Code* came out with the 9/11-conspiracy-theory-pagan-goddess Jesus. A Jesus who wasn't God, who married Mary Magdalene and had children while worshiping goddess religion. Reflecting the postmodern-Internet-rumor-Wikipedia version of secret history that our society has fallen prey to, *The Da Vinci Code* Jesus provided the millions of others who hate the Jesus of the Bible with a fictional Jesus created in their own image. But we'll examine this movie closer in the next chapter on Christianity in the movies.

CONCLUSION

The power of dramatic cinema is undeniably helpful in visualizing such an influential figure in Western civilization as Jesus the Christ. And the various depictions of the Son of Man/Son of God have surely been reflections of the cultural biases of their respective eras. To see the miracles brings his divinity to light. To see Jesus laugh and love and cry brings his humanity to life. This battle of the flesh and the spirit has always been the issue for filmmakers and has resulted in the balance tipping one way or the other in the history of Jesus in the movies. The emphasis of the divine over the human has resulted in mystical and unapproachable Messiahs removed from the common man's reality. The emphasis of the human over the divine has resulted in impotent and reluctant Messiahs removed from God's reality. But one thing is for sure, any Christlike figure is a powerful metaphor, indeed incarnation of the ultimate hero, fulfilling the inner desire of humanity to be rescued from ourselves.

WATCH AND LEARN

Have your movie-watching group watch the film *Les Misérables*. Discuss what ways Valjean and Javert symbolize different worldviews. How does this contrast between these two men reflect a biblical contrast of grace and law? What examples of the Christ story do you see in this film? How are grace and law, and their consequences, portrayed throughout the film?

8

CHRISTIANITY

In *Hollywood Versus America* Michael Medved aptly detailed the assault on the Judeo-Christian faith by some in the Hollywood community. He describes how studios willingly create negative images of religious people without a corresponding balance of positive treatments. Medved details how many movies of the 1980s created stereotypical images of Jews and Christians by casting them as buffoons, hypocrites, repressed adulterers, killers and the like.[1]

And that approach to representing Christians has not ceased since the publication of Medved's book. Movies continue to portray Christians as crazed, Bible-quoting killers. Christianity is often depicted as a dangerous belief that breeds and feeds murderous hearts.

In *The Cell*, as discussed earlier, the heroine tracks down a demented killer of women whose twisted acts of evil are tied to his Christian upbringing. His method of drowning his female victims is based on his fa-

---

[1]Michael Medved, *Hollywood Versus America* (New York: HarperCollins, 1992), pp. 50-90.

ther holding him down too long when he was baptized, an act that symbolizes the forceful oppression of Christianity. The scene shows a crowd of hand-waving evangelicals "praisin' the Lord." And in true stereotypical fashion, the religious father was also criminally abusive to his family. So Christianity is at the heart of the problem of this maniacal killer.

In *Quills* playwright Doug Wright portrays the sadistic reprobate Marquis de Sade as an oppressed victim of a puritanical religious society. Of all the debauched perversions in the movie, the most heinous sexual sin, that of necrophilia (sex with a corpse), is engaged in by the Catholic priest who is trying to rehabilitate the Marquis. The despicable act is only a nightmare of the priest's, but the point is still made with spite: Christians are the most vile of sinners because they "repress" their desires, which results in oppressive morality.

According to some Hollywood movies, Christianity does not merely lead to mental breakdown in serial killers; it also leads to a breakdown of society. In the secular mindset, restraining immorality unleashes the very thing it tries to stop. Repressing our desires is bad; indulging them is good. Thus saith Freud. In this view, Christian faith is part and parcel of sexual intolerance *(Kinsey, Saved!)*; sexual intolerance *and* racist repression *(Pleasantville)*; sexual intolerance, racist repression *and* the subjugation of women (*Titanic, The Stepford Wives* [2004]); fear-driven, self-imposed ignorance about life *(I Heart Huckabees, The Mist)*; and useless twelve-step spiritual therapy that utterly fails to change a person *(21 Grams, Snow Angels)*. Commitment to biblical law leads to lawlessness, like that of the legalistic, Bible-thumping warden of *The Shawshank Redemption.*

In *The Mist,* a horror movie adapted from a Stephen King novella, a strange mist covers a small town, bringing with it bizarre prehistoric creatures. The townsfolk hide in a supermarket, and one of the women talks about the book of Revelation and God's judgment. The truth is that the mist is the result of a secret military experiment, but many of the townsfolk believe the prophecy-obsessed woman. She justifies sacrificing someone to God by repeatedly shouting the term *expiation*, which means "the satisfaction of God's wrath." (Jesus Christ was an expiation for our sins.) The movie thus portrays God as cruel and barbaric, and his people as violent lunatics. In this view, religion leads to the breakdown of society.

According to the gospel of some in Hollywood, reinforcing Christian moral codes in society leads to intolerance, violence, wife beating, the oppression of women and murder as in *The Scarlet Letter, The Crucible* and *Chocolat.* Ancient or futuristic dystopias are often depicted as being led by religious priests who, if they are not explicitly "evil controlling" Christians, they act and sound just like Christians.

DYSTOPIAN OPPRESSORS WITH CHRISTIAN MARKINGS
The Handmaid's Tale
Kingdom of Heaven
King Arthur
V for Vendetta
Chronicles of Riddick
Sky Captain and the World of Tomorrow

To the religious bigots of La-La Land, Christian commitment to marital fidelity strangles "true love" as in *Jude, The Scarlet Letter* (1995), *The Crucible* (1996), *The Magdalene Sisters, Kinsey* and *The Stepford Wives* (2004). The attempt to redeem others through missionary efforts leads to their enslavement and destruction as in *Black Robe, At Play in the Fields of the Lord, Jude, Oscar and Lucinda, Saved!* and *There Will Be Blood.* Christians are portrayed in these movies as ignorant, puritanical oppressors of those they seek to convert—and as more in need of conversion themselves.

At Play in the Fields of the Lord, by Hector Babenco, portrays Christianity as powerless against the glories of primitive animistic religion. It is the story of naive small-town missionaries who enter the Amazon to try to convert one of the indigenous tribes of natives untouched by civilization. The task becomes too formidable, and one missionary woman goes insane because her self-righteous faith cannot cope with the primal jungle. Her husband changes his original intentions and concludes that it would have been better for the natives if they had never met the evangelists. Another missionary accepts the temptation of lust as more desirable than her spiritual pursuit. In a complete reversal of Genesis, she confesses to another missionary that she was seduced by a certain man after bathing in the river and she felt "naked and *not* ashamed." The lead missionary is a self-righteous hypocrite who slips into a TV evangelist mode of delivery when he tries to preach the good news, all the while remaining entirely irrelevant and entirely ignorant of the people's true needs. And they all bring death, disease and destruction to the very people they are trying to save—not without blaming the Christian God for it all and likening Jesus to the devil.

David Franzoni's *Amistad* is a revisionist portrayal of the 1839 revolt of Africans on a slave ship and their subsequent trial on American soil. The historically dominant force of the abolitionist movement, the Quakers, are relegated to the background role of kooky, irrelevant protesters. Despite this negative portrayal, however, *Amistad* contains one of the most thorough descriptions of the gospel ever shown in a movie. In a long, powerful scene, a couple of the slaves get a picture Bible and "read" the gospel in pictures. The scene transcends the political message forced upon it by the filmmakers.

Oscar and Lucinda, written by Laura Jones from Peter Carey's novel, stars Ralph Fiennes and Cate Blanchett in the title roles. This is a story about two star-crossed lovers who are addicted to gambling. The problem is that Oscar is also an Anglican minister who is tormented by his Christianity. Oscar's father is portrayed as an intolerant, legalistic, pleasure-hating Plymouth Brethren who won't let Oscar enjoy Christmas pudding because desserts are "the food of Satan." Then Oscar's Anglican adoptive father turns out to be a repressed gambler himself, who ends up committing suicide. And every denomination is intolerant of the others.

In this film Christianity is a guilt-inducing faith that haunts Oscar and Lucinda all their lives. Oscar becomes so obsessed with guilt that by the end of the film he is asking for forgiveness of sins committed by others against him! He tries to deliver a glass church, on behalf of his love for Lucinda, to a minister in the uncharted wilderness. It is floated upstream on a raft, and one day, after he has prayed inside the church (which looks like a large cage), it starts to sink into the river with him locked inside. He drowns in it as it reaches the bottom, and the point is made through metaphor that Christianity is a cage that suffocates and drowns its adherents with unnecessary guilt and intolerance.

One of the few movies critical of Christians that is worthy of some respect is *The Big Kahuna*, written by Roger Rueff. It's a movie about three salesmen who come together at an industrial lubricant convention in order to wine and dine a "big kahuna" prospect into placing an order for their product, a sale that will save their floundering company.

Danny DeVito's character, Phil Cooper, has gotten to the point in his life where he is encountering the meaninglessness of his existence and his wrecked marriage. He's searching for a reason to live. Larry Mann, played by Kevin Spacey, is a spiritually void, soulless, manipulative salesman, who also happens to be a devoted friend to Phil. Out of his own spiritual vacuum he gives worthless advice to the empty, soul-searching De Vito—but he cares.

Another coworker, Bob Walker (played by Peter Facinelli), is there for his first convention. He is a young, inexperienced salesman but also a Christian who boldly shares his faith and values with others. Unfortunately, his youth betrays a judgmental spirit toward the godless. The worldly Spacey and spiritual Facinelli are soon battling for De Vito's soul and arguing over the answer to his emptiness as well as the ethical dilemma of manipulating their potential buyer into a sale. They escalate to the point of a fight and break up. The story ends with De Vito, even in his state of despair, teaching the kid a lesson that Jesus is not a product to sell to people. If you believe you have what people need, you've got to care about them if you want them to listen to what you have to say. In a sense, the young man's witnessing practices are no different than Spacey's opportunistic manipulation of the sale. We are not salesmen for Jesus; we are doctors of the soul.

In 2004, another case of anti-Christian hysteria came to the screen in Brian Dannelly and Michael Urban's black comedy, *Saved!* The story is about a young girl, Mary, at a Christian school who tries to "save" her boyfriend from turning gay by sleeping with him. When she gets pregnant, she has to hide her shame and deal with the "queen Christian" in the school, self-righteous Hilary Faye (an obvious reference to Tammy Faye Bakker) played by Mandy Moore. Mary hangs out with the rebels, a crippled non-Christian and the lone Jewish girl at the school who is there only because her other choice was home schooling. Mary eventually gives up her evangelical faith for a humanistic faith in herself and her feelings.

These filmmakers have clearly had some experience either in the evangelical subculture or know some who are in it because the movie captures some of the bad side of said subculture rather well: prayer as a weapon of gossip, "God told me" excuses, using Jesus as a cover for every kind of selfish pursuit, Jesus marketing, frauds and hypocrites. I actually agree in part with the critique that the evangelical subculture has become a fraudulent marketed substitute for secular culture covered over in platitudes and rationalizations. But the film's bigotry lies in not having a single genuine authentic Christian in the story. They are all portrayed as losers, liars, hypocrites or frauds, the classic rhetorical trick of propaganda and hate speech (remember the Nazi films portraying Jews as snively greedy sleazebags?).

CHRISTIANITY AS DESTRUCTIVE

Poltergeist II
The Handmaid's Tale
The Rapture
Cape Fear
Guilty as Charged
Copycat
Seven
The Cell
The Pledge
Sky Captain and the World of Tomorrow
Sin City
Silent Hill
The Mist
The Golden Compass

The movie mocks good things as if they were bad. It mocks secondary virginity, recovery from destructive behavior, clean lifestyles, home schooling, prayer, faithfulness in marriage, worship music, interventions, etc. As an adulterous woman tells her sexually fallen preacher (another cliché of anti-Christian agitprop), "Why would God give us these feelings if what we are doing is wrong?" The heroine Mary, at the end of the film says, "Life is perfect. There has to be a God out there—or in us. You just have to feel it."

The homosexual is affirmed in his feelings, the adulterers are affirmed in their feelings, the fornicators are affirmed in their feelings, and rebels are affirmed in their feelings. Everyone is affirmed in their feelings, except of course the Christians. Their feelings are not legitimate. The problem with this common argument of feelings determining legitimacy of behavior is that, if applied consistently, one would have to morally accept pedophilia, necrophilia, zoophilia, polygamy, rape and every other "sexual orientation" as legitimate because it arises *from feelings*, just as the homosexual, adulterer and fornicator claim their orientation is legitimate because it arises from their feelings. To see the absurdity of this argument, simply place it in the film's own words, "Why would God give us these feelings of wanting sex with children or sex with animals if what we are doing is wrong?" Unlike what the movie *Saved!* suggests, Christianity is not a sexual fun spoiler, it's the only prophylactic against self-destruction.

> Woe to those who call evil good, and good evil;
>   Who substitute darkness for light and light for darkness;
>   Who substitute bitter for sweet and sweet for bitter! (Is 5:20)

PAGANISM IN THE MOVIES

One of the most hate-filled attacks against Christianity to ever reach the silver screen was produced by Ron Howard and Brian Grazer of Imagine Entertainment, and penned by Akiva Goldsman. That movie was *The Da Vinci Code*, based on the mega-bestselling novel by Dan Brown. It is a thriller about a cryptologist (played by Tom Hanks) and a symbologist (played by Audrey Tautou) who stumble upon a conspiracy to hide the "truth" of long-held secrets about Jesus, which ultimately deny the foundational beliefs of the Christian faith. These include accusations that the Bible is not true, that Jesus was not God, that he fathered children with Mary Magdalene and embraced pagan goddess religion. It also depicts the Roman Catholic Church in specific, and Christianity in general, as attempting to cover up these alleged "truths" with a diabolical web of lies and murder. In short, the movie concludes that God is a woman and Christians are cold-blooded murderers who want to keep people from having fun—especially women.

In point of fact, these kinds of claims are not new. Christian-haters have been spinning conspiracy theories from the first day of the resurrection when the chief priests started a whispering campaign that Jesus' disciples stole his body. Nero pinned his burning of Rome on the Christians in a first-century conspiracy theory. And in an ironic reflection of modern-day America, these ancient believers were called "haters of the human race" by the Neronic Romans who hunted them down and persecuted them with loving zeal.

The Da Vinci Code is not unlike another conspiracy theory created in the late nineteenth century, The Protocols of the Elders of Zion. This hate-filled hit piece was written by an anti-Semite to "expose" a conspiracy of a cabal of Jews to take over the world. It's intent was to demonize Judaism and feed irrational bigotry against the Jews. Millions in the Muslim world still believe it today which props up their hatred of Jews. So The Da Vinci Code veils its hatred behind a fictional conspiracy that demonizes Christianity.

When the movie first came out, I decided to do a different kind of movie review. Instead of pointing out the exhausting myriads of lies in the movie, I decided to illustrate the absurdity of the story by simply returning the favor of conspiracy theorizing. I took factoids I found on the Internet and mixed them with fiction to weave my own conspiracy theory about The Da Vinci Code's filmmakers, Ron Howard, Brian Grazer and Akiva Goldsman.

For example, I "discovered" that the word Imagine was an anagram for "I in Game," which was linked to a long historical line going back to the Ku Klux Klan, Nazis and even Nero Caesar. It stands for "I am in the game of killing Christians," and its goal is to spread hatred for Christians so that people will rise up and imprison them in a new wave of religious persecution like in the Coliseum in Rome. The fact that there is no documentation for this conspiracy is the greatest proof for it because it proves how secret they are.

The accusations continued, one more outrageous than the last. In response to the charge that this was mean-spirited libel, I retorted with Dan Brown's own words—"My story here is only fiction. But every detail is based on facts." Try to nail me down on that one. The point of this exercise in sarcasm was that slander and hatred seem to be acceptable only when aimed at Christianity, Christians or their institutions. As Tom Hanks's character, Langdon, says in the movie, "The only thing that matters is what you believe," not, evidently, the factual truth.

The 2000 Academy Award winner Gladiator makes a subversive attack on Christianity by replacing it with a positive portrayal of pagan religion. Writer David Franzoni has said that he deliberately wanted to offer a contrast with the sword-and-sandal epics of yesteryear:

> The film is about a hero who has morality, but that morality is a secular morality that transcends conventional religious morality. In other words, I believe there is room in our mythology for a character who is deeply moral, but who's not traditionally religious: I loved that he was a pagan, not Christian or any other traditional/established religion. All those Roman Empire movies from the '50s and '60s were religious morality plays, and had to maintain the Christian status quo, it's all very conventional. You would never have been able to portray a pagan afterlife back then, either. Maximus is a man who will die for his family, and he will die for what's right.[2]

Apparently, the contradiction of a "secular morality" derived from Roman paganism does not bother Franzoni. Maximus does "what is right" as his religion conventionally defines it for him.[3] So Franzoni has replaced the Christian convention of morality with another religious convention, that of Roman paganism, thinking that this somehow points to a secular morality that transcends them both.[4] Be that as it may, Maximus's pagan heaven was depicted as real, which is extremely rare in a

---

[2]Quoted in John Soriano, "WGA.org's Exclusive Interview with David Franzoni," WGA <http://www.sois.uwm.edu/xie/dl/Movie%20Project%20Team%20Folder/Movie%20Project%20Team%20Folder/Writers/David%20Frazoni-%20Gladiator.pdf>. The interview has been removed from WGA.org since publication of the first edition of this book.

[3]There was nothing more conventional in Rome than the *religious* belief in Elysium and in strength and honor.

[4]"Transcendent secular morality" is an oxymoron. Secularity cannot be transcendent, because by definition it is immanent, that is, of the world rather than of the transcendent spiritual realm. From Aristotle to Wittgenstein, if there is one thing that the history of the secular philosophy of ethics illustrates, it is that when people reason "secularly" (from themselves), rather than from the transcendent God, they can only end in subjectivism (each person decides for himself or herself), and that is certainly not transcendent. Without a transcendent absolute standard, this secular moral relativity reduces to the will to power—whoever is in power (the majority) defines what is right and wrong for the rest (the minority). This will to power is the essence of Rome, and it is the same will to power that was embodied in the German Nazi state of the 1930s and 1940s. The director Ridley Scott understood this, and that is why he modeled the look of the Roman cult in *Gladiator* after the fascist imagery of Leni Riefenstahl's Nazi propaganda film *Triumph of the Will*.

mainstream movie of such prominence, and it marks the cinematic postmodern openness to religion—as long as it is *not* Christianity.

Franzoni seems to have a hate affair with Christianity that finds its way into several of his works. Another movie that illustrates his hostility is *King Arthur.* This epic about the alleged true origins of the King Arthur legend and his Round Table knights suggests that it was based on Sarmatian warriors during the collapse of the Roman Empire around A.D. 400. The Roman Church is depicted as already more barbaric and cruel than the marauding Saxons. The "uncivilized" pagans of the woods are even more noble than the Christians and end up allying with Arthur in his personal quest of redemption.

Arthur starts out as a Christian thinking Rome is where "the greatest minds in all the world come together in one place to help make mankind free." But by the end of the story, he concludes that "the home we seek is not in some distant land [read: heaven] but in our hearts. As free men, we choose to make it so." He concludes by giving up that faith of his fathers to marry a hottie-pagan wench in a pagan ceremony in the midst of a minipagan Stonehenge.

That is the power of subversive drama. Make the hero a committed loyal member of the worldview you want to discredit (in this case, Christianity), so that by the end of the story, when the hero changes his view about the world, it gives the audience the affirming encouragement to do so as well. After all, the hero is the good guy, right? And we want to cheer on the good guy, right? So, before you know it, you are cheering on leaving the Christian faith because of how cruel it is—or rather how cruel it has been *portrayed.*

The movie also cleverly embodies its egalitarian theme of political and religious freedom in a true historical character, the arch-heretic Pelagius, whose teachings Arthur follows (the director's cut contains more scenes of this character Pelagius). Pelagius is a hero championing "individual rights," teaching that all men are free to choose their own destinies and free from the authority of others (especially from God). Pelagius denied the biblical doctrines of original sin and the sovereignty of God. He ultimately believed that man saves himself through his own works of righteousness because his will is the ultimate control over his life, not God's.

Augustine rightly condemned Pelagius as a heretic of Christianity, but *King Arthur* canonizes him as a saint of Franzoni's humanism.

Other movies that display the superiority of pagan religious beliefs over Christianity are *The Missing* and *Hidalgo*, both of which show "Christians" as intolerant, arrogant bigots and the American Indian pagan religion as superior in power to Christianity. As explained in the previous section "Nietzsche in the Movies," *Beowulf* complains that the coming of Christianity ruined the full-blooded hearty and passionate heroism of paganism by replacing it with "martyrs, weakness and shame."

CHRIST-AFFIRMING FILMS

Although films portraying Christians in a negative light are all too common, there are films in recent memory that deserve recognition for their honest or fair portrayal of the faithful. In this postmodern milieu of anti-Christianity, the simple act of portraying a church community as positive and loving rather than oppressive and intolerant is a massive accomplishment. Some movies that have done this more recently are *Woman, Thou Art Loosed, Junebug, The Gospel* (2005), *Amazing Grace,* and *Lars and the Real Girl.*

Some movies of the past, like *Chariots of Fire* and *The Mission,* redeem the Christian missionary as an honorable soul with a virtuous heart who brings redemption—not destruction—to the lost. Others, like *The Apostle,* show the believer as flawed but sincere. *Shadowlands* portrays Christianity as a belief of strong intellects like C. S. Lewis, and *Les Misérables* characterizes Christian forgiveness as "muscular faith" rather than weak capitulation. Some, like *The Apostle,* are a mixed blessing of positive and negative understandings of the faith. A survey of some of these daring films will help offset the winds of bigotry blowing hard against the gates of heaven.

Les Misérables, starring Liam Neeson as Jean Valjean, is one of the most robust stories of Christian redemption ever allowed to grace the cinema. It was adapted by Rafael Yglesias from the classic Victor Hugo novel and is through and through a parable of the nature of grace and forgiveness. Valjean is a man haunted by "the law" as embodied in Javert, played by Geoffrey Rush.

In the beginning of the story Valjean is a paroled ex-convict who restarts his life of crime by stealing a cleric's silver. When he is caught and brought back, the cleric denies it was theft and offers Valjean the silver candle stands as well. The cleric leans in and whispers to Valjean that with that silver he's ransomed him from fear and hatred, and now he must live his life for God. Because of this encounter with grace and forgiveness, reminiscent of Christ's own ransom for us, Valjean's life is forever changed. Grace is something that we do not ask for or even have the power to accept; rather, it is something that is done to us and to which we respond with repentance.

Valjean reforms and becomes a productive economic, civil and moral force in his city. But his attempt to put his past behind him is endangered by the appointment of Javert to the position of police captain in his city. Javert soon recognizes Valjean and spends the rest of the story seeking out ways to bring him down. Near the end, Valjean captures Javert but then lets him go in mercy. And in the final confrontation, when Javert has captured Valjean, he cannot kill him, because of the mercy that he had received. Javert says to Valjean, "I have tried my whole life to keep every law." Then Javert lets Valjean go, handcuffs himself and drowns himself in the river. Javert is clearly the symbol of works righteousness and the law's relentlessly condemning power (God's law, that is), along with its inability to redeem people. *Les Misérables* is a parable of what the apostle Paul meant when he said,

> Therefore there is now no condemnation for those who are in Christ Jesus. For the law of the Spirit of life in Christ Jesus has set you free from the law of sin and of death. For what the Law could not do, weak as it was through the flesh, God did: sending His own Son in the likeness of sinful flesh and as an offering for sin, He condemned sin in the flesh, so that the requirement of the Law might be fulfilled in us, who do not walk according to the flesh but according to the Spirit. (Rom 8:1-4)

One movie that in recent years has attempted to give a positive spin on Christian faith is *The Apostle*. Robert Duvall took more than ten years to get the movie made and has explained in interviews that he was deliberately trying to break the Elmer Gantry stereotype of Christian preachers in the South. And in fact, this interesting and faithful portrayal of south-ern Pentecostals is one of the few films that manage to capture the uniqueness of a Christian subculture's adherents without mocking or deriding them. Characters may be eccentric or lovable and humorous, but not laughable. The movie conveys a genuine respect for the subculture.

The story is about Eulis ("Sonny") Dewey, a preacher in Texas whose safe life is shattered when he discovers that his wife is having an affair with the local youth minister. Sonny responds by beating his wife's lover with a baseball bat, putting him in a coma. Sonny becomes a fugitive, fleeing to Louisiana, where he starts preaching under a false name and baptizes himself as an "apostle" of the gospel.[5] He struggles with God and with his conscience but continues to do the one thing he is gifted at: preaching the gospel.

Sonny helps rebuild an old church and even brings a local racist (Billy Bob Thornton) to his knees in repentance in one of the most moving Christian conversion scenes ever filmed. This film would be a strong picture of true Christian repentance, had it not been for its ending. Sonny never repents for his criminal act of violence done in the beginning. He is ultimately tracked down and caught and willingly goes to jail, *but he never repents*. True repentance requires that he hand himself in, thus displaying true integrity of faith and redemption. But as the movie stands, Sonny goes to jail and starts preaching the gospel there as well. No matter where he is, it comes out of him like honey from a bee. Duvall seems to be saying that the man has flaws, but at least he is sincere in his beliefs. And sincerity is the real judge of character in this fallen world. Sadly, *The Apostle* communicates a morality that doesn't affirm repentance but ultimately rewards bad behavior in the name of sincerity.

With the financial bonanza of *The Passion of the Christ*, there was an opening of studios to the lucrative potential of mainstream films with positive Judeo-Christian worldviews in them. *Bruce Almighty*, and its sequel, *Evan Almighty*, may have been made possible because of this

---

[5]Claiming apostleship in this postapostolic era is something the Bible doesn't allow individuals the authority to do (Acts 1:21-22), but Sonny's behavior points up the length to which self-deception will go when rationalizing our sin and pride.

opening. The worldview presented in these movies is a mixture of good and bad, containing a generic positive affirmation of Judeo-Christian images and ideas mixed in with bad theology.

Bruce Almighty, written by Steve Koren, Mark O'Keefe and Steve Oedekerk, stars Jim Carey as Bruce, a selfish news reporter so upset with his unlucky circumstances that he shakes his fist at God, arguing he could do a lot better with his life if he was in control. God shows up in the form of an irreverent Morgan Freeman and gives Bruce exactly what he prays for: God's almighty powers for a short time.

In the course of this humorous setup, Bruce realizes that God really does have a lot on his plate in ruling the universe, which is far too much for any human to handle, and that Bruce really doesn't know better after all. In other words, the story is a parable that proves we are not in control, and God knows better for our lives. At the climactic moment of the movie, Bruce realizes his hubris and falls to his knees proclaiming, "I don't want to do this anymore. I don't want to be God. I want you to decide what's right for me. I surrender to your will!"

This quintessential definition of repentance, however, is hampered by the almost total lack of Jesus in the film (outside of a couple jokes), as well as some New Age religious notions like the "divine spark of God within all of us." In *Bruce Almighty*, it seems God is not quite almighty after all, since there are some things even he can't control. The movie is a step in the right direction, but a very awkward staggering step.

Another positive portrayal of Christianity can be seen in Sylvester Stallone's sequels *Rocky Balboa* and *Rambo*. Evidently mirroring a spiritual change in his own life, his last Rocky installment brings a subtle spiritual aspect to Rocky's life when he prays to put himself in the hands of God and quotes the Bible before his big fight with the heavyweight champion. *Rambo* becomes even more explicit about a positive Christian faith when John Rambo is hired to liberate some Christian missionaries held captive by mercenaries in Thailand. Lo and behold, the missionaries are actually good people concerned with the human rights of the Karen people oppressed by the Burmese military. Rambo begins the story as a cynical nihilist believing there's nothing worth living for, only to learn by the end of the movie that there are still some things worth dying for.

SUBSTITUTIONARY ATONEMENT

One of the most important truths of the Christian faith is Christ's death on the cross paying for the sins of his people. Christ is our substitute, who atones for our sin by taking our place in receiving God's judgment against our sin. This beautiful scriptural truth is sometimes called substitutionary atonement.

> Surely our griefs He Himself bore,
>   And our sorrows He carried;
>   Yet we ourselves esteemed Him stricken,
>   Smitten of God, and afflicted.
> But He was pierced through for our transgressions,
>   He was crushed for our iniquities;
>   The chastening for our well-being fell upon Him,
>   And by His scourging we are healed.
> All of us like sheep have gone astray,
>   Each of us has turned to his own way;
>   But the LORD has caused the iniquity of us all
>   To fall on Him. (Is 53:4-6)

The most well-known example of substitutionary atonement in filmdom is now *The Lion, the Witch and the Wardrobe*, adapted by Andrew Adamson, Ann Peacock, Christopher Markus and Stephen McFeely from the classic children's series by C. S. Lewis. When the White Witch demands Edmund's life due to the Deep Magic that demanded such punishment for treachery, Aslan appeals to a deeper magic and takes Edmund's place. Aslan is then tortured and killed at the stone altar (a metaphor for the cross), and mocked by the minions of evil, just as the demonic powers mocked Christ on the cross. But Aslan's substitutionary sacrifice is what frees them all and leads to the children being crowned with glory at the end (see Col 2:13-15).

Brian Helgeland's film adaptation of the novel *Man on Fire* incarnates a Christian notion of substitutionary atonement. Burned-out ex-CIA assassin Creasy (Denzel Washington) is hired to guard the daughter (Dakota Fanning) of a rich Mexican industrialist. When the girl is kidnapped, he goes on a rampage, killing everyone connected to the kidnappers, right on up to the kidnapper's brother. But when Creasy discovers the girl is alive and will be allowed to go free if he takes her place, he realizes that he will find justice not by vengeance but by sacrificing himself.

To End All Wars, which I adapted from the book by Ernest Gordon, contains at its heart the notion of substitutionary atonement. It is the true story of Allied prisoners of war suffering under the Imperial Japanese in Thailand during World War II. As the POWs are tortured during their captivity, one man, Major Campbell, plots a coup d'état to take over the camp and kill their Japanese captors. He is hampered by a Christian, Dusty, who seeks to teach love of their enemies to the captives. Campbell betrays Dusty and moves ahead with his plans. But when he fails and is about to be executed, Dusty intervenes and takes the Major's place, the innocent for the guilty, in a Christlike sacrifice. The lives of all the men in the camp are changed by this act of redemption.

But blood atonement is not the sole province of Christianity. Even paganism has its version of substitutionary sacrifice, as in the Oscar-winning Pan's Labyrinth by Guillermo del Toro. It's an adult fairy tale of a little girl coping with the violent reality of 1944 fascist Spain fighting the communists. She is taken in by her new stepfather, a sadistic military captain. In her desire to see her real father, she creates a complex surreal fairy tale in her mind that includes fairies and a faun, centered around a labyrinth of the famed pagan deity Pan. She accomplishes three quests of maturity given her by the faun but ends up being shot dead by her stepfather while protecting her baby brother. As her blood drips down into Pan's labyrinth, it becomes the life force that opens the portal for her to see her father in Paradise. The little girl's own shed blood in sacrifice becomes her redemption—a paganized version of substitutionary atonement.

THE SOVEREIGNTY OF GOD

Another key linchpin in orthodox Christian theology is God's sovereignty. Jesus proclaimed that nothing happens apart from God's sovereign will, not even the death of the most insignificant sparrow (Mt 10:29). The rise and fall of kingdoms, people's wisdom and people's foolishness, the actions of both kings and paupers, everything in history, both big and small is sovereignly ordained through God's will (Job 12:16-25)—

even the good, the bad and the ugly are under his control (Is 45:7; Job 2:10; Lam 3:37-38).

Simon Birch, a movie about a boy born with a disease that made him small and deformed, is a virtual sermon of how God has a plan and purpose for everyone, even those we would consider to be unlucky or unblessed. While everyone around him sees his physical deformity as a curse from which no good can come, little Simon states repeatedly that he believes God has a plan for his life, and he seeks to find out what that is. Even his pastor states, "It's wonderful to have faith, Simon, but let's not overdo it." But Simon does show everyone God's plan for him: because of his small size and special abilities, he is able to save a busload of kids. What we think is only evil, God determines for good (Gen 50:20).

Signs, M. Night Shyamalan's original creation, is a movie about God's sovereign control of all events. Mel Gibson plays a backslidden minister, Graham Hess, who loses his faith when he loses his wife in a car accident. The metaphor of signs is used with a double meaning in this story: Not only are signs of alien invasion burned into farm fields around the planet, but it also represents the signs that God gives us, if we have eyes to see and ears to hear, that indicate his invasion of our reality. Thus, the same providential determination of the bad (Graham's wife's death and his son's asthma) is used by God to bring about their rescue later in the story. His son's asthma saves him from deadly alien fumes, and his wife's dying statement inspires Graham's brother's special God-given talent to stop an attacking alien. All of these draw Graham back to faith in the end.

Magnolia, by Paul Thomas Anderson, is a film that addresses the issue of providence and freedom in a memorable and biblical way. Starring Tom Cruise, Julianne Moore and Jason Robards, it's the story of twelve-plus people whose lives intersect on one fateful evening during a storm of raining frogs. Each of them is embroiled in his or her own dysfunctional attempts to make sense of life and find some solace, as they are haunted by past pain and sins. The theme is revealed through a repeated phrase in the film: "We may be through with the past, but the past is not through with us." The power of the story lies in the reference to the underlying providence that drives them through apparent coincidences and into their respective redemptions.

The movie begins with a dramatization of several bizarre coincidences of true history. Freakish accidents ripped from the pages of Ripley's Believe It or Not! The narrator then explains in voiceover how he doesn't think these are coincidences at all. Rather than affirming some kind of impersonal fate, Anderson goes out of his way to express *biblical* providence.

References to Bible verses occur throughout the movie. They are planted on billboards, whispered randomly by characters and even plastered on signs in a TV show audience. One is Exodus 34:7, which states, "[The LORD God] keeps lovingkindness for thousands, . . . forgives iniquity, transgression and sin; yet He will by no means leave the guilty unpunished, visiting the iniquity of fathers on the children and on the grandchildren to the third and fourth generations." The other is Exodus 8:2 which states, "If you refuse to let them go, behold, I will smite your whole territory with frogs."

The entire film is about characters suffering under the negative effects of the sins of their fathers, which directly affect their own lives: overachievement, unfair expectations, abandonment, even incest. One of the two pure-hearted souls in this story loaded with foul-mouthed reprobates is a bumbling yet ultimately sincere Christian cop (the other one a compassionate nurse). Most of the other characters avoid facing their own culpability in the process. That is, until a freak rainstorm of frogs occurs that operates as a divine intervention in all their lives with intersecting velocity.

Ironically, when one considers Anderson's own explanation of why he chose the biblical imagery of frogs as well as the Bible verses to support it, one can only conclude that the making of this movie is an example of human freedom and divine determination. As Anderson explains:

> There's certainly a biblical reference there, but I'd be a liar if I said to you it was written initially as a biblical reference. I truthfully didn't even know it was in the Bible when I first wrote the sequence . . . but maybe there are certain moments in your life when things are so . . . confused that someone can say to you, "It's raining frogs," and that makes sense.

That somehow makes sense as a warning; that somehow makes sense as a sign. I started to understand why people turn to religion in times of trouble, and maybe my form of finding religion was reading about rains of frogs and realizing that makes sense to me somehow. And then of course to discover it in the Bible and the reference that it makes there just sort of verifies it, like, "Hey, I guess I'm on the right track."[6]

Anderson's rejection of chance and his use of biblical providence is more arbitrary cultural imagery than true Christian devotion. Nevertheless, *Magnolia* is a film that illustrates that life is not a random sequence of unfortunate events but rather a providentially directed, divinely redeeming story. So it appears that Anderson is as much a subject of God's providence as are the characters in his own movie. *Magnolia* is a strong example of art imitating life.

A movie that seeks a heterodox view of free will and God's sovereignty more in line with open theism is *Minority Report*. This movie was adapted by Scott Frank and Jon Cohen from Philip K. Dick's short story about a "pre-crime unit" of cops in the future of 2054, who use the precognitive (foreseeing) visions of several individuals to stop crime before it happens. When the hero, a cop played by Tom Cruise, is accused of committing a crime in the future, he goes on the run to exonerate himself, because as a religious open theist character claims, the precogs are not always right, leaving the future to be open and unpredictable with alternate quantum possibilities.

Other sci-fi movies that deal with precognition and man's free will to change the future are *Paycheck*, *The Butterfly Effect*, *A Sound of Thunder* and *Next*.

FATE: A GOD SUBSTITUTE

When storytellers don't want to admit their Creator into their worldview, and yet don't want to face the horror and meaninglessness of the random universe they are left with, they substitute fate for the living God. The benefit of this tactic is that it gives the storyteller all the benefits of a

---

[6]From an interview with Paul Thomas Anderson for *Creative Screenwriting Magazine*, posted on P. T. Anderson's website <http://www.cigarettesandredvines.com/articles/display.php?id=M16>.

personal loving God, complete with a happy ending, but none of the moral accountability. As C. S. Lewis eloquently stated:

> When you are feeling fit and the sun is shining and you do not want to believe that the whole universe is a mere mechanical dance of atoms, it is nice to be able to think of this great mysterious Force rolling on through the centuries and carrying you on its crest. If, on the other hand, you want to do something rather shabby, the Life-Force, being only a blind force, with no morals and no mind, will never interfere with you like that troublesome God.[7]

Cast Away, written by William Broyles Jr., is an example of fate as a God substitute. It's a thought-provoking story of a FedEx employee named Chuck Noland (played by Tom Hanks) whose life is dictated by his time schedule and whose plane crashes in the ocean, resulting in him washing up on a deserted island. The entire middle of the film is a contemplative series of scenes of a man facing his helpless solitude—a good examination of how so many things we consider important fall away when we lose the conveniences and distractions of modern life. We have allowed ourselves to become tyrannized by time and therefore miss out on what's really important all around us.

This survivor relives the so-called evolutionary stages of humankind as he learns to find shelter, create tools, build fire and ultimately seek companionship. God is conspicuously absent from the entire search, unlike its classic literary predecessor, *Robinson Crusoe*. Not once does this shipwrecked victim ever consider his Creator, even to lash out at him for his predicament. He is all alone in a naturalistic universe.

There are a few spiritual symbols that are secularized into subtle metaphors for his quest. A set of wings (angel?) on a FedEx package becomes Chuck's sailboat symbol. He uses his own blood to make a face on his volleyball friend, Mr. Wilson ("bone of my bone, flesh of my flesh"?). And after Chuck sets out to sea to find civilization, he encounters a whale at night that stares at him (a reference to the biblical Jonah?).

At the end of the film, Chuck finds his way back to civilization. The woman whose angel-wings mail package washed up on shore and kept

---

[7]C. S. Lewis, *Mere Christianity* (New York: Macmillan, 1960), p. 35.

him going in his darkest hour just happens to be a beautiful and available woman for our lonely returned hero—a substitute for the woman he had lost. So humanity finds meaning in hope for another human being, and the benevolent impersonal fate will work it all out for us in the end.

A negative version of fate can be found in David Webb Peoples's *Twelve Monkeys*. This time-travel picture is crafted like a Greek tragedy of fate on the level of *Oedipus*. The hero, in trying to save the world from biological warfare, is trapped in the never-ending time loop of seeing himself as a child observing his own death as an adult and failing to save the world (echoes of Nietzsche's "eternal recurrence").

Wanted, written by Michael Brandt, Derek Haas and Chris Morgan, based on the graphic novel of the same name, illustrates another God-substitute version of impersonal fate. In this festival of violence, James McAvoy plays a recruit to a secret society of assassins who have preternatural abilities to curve the trajectory of bullets, and turn their flight-or-fight mechanism into hyperdrive. Played by Morgan Freeman, the leader of the conspiracy has a huge paranormal loom that foresees history and codifies names in the weaving of the fabric, indicating the assassins' next targets. One of the issues in the film is "faith" in trusting the loom's authority. How do they know these people they are killing are really bad people who would end up doing evil in the world? Angelina Jolie plays an assassin and true believer whose zealous dedication to the "loomic" prophecies amounts to a secular version of religious fanaticism. The resignation to an impersonal fate is finally embraced by the hero, and no doubt by many in the admiring audience as well.

PROVIDENTIAL ENSEMBLE

Pulp Fiction, discussed in an earlier chapter, is not a "fate" film, because it actually addresses the idea of God using miracles to bring redemption into a criminal's life. But it spawned a whole subgenre of films after its own image that *would* embrace fate rather than God within a quirky postmodern context of criminal chic.

One of the redeeming features of *Pulp Fiction*'s celebration of underworld depravity is its wrestling with God. Samuel L. Jackson's hit man character, Jules, recognizes the "touch of God" when he and fellow killer

Vincent are miraculously unscathed by a surprise gun attack. All five bullets of a revolver shot at them at point-blank range completely miss them.

Jules argues with the skeptical Vincent that God stopped the bullets by divine intervention. Jules says to his compadre in crime, "What happened here was a miracle, and I want you to acknowledge it." Vincent refuses to do so, thinking he merely witnessed a "freak occurrence." But Jules knows better and decides that his killing days are over. He is going to quit "the business" and walk the earth "like Caine in *Kung Fu,* till God puts me where he wants me to be."

Before Jules would kill his victims, he would quote an amalgamation of Bible verses in cold-blooded mockery:

> The path of the righteous man is beset on all sides by the inequities of the selfish and the tyranny of evil men. Blessed is he who, in the name of charity and goodwill, shepherds the weak through the valley of darkness, for he is truly his brother's keeper and the finder of lost children. And I will strike down upon thee with great vengeance and furious anger those who would attempt to poison and destroy my brothers. And you will know my name is the Lord when I lay my vengeance upon thee.

But when Jules has his newfound revelation, the true meaning of those verses comes alive to him. He repents of his own "tyranny of evil" and becomes a man of grace, a shepherd to help the weak.

Contrarily, Vincent, who refuses to see the handwriting on the wall, continues on living by the gun and therefore dies by the gun—at the hands of his enemy. These contrasted destinies are rather profound expressions of a biblical truth:

> They shall eat of the fruit of their own way
> And be satiated with their own devices.
> For the waywardness of the naive will kill them,
> And the complacency of fools will destroy them.
> But he who listens to me shall live securely
> And will be at ease from the dread of evil. . . .
> So you will walk in the way of good men
> And keep to the paths of the righteous.
> For the upright will live in the land

And the blameless will remain in it;
But the wicked will be cut off from the land. (Prov 1:31-33; 2:20-22)

Because of the success of *Pulp Fiction,* there is a new subgenre of films on the rise that I call "providential ensemble," based on the *Pulp Fiction* paradigm. They are often smaller, independent films that contain multiple story lines of different people who are unconnected to each other, but through some wild, complex twists of fate end up intersecting all in one moment or day in such a way that all their stories are resolved together. This technique has the effect of illustrating the interconnectedness of all things. The main characters in these stories are usually small-time criminals who are portrayed as making bad choices rather than as being bad people. By the end of the story, the trouble that these misdirected souls have gotten into is resolved perfectly, and most of the *really* bad guys are punished— and all of this because of the intricate workings of an impersonal fate.

Like *Pulp Fiction* and *Magnolia,* these fate films have the same kind of perfect foreordination of every little event working toward a final purpose, but altogether without God. They often use the postmodern storytelling device of showing nuances of difference between each person's perception of events. Let's take a look at some of these providential ensembles.

PROVIDENTIAL ENSEMBLE FILMS

Short Cuts

2 Days in the Valley

Lock, Stock and Two Smoking Barrels

Payback

Go

Small-Time Crooks

13 Conversations About One Thing

The Mexican

One Night at McCool's

The Score

Sexy Beast

Snatch

Between Strangers

11:14

Crash

Running Scared

Lock, Stock and Two Smoking Barrels from British writer/director Guy Ritchie takes four different stories and weaves them together into one karmic blend. Four wide-eyed young Cockney card-playing lads of London want to join an illegal, high-rolling card game. The leader of that little game is a gangland boss who is in search of two antique shotguns that have been stolen. A drug lord is growing pot in a house that is about to be raided by some robbers, who just happen to live next door to our four young lads.

When the card players get in life-threatening debt over the rigged card game, they try to make up the money by stealing the drug robbery job away from their next-door neighbors. So the gangland boss sends a killer to take out the kids, the druggies are after the kids to get back their stash, and the intended robbers are after the kids to regain their dignity.

All their plans go awry, and all the bad guys descend upon each other unwittingly in one huge gun battle in which they all die, leaving the young kids alive and debtfree. It's a perfect circle: the bad guys kill each other; big crimes may not pay, but small ones do; and it all works out for "the good" in the end.

Paul Haggis's Oscar-winning *Crash* is another version of the providential ensemble. The movie portrays the ubiquitous presence of racism within American culture by following the lives of a dozen different people in different socioeconomic parts of Los Angeles over two days. Most of the characters do not know each other, indeed have nothing to do with each other, but the story shows how their bigoted actions and attitudes ultimately connect them all and affect each other. A pair of black car thieves from the ghetto, a white district attorney and his pampered suburban wife, a white racist city cop and his liberal young partner, a successful black Hollywood director and his mulatto wife, a Persian immigrant store owner and his educated daughter, a black cop and his South American lover, and a Hispanic locksmith with his daughter are all brought together in a providential web of interconnectedness and irony not present at the beginning of the story.

THE SPIRIT OF TRUTH

As we have seen throughout this chapter, our secular society is actually a very religious one underneath. Many movies deal with spiritual themes and issues, even those of a Christian nature. Some of these Christian elements are genuine, capturing a truthful portrait of authentic Christianity. Other spiritual elements are deconstructed or reinterpreted through countervailing worldviews, but they are not ignored. The argument could be made that movies that ignore God or the spiritual side of humanity are far more dishonest than those that attack God. For when a story attacks God or tries to redefine him, it is at least admitting that he is an issue, whereas ignoring him leaves the impression that he is a nonissue, irrelevant to our reality—and those may be the most detrimental stories of all.

WATCH AND LEARN

1. Watch *The Big Kahuna* with your church small group. Discuss what you think the theme of the movie is. Discuss how accurate or inaccurate the depiction of the Christian in the movie is. Reflect and discuss in what ways you are guilty of preaching Jesus out of salesmanship rather than out of genuine concern for people's souls. What kind of things can you do to continue sharing your faith without succumbing to salesmanship? Read John 4, and discuss how Jesus approached the woman at the well with the gospel. Do you think he was opportunistic? Does the Master's approach correlate in any way with a salesman's approach? How does it differ?

2. Watch *Les Misérables* with your church small group. Discuss the ways in which Valjean represents grace and Javert represents law or legalism. How is justice balanced with mercy in the Bible and in the movie?

9

FAITH

The existential leap of blind faith has already been discussed in chapter four. But this leap is not merely confined to the rejection of reason. It bleeds into the realm of science as well, ultimately reducing faith to a belief in something that we think is factually untrue. As indicated earlier, this kind of faith is belief in spite of or against the evidence. In order to understand just how influential this definition of faith is on movies, we need to know where it came from and how it came to us. Then we can see how specific movies illustrate this "faith" in its various aspects.

A NECESSARILY OVERSIMPLIFIED BRIEF HISTORY OF THE SENSES

In the year 1620, during the Renaissance in Europe, English jack-of-all-trades Francis Bacon published the *Novum Organum,* in which he proposed the inductive method as the basis for scientific knowledge. This procedure of inferring general laws of nature (regularity) from empirical observation and repeatable experimentation would soon prime the explosion of what we know as modern science.[1]

With the coming of Sir Isaac Newton and the British empiricists, humanity's faith in empirical observation would soon eclipse all other belief systems. Of course many still believed in God as the Creator of that observable order. In fact, as historian of science Alfred North Whitehead has stated, it was the Christian worldview that provided the philosophical foundation for the birth of science.[2] Because God is rational, his creation reflects that same rationality and law-like regularity. We can trust that the future will be like the past ("natural laws") because God himself sustains the regularity of nature by his omnipotent power.

In the 1700s the skeptical empiricism of Scottish philosopher David Hume established doubt about the knowability of reason and morals, and even the justification of causality itself, relegating them to the realm of unjustifiable beliefs. The German thinker Immanuel Kant attempted to solve this skeptical dilemma by proposing that our mind uses reason and value as tools to organize our experiences. We actually have no way of knowing whether the categories of the mind actually correspond to ultimate reality, but it is convenient for us to believe so.

The bifurcation of our experience and our mind would soon evolve into a dichotomy of "fact" and "value," facts being those things that we can empirically verify with our senses and values being those things the mind attributes abstractly to its experiences. In this view gravity is a fact, implying objective reality, while morality is a value, implying subjective relativity. We can prove facts, but we can't prove values. This dichotomy of fact and value would soon turn into a battle for social dominance in which so-called fact would eventually come out on top and keep pushing

---

[1]Bacon proposed that making logical inferences from what we observe in the world is more reliable than formulating ideas about the world apart from investigating it. If we want to know, for example, whether light is important for the growth of green plants, then we can test it. We can put some plants in darkness and others in light, and then we can see what happens. This process of observation, hypothesis, experimentation and conclusion is what became known as the scientific method. Thanks to Stephen Ross for this clarification.

[2]And not merely the Christian worldview in principle, but the *medieval* Christian worldview in historical practice. The medieval period was the very era that Enlightenment thinkers consider to be the "Dark Ages." See Stanley L. Jaki, *Chance or Reality and Other Essays* (Lanham, Md.: University Press of America, 1986), p. 152.

values to the point of irrelevancy, where they are now regarded as mere myth or cultural interpretations.

In the nineteenth century Auguste Comte had completely rejected metaphysics and theology ("values") as an adequate "means of knowledge." He developed what he called "positivism," a philosophy based on empirical knowledge and experience. By the mid-1930s, the logical positivist school had become a dominant force in society. Led by thinkers such as A. J. Ayer, Morris Schlick and Rudolph Carnap, this school relegated all metaphysical notions (including religion and morals) to the scrap heap of meaninglessness.

There was a place for believing in such things as God, doctrines and ethics, but they were not verifiable through empirical observation, the scientific method or sense perception, and were therefore quite literally "non-sense" to these men. In fact, this supreme faith in our sense perception would balloon to such proportions that it is currently assumed as true that facts are "provable" things and values (morals, religion, truth) are matters of "faith" without factual support.

Fact and faith are often perceived as eternal opposites in our culture. People tend to think that what they can experience with their five senses is the most reliable knowledge and that religion is arbitrary, unproven belief. If a scientist says something, there is instant credibility; if a religious leader says something, well, that's true for him but not necessarily true for me. So, when the Son of Man comes, will he find faith in the movies? Religious faith plays an important role in many modern secular movies. Because of this influence of empiricism on the Western mind, faith is usually dealt with in one of three different ways: faith versus proof, the individual versus the institution and doubt versus faith.

BLIND FAITH VERSUS PROOF

In the film *Keeping the Faith,* Father Brian Finn (Edward Norton) defines faith as "not about having all the right answers. Faith is a feeling. Faith is a hunch. It's a hunch that there is something bigger connecting it all, connecting us all together. And that feeling, that hunch is God."

Indiana Jones and the Last Crusade, written by scribe Jeffrey Boam, is a movie about faith. It brings an occult angle to Christianity as a religion of mystically powered relics but weaves it together with the notion of faith as trust (very often, blind). As Indiana's lightheaded sidekick says, "The search for the cup of Christ is the search for the divine in all of us." That's occultism. And faith is ultimately a part of the nonfactual realm. As Indiana tells his class, "Archaeology is the search for fact—not truth."

At the end of the story, when Indiana is following his map to the Holy Grail, he finds himself at the edge of a great precipice. The only way to cross the chasm to the other side is to follow the drawing of a knight stepping out into midair. Indiana decides to follow this drawing by stepping into the chasm with faith, only to find there an invisible bridge that allows him to cross. Faith is here affirmed as a blind leap, or at least a blind step.

The positive side of this tale is that Indiana begins as a skeptic telling his class, "We cannot afford to take mythology at face value," but ends up a true believer in the factual origins of such myths. And Indiana's father, played by Sean Connery, says at the end that "finding the Grail is not about finding a prize, but about illumination."

An interesting flip-flop of science as a leap of faith occurs in the movie *O Brother, Where Art Thou?* by the eccentric brothers Coen (Ethan and Joel). In this amusing tale, which is based very loosely on Homer's *The Odyssey* but told using Christian symbols and spirituality, the accusation of blind and even ignorant faith is leveled at the empiricist, the one who denies that there is a supernatural world that transcends our physical senses.

O Brother is the story of three escaped convicts from a Mississippi chain gang in the Depression-era South led by Ulysses Everett Gill (played by George Clooney). While on the lam, they encounter an old-fashioned, fundamentalist baptism at a river. But unlike in most movies, these Bible belt people are mocked only through the eyes of the skeptical Everett, not the others. Angelic singing permeates the area with peace, and two of the convicts decide to repent and get cleansed from their past life of sin. But Everett, good ole empirical scientist that he is, believes there is a natural explanation for every religious "superstition." He refuses to join in the conversion and chalks it up to the belief that tough times bring out the weakness in people.

Everett's empiricism is ultimately shown to be blind faith itself because he keeps explaining away all the fortuitous events that happen to the two fellows. Everett's lack of spiritual understanding and his belief in the inherent goodness of humanity also keep him from recognizing real evil when faced with it. A big, one-eyed pseudo-Bible salesman (Cyclops) hoodwinks two of the convicts and robs them. The Christian convict tries to fight the ogre right in front of Everett because he has discerned his evil intentions, but the blissfully unaware Everett never catches on.

Earlier in the story, the three men hear a black man prophesy that among "many startlements" they will encounter are a flood and a vision of a cow on top of a cotton house. Everett is not in awe of such "mystery."

> The blind are reputed to possess sensitivities compensatin' for their lack of sight, even to the point of developing paranormal psychic power. Now, clearly seein' the future would fall neatly into that ka-taggery. It's not so surprisin' then.

Everett keeps on a-scoffin' at this and other spiritual things until he is on his knees at the climax of the film, about to be shot by the bad guy, and belts out a sinner's prayer to God quicker than you can shake a stick.

But when a flood sweeps through the valley and saves the convicts from their execution, they float to the top, and the men yell out that God has pitied them in response to their prayers. Everett remarks with contempt that his hayseed brethren are just showing their "want for innalect." "There's a perfectly scientific explanation for what just happened," he opines. But when challenged that he has suddenly changed the tune he was just a-singin' back at the gallows, he promptly derides, "Well, any human being will cast about in a moment of stress." His foxhole conversion proves counterfeit. Just then they see a cow on a cotton-house roof, as the oracle prophesied, and Everett looks the other way in denial, remaining truly blind in his empirical faith in "scientific facts."[3]

---

[3]Even if we accept the validity of science, what the average Everett doesn't comprehend is that there are as many versions of "science" as there are Christian denominations. Even what scientists have considered to be reliable scientific knowledge has often turned out to be in error. Some have even noted that "science," as a monolithic unity of knowledge, simply does not exist. And in fact, different sciences are driven and changed by philosophical commitments and prejudices just as regularly as any other metaphysical system

The issue of blind faith in science is also explored in the movie *Contact*, adapted by James V. Hart and Michael Goldenberg from the famous Carl Sagan novel about extraterrestrial life contacting earth through radio waves. In this movie the similarity of religious faith and scientific faith is explored through the contrast of characters Palmer Ross (played by Matthew McConaughey), a political lobbyist and "man of the cloth without the cloth [and the morals]," and Dr. Eleanor "Ellie" Ann Arroway (played by Jodie Foster), an atheist research scientist who establishes contact with extraterrestrials.

In a spirited discussion Ellie questions the validity of faith in things one cannot see. She challenges Palmer to prove the existence of God. Unpredictably, Palmer turns Ellie's own argument against her and challenges her, "Do you love your father?" "Yes, very much," she replies. "Prove it," demands Palmer, and for one rare moment in film history, the scientist is the one without a response.

True to Sagan's devoted faith in science, *Contact* explores the actual religious foundations of modern science's quest for ultimate answers. No longer are scientists content in dealing with physical phenomenon, but they are now engaged in the metaphysical quest for truth and the ontological cure for loneliness. Ellie thinks that finding extraterrestrial life somehow supplies this answer.

> For as long as I can remember, I've been searching for something, some reason why we're here. What are we doing here? Who are we? If this is a chance to find out even just a little part of that answer . . .

After Ellie makes contact with an alien in the guise of her dead father, the alien tells her the "wisdom of the ages."

> You're an interesting species, an interesting mix. You're capable of such beautiful dreams and such horrible nightmares. You feel so lost, so cut off, so alone, only you're not. See, in all our searching, the only thing we've found that makes the emptiness bearable is each other.

---

or religion (Thomas Kuhn, *The Structure of Scientific Revolutions* [Chicago: University of Chicago Press, 1996]). The famous quantum physicist Max Planck voiced the dirty little secret that most modern scientists refuse to admit: "Over the entrance to the gates of the temple of science are written the words: 'Ye must have faith'" (Max Planck, *Where Is Science Going?* [Woodbridge, Conn.: Ox Bow, 1981], p. 214).

The Search for Extraterrestrial Intelligence (SETI) reduces to the search of lonely sentient beings for other lonely sentient beings with which to be lonely together. In an ironic twist *Contact* deconstructs SETI's search for alien life forms into a faith commitment itself. When young Ellie asks her dad if he thinks there are people on other planets, he responds, "I don't know, Sparks. But I guess I'd say if it is just us . . . seems like an awful waste of space."

And Ellie's experience with aliens is also likened to a faith encounter. She stands before a congressional committee to try to explain her worm-hole space travel, and she winds up looking like any other religious person trying to explain her "testimony" or religious faith encounter. What is normally criticized by atheist scientists as the arbitrariness of faith is now employed by the atheist-science poster girl herself.

> Look, all I'm asking is for you to just have the tiniest bit of vision. You know, to just sit back for one minute and look at the big picture. To take a chance on something that just might end up being the most profoundly impactful moment for humanity, for the history . . . of history.

In other words, she's asking them to have *faith,* to *believe* that her experience was real and to keep searching for that for which there is no evidence (except an awful lot of wasted space) in order to make the emptiness more bearable.

Proof, adapted by David Auburn from his play, is another example of the epistemic wrestling match between faith and proof. It's about a brilliant mathematician (Gwyneth Paltrow) who must take care of her brilliant mathematician father (Anthony Hopkins) who is losing his mind to Alzheimers disease. A colleague must investigate her because she claims to be the writer of a notebook full of breakthrough mathematics attributed to her father.

The dramatic question of the movie is: did she write the notebook full of breakthrough mathematics during her father's brief remission, or did he write it? The philosophical question posed by the film is: how do we prove what is true? The stock answer of reason and observation is ultimately undermined because when it comes down to it, *all investigation and evidence is based on faith in one source or another.*

The father's Alzheimer's is an effective indictment of the Enlightenment metaphysic that reduces reality or truth to a mathematical theorem. As Chesterton wrote, "Poets do not go mad; but chess-players do. . . . The madman is not the man who has lost his reason. The madman is the man who has lost everything except his reason."[4]

THE INDIVIDUAL VERSUS THE INSTITUTION

The image of pioneers braving the cold, cruel frontiers all alone is an American myth (discussed earlier) that has entrenched itself in every aspect of our culture. And that mythology is all about individualism.

Much good has come from individualism, but so has much that is questionable. We Americans think we can do everything on our own from starting our own businesses to starting our own religions, and we distrust institutions as big, bad corporate entities headed by power-mongering "suits" who want to use the institution to tromp on the little guy. We love the underdog, the one person against the system, which is collectively referred to as "the man." But we also elevate "individual rights" to the exclusion of personal responsibility and in the name of freedom impose those rights on others through massive litigation. We end up with a tribalist society of warring factions—and all of it under the guise of respect for individual rights.

Individualism has also resulted in relativism and a breakdown of tradition—not just bad tradition but all tradition. Americans question *all* authority, because after all, "No one is the boss of me." This rejection of authority and institutions, or the many in favor of the few, has become a staple of religion as well. Transfers of church membership are more often attributable to personality differences than justifiable biblical separation.[5] The elevation of the individual to a nearly absolute status has affected American Christianity to the detriment of true biblical community and accountability. Everyone tends to do what is right in his or her own eyes.

Rebellion against authority plays well in American movies. Stories with a lone hero who stands against the system or doesn't fit in are more

---

[4]G. K. Chesterton, *Orthodoxy* (New York, N.Y.: Doubleday, 2001), pp. 10, 13.
[5]Rather than follow the apostle Peter's command to "submit yourselves for the Lord's sake to every human institution" (1 Pet 2:13), and especially to one's church elders (1 Pet 5:5), most Christians will usually just up and leave their church to find a new one that "ministers to them."

conducive to storytelling than are ensemble pieces, and they can ring true when the individual is right and the collective is wrong. But rare will be the occurrence of a hero who realizes that he is a rebel and is wrong in his individualism. It just doesn't fit our mythology of individualism. This is why most institutions of faith are portrayed in a negative way. They are usually filled with power mongers set on control and destruction, or with boring, stuffy keepers of dead traditions.

OPPRESSIVE INSTITUTIONS

1984

Brazil

Dead Poets Society

Demolition Man

Gattaca

The horror film *Stigmata* features a young New York hairdresser (Patricia Arquette) who begins receiving the wounds of Christ on her body. The Roman Catholic Church is shown as a nefarious conglomerate of religious leaders trying to suppress a secret document that contradicts the New Testament:

> The kingdom of God is within you and all around you. It is not within buildings of wood or stone. Split a piece of wood and you will find me. Look beneath a stone and I am there.

The real-life source material of this fictional text is the Gospel of Thomas from the Nag Hammadi library, a collection of Gnostic literature written sometime after the first century. At the end of the movie a title scroll says that the "Gospel of St. Thomas has been claimed by scholars around the world to be the closest record we have of the words of the historical Jesus" and that "the Vatican refuses to recognize this gospel and has described it as heresy." Supposedly, the Vatican is ignorantly denying what most scholars have proved.

The fact is, the Gospel of Thomas and dozens of other Gnostic texts are available and have been studied by scholars for many years. They were rejected when the biblical canon was formed because they failed to meet the rigorous criteria of Scripture that other books also had to meet.

There *are* negative institutions that oppress the freedom and rights of individuals. There *are* dark corridors of power and evil religious leaders. But in focusing exclusively on anti-institutional storytelling and negative authority figures, without a balance of proper authority or submission, movie culture amounts to propaganda that breeds anti-authority lawlessness and bigotry in audiences. As C. S. Lewis wrote, "We make men without chests and expect of them virtue and enterprise. We laugh at honor and are shocked to find traitors in our midst. We castrate and bid the geldings be fruitful."[6]

But not all challenge to authority is wrong. *How* a person brings change is the moral question. Defying rules *without respect or submission* breeds anarchy, with everyone a law unto themselves. Both extremes—oppressive institutions *and* rebellious individuals—are wrong.

One is hard pressed to find a recent film that extols the virtues of accountability to the community. One such film is *White Squall*, adapted by Todd Robinson, depicting a boatload of typical, individualistic young boys who sign up for a sail across the ocean, only to be capsized by a huge wave. Their very survival is dependent upon their following the rules and order laid out by the captain (played by Jeff Bridges) and working together by subordinating their individuality for the greater good of the group.

In *Miracle* a hockey team succeeds in the Olympics because its players put aside their individual glory and become a team, communicating the same communitarian redemption. Some military movies, like *Heartbreak Ridge, Hanoi Hilton, Rules of Engagement, Black Hawk Down* and *We Were Soldiers*, illustrate this team-oriented discipline and the subordination of the individual as well.

DOUBT VERSUS FAITH

The issue of doubt and faith is not unknown in contemporary cinema. In fact, it's probably the approach most favorable to the postmodern dilemma. By facing doubt, we can sometimes face our own arrogance and discover that we are asking the wrong questions after all. And the internal struggle of a hero trying to discover the truth under his or her own personal crisis is the stuff of great drama.

Shadowlands—William Nicholson's film adaptation from his play of C. S. Lewis's struggle with love and suffering—is a rather positive portrayal of the Christian life in the face of doubt. It is the love story be-

---

[6]C. S. Lewis, *The Abolition of Man* (New York: Macmillan, 1955), p. 35.

tween Lewis (played by Anthony Hopkins) and Joy Davidman (played by Debra Winger) and her subsequent battle with cancer. Lewis is portrayed as an intellectual who is so absorbed in books and ideas that he lacks the experience of real-life suffering about which he writes so articulately. In fact, he is a bit arrogant because he always wins arguments. In short, he is a know-it-all who has never really experienced loss.

But it is one thing to write clever words of advice and quite another to live them out in flesh and blood. And that is what his journey becomes. The key repeated phrase in the film is "Pain is God's megaphone to a deaf world." And megaphone it is for Lewis as he is surprised by the pain of losing the woman he loves, which leads him to question his faith. This is an honest struggle portrayed with sensitive sympathy as he rediscovers God's severe mercy in the midst of suffering.[7]

Another movie that expresses the goodness of God's will in the face of human doubt is *Commandments* (1997). Aidan Quinn plays a young man who loses his job, his house, his health and, most precious of all, his wife. He embarks on a quest to break the Ten Commandments one by one until God explains himself. He is miraculously rescued from suicide and resigns himself to the fact that God is in control, only to find peace and happiness in a twist of events ordained by his Creator, which give his life back to him.

The End of the Affair—adapted by Neil Jordan from the novel of the same name by the famous author Graham Greene—is a story of attempted fidelity to God in the midst of suffering. Set during World War II, this movie presents a successful writer named Maurice who has an adulterous affair with Sarah, his friend's wife. But then one day, after his home is bombed and he has a near-death experience,

---

[7]Unfortunately, even though the film deals with Lewis's faith, it pulls way back from the boldness in the original play, diluting its power. And one tiny line change from the play to the movie stains a potentially great finale. At the end of the film after Lewis has been humbled in his intellect, he is walking away, and we hear his voice-over narrate that he doesn't have "any answers," but he has learned that "the pain now is part of the happiness then—that's the deal." The original line was that he didn't have "all the answers." This subtle difference between "all" and "any" makes all the difference in the world because it transforms his faith from a humble submission to a reasonable God into an existential leap without rational foundation. It seems the filmic Lewis, unlike the real one, went from one wrong extreme to another.

Sarah leaves his life and never tells him why.

Maurice decides to investigate and discovers that she had promised God to stop the adultery if he would save Maurice's life at the bombing. This enrages his atheistic sentiments, and he pursues her until she can no longer remain true to her promise and gives in to his seductions again. But then she gets a terminal illness and on her deathbed repents of it all. This enrages Maurice, who cannot accept a God who wields such power over people's destinies. As he writes a letter of hatred about God, we see the bitter fruit of unbelief in the life of the unrepentant.[8]

NEGATIVE PORTRAYALS OF INSTITUTIONAL FAITH

The Handmaid's Tale

The Scarlet Letter

The Crucible

Chocolat

Quills

Sister Act

Oscar and Lucinda

The Da Vinci Code

Doubt

The Body is worthy of special attention because it brims with every aspect of faith discussed in this and previous chapters: good Christians, bad Christians, insane Christians, blind faith versus proof, individual versus institutional faith, and the battle between doubt and faith.

Antonio Banderas plays Matt, a Jesuit priest who is sent from the Vatican to investigate the alleged discovery of the bones of Jesus Christ in an ancient Jewish grave found by Jewish archaeologist Sharon (played by Olivia Williams). Needless to say, if these bones are of the Son of Man, this could topple one of the three biggest religions of the world—and you can bet all three have their motives for getting involved.

Vatican officials are intent on suppressing the discovery and are represented as institutional despots. Matt's superior tells him, "We are counting on you to protect the Church." "You mean the faith," replies Matt. "The Church *is* the faith," retorts his superior. Matt asks, "What if this is—" His superior interrupts him by saying, "This is *not* the body of Christ," thus sealing the Catholic leaders as unwilling to face the truth if it contradicts their religious beliefs and as willing to do anything to stop that truth from getting out.

---

[8] I consider the sex scenes in this otherwise thoughtful film sexually exploitative and therefore a hindrance to its integrity as an examination of the issue of faith and fidelity.

Matt is more genuine and, along with another priest (played by Derek Jacobi), goes through a crisis of faith. The lines of evidence converge to indicate that these are indeed the bones of Christ: rich man's tomb, coins dated from Pilate's reign, crucifixion marks, spear wound on the rib cage, legs unbroken, thorn-like damage to the skull. While the older priest commits suicide after going insane because he could not handle the ramifications, Matt suffers psychic torment because, as he says, Jesus is God, so "if you take away the resurrection, you kill the God, Jesus." He painfully contemplates the conclusion that if Christianity is wrong, then oblivion awaits us when we die.

This is a stunningly biblical truth reiterated by the apostle Paul when he wrote:

> If Christ has not been raised, then our preaching is vain, your faith also is vain. Moreover we are even found to be false witnesses of God, because we testified against God that He raised Christ, whom He did not raise, if in fact the dead are not raised. For if the dead are not raised, not even Christ has been raised; and if Christ has not been raised, your faith is worthless; you are still in your sins. Then those also who have fallen asleep in Christ have perished. If we have hoped in Christ in this life only, we are of all men most to be pitied. (1 Cor 15:14-19)

Sharon, in a display of scientific arrogance, tells Matt, "My archaeological facts are going to conflict with your religious beliefs."

A Jewish leader wants to use the bones as a bargaining tool with the Vatican for political acknowledgment of the state of Israel. This guy doesn't really care whether it's true or not, because according to his postmodern understanding of faith, he says, "Religion does not exist based on a rational system of proof but because of man's need." He thinks Christian faith will survive because people will still believe contrary to the evidence anyway.

Finally, Muslim terrorists want the bones so that they can blackmail both Israel and Christianity to give them land in Jerusalem.

By the end of the story, Matt discovers the last piece of evidence that proves the bones are a later Christian burial of a man named David and not Christ's own bones. He goes back and quits the Vatican with an inspiring speech of honesty, integrity and *individualistic* faith:

I went to prove it was *not* the body of Christ, whether it was true or not. I thought I had lost my faith in Christ my savior, my friend. But I have lost my faith in men like you who serve God for their own material agenda.

In a personal-versus-institutional battle for his soul he concludes that he will now serve God "in his own way."[9]

TO BELIEVE OR NOT TO BELIEVE

After considering this sampling review of the nature of faith in film, it should be clear how often spiritual beliefs are worked out through storytelling. For good and bad, movies are a powerful medium for religious expression. Though authentic biblical spirituality is often hard to come by, there is still the kernel of it everywhere, even in the bad Christian movies, and anti-Christian movies. Whether it's blind faith versus reasonable faith, individual versus institutional faith or even the confrontation of doubt with faith, filmmakers seem to provide a mixed bag of truth and error when dealing with faith and the human condition.

WATCH AND LEARN

1. Watch a movie about a historical person of faith (such as *Shadowlands* or *Romero*). How does the movie portray that person's Christian faith? What aspects of faith are ignored or downplayed? What aspects of faith are emphasized? How is the character's faith related to his or her redemption in the story?

2. Watch the movie *Contact*. Compare and contrast how the movie characterizes faith and science. What do you think the movie is saying about the proper relationship of science, faith and society?

---

[9]A rather positive aspect of *The Body* is that the priest never fornicates with the woman, unlike the typical exploitative tactic in stories that explore the relationship of doubt and faith *(The Third Miracle, Simon Birch)*.

SPIRITUAL WARFARE

A hallmark of "Christian" filmmaking is its obsession with the end of the world. One would think that the book of Revelation is the only creative element of Christianity.

It all started back in 1972 with *A Thief in the Night,* which gave us scenes of the one-world government chasing after Christians in one-world-government vans to bring them to the guillotine. But it soon grew to monstrous, blob-like proportions with dozens of antichrist movies and the granddaddy end-times moneymaking phenomenon of all time, *Left Behind,* turned into a movie in 2001. This adaptation of the mega-million bestselling series that began as a trilogy and soon mutated into a twelve-book series brought the book of Revelation to the forefront of popular interest.

The difficulty with this focus on end-times scenarios is the speculation that is unavoidable with such interpretations. A careful viewer who takes the time to consider these interpretations will soon discover that every interpretation of the key prophetic elements of the end times has changed so often over the years as each fails to be predictive of historical events that it is quite embarrassing.[1] Though many have surely been scared into the kingdom of God through these fantastic doomsday predictions, nevertheless, too many others have seen their unreliability and have confused the fallible interpretations of people with the infallibility of God's Word.

PIN THE TAIL ON THE ANTICHRIST

Christians do not have a corner on the market of antichrist movies. The classics *Rosemary's Baby* and *The Omen* (1976) were among the most truly scary movies about Apollyon come in the flesh. But the arrival of the new millennium seemed an acceptable time to march out new movies about the apocalypse—Hollywood-style.

The Devil's Advocate, written by Jonathan Lemkin, is about a ruthless, hotshot attorney, played by Keanu Reeves, who has never lost a case and is recruited by the most powerful law firm in the world in New York. And this citadel of power just happens to be headed by Satan himself, played by Al Pacino and named John Milton (an ironic jab at the seventeenth-century Christian author of the epic poem *Paradise Lost*). Of course the young lawyer doesn't know this little factoid and gets sucked in. What begins as a noteworthy Faustian bargain parable about the temptations of pride and power ultimately degenerates into an implausible tale of Satan trying to breed the antichrist through the young hero, who it turns out is the offspring of his mother's sexual tryst with Satan.

But despite this preposterous premise, Pacino gives a rousing performance of a blame-shifting monologue worthy of the Father of Lies himself:

> Let me give you a little inside information about God. God likes to watch. He's a prankster. Think about it. He gives man *instincts!* He gives you this extraordinary gift, and then what does he do, I swear for his own amusement, his own private, cosmic gag reel, he sets the rules in opposition. It's the goof of all time. Look but don't touch. Touch but don't taste! Taste, don't swallow. Ahaha! . . . He's a sadist! He's an absentee landlord. Worship *that? Never!*

[1]Dwight Wilson, *Armageddon Now: The Premillennarian Response to Russia and Israel Since 1917* (Tyler, Tex.: Institute for Christian Economics, 1991).

The most profound revelation of the villain is often what comes out of his own mouth, and *The Devil's Advocate* renders a truly accurate and insightful portrayal of the kinds of lies Satan may use to convince people of their innocence and rationalize their pride, avarice and vanity. At one point Milton says, "Vanity. Definitely my favorite sin. . . . Freedom, baby . . . is never having to say you're sorry."

Although not strictly an "antichrist" movie, *Bedazzled* is a modern Faustian parable in the vein of *The Devil's Advocate* written by Larry Gelbart, Harold Ramis and Peter Tolan. It stars model/actress Elizabeth Hurley as a female incarnation of the Dark Lord of Sheol who tempts innocent Elliot (played by Brendan Fraser) with seven wishes in exchange for his soul. As each wish for wealth, fame, sensitivity and intellect is ruined by unexpected complications, Elliot learns that in order to be a self-actualized person, and in order to get the girl of his dreams, he needs to engage in "selfless acts of redemption" rather than selfish pursuits of power.

ANTICHRIST MOVIES

A Distant Thunder

Image of the Beast

The Prodigal Planet

Revelation (1996)

Apocalypse: Caught in the Eye of the Storm

The Omega Code (1999)

Revelation (1999)

Tribulation

Apocalypse IV: Judgment

Megiddo: The Omega Code 2

Deceived

The Moment After

The Gathering

Six: The Mark Unleashed

This parable lucidly points out the seductiveness of temptation (Satan disguising himself quite appropriately as a female angel of beauty) and the emptiness of vanity and power with all its accouterments (à la Ecclesiastes). Unfortunately, it also ends up secularizing God into Zen-like terms as "that universal spirit that animates and binds all things in existence."

After Elliot overcomes the Hurley she-devil and they become chums (the devil knows when she's lost fair and square), she lets him in on a "little secret":

> The whole good and evil thing. You know, Him [God] and me. It really comes down to you. You don't have to look very hard for heaven and hell.

They're right here on earth. You make the choice.

And thus the spiritual reality of temptation and eternal punishment or bliss is replaced with a humanistic substitute of heaven and hell right here and now. But then again, remember who just said that line—the Father (or in this case, Mother) of Lies.

End of Days, an Arnold Schwarzenegger vehicle, has a couple of positive twists on an otherwise predictable film about the devil. A sect of priests vow to protect a girl from a dark cabal of Jesuits, and the filmmakers consulted with several Christian ministers solicited by Schwarzenegger and focused on the power of faith alone to defeat the devil. Arnold remarkably puts down his weapon and submits to God, defeating the devil through faith, sacrificing himself to save the day.

FEARING WHERE ANGELS TREAD

Angels have always been a great tool in movies to help bring wisdom to mortals. With the success of the hit television series *Touched by an Angel,* as well as the New Age fascination with these ethereal heavenly beings, come some recent additions to the catalog of divine celluloid assistants.

City of Angels, starring Nicolas Cage and Meg Ryan, was rewritten by Dana Stevens from the original, *Wings of Desire*, created by critically acclaimed born-again German filmmaker Wim Wenders. The story is about an angel who longs to experience the joys of flesh and blood, falls in love with a woman, and seeks his transformation into a mortal in order to consummate those desires. It has insightful thoughts about the struggle of flesh and blood with spirit as well as some lucid images of frock-coated guardian angels doing their duties, unseen and unappreciated by their patrons.

A particularly moving scene shows an ensemble of these spiritual servants lined up on the beach watching and *hearing* the beauty of the sunrise. This is one of screendom's most beautiful visualizations of the unseen world and its inhabitants.

Seth, the angel, asks his human love interest, Maggie, to describe the taste of a pear because he can't taste such physical things. She tries and fails to do it adequately. Then he encourages her to describe it like Hemingway, because the power of words can come so close. She finally says, "Sweet, juicy, soft on your tongue, grainy like a sugary sand that dissolves in your mouth. How's that?" He replies, "It's perfect." Watching the film reinvigorates the soul to appreciate every life experience, even the simple ones like the taste of a pear, with a thankful heart, because life is short.

The downside to *City of Angels* is its humanistic worldview. According to the Bible, the "things into which angels long to look" (1 Pet 1:12) are not the experiences of being physical but the eternal gospel of salvation, which had been prophesied but hidden for centuries. *City of Angels* devalues spiritual value and elevates physical humanity as the highest order of experience (remember the similar sentiment of "The gods envy us" from *Troy?*). And the act of sexual intercourse becomes the highest experience in this humanistic parable of the priority of this life over the next.[2] Seth says of his desire for physical connection with Maggie, "I would rather have had one breath of her hair, one kiss from her mouth, one touch of her hand, than eternity without it." Thus the highest love in life is the love of another human rather than the love of one's Creator.

A more recent movie that plays like a virtual remake of *City of Angels* is *Angel A*, by Luc Besson. Only in this movie, the angel who falls in love with the human is a beautiful supermodel woman, and the human is a pathetic portly yet cute French version of white trash. And this movie concludes with the angel being able to become a human.

Michael, writer-director Nora Ephron's excursion into angelology, is another example of the exaltation of romance as religion. John Travolta plays the archangel with a twist. Rather than a blindingly bright, glorious creature, he is a fat, slobbish, cigarette-smoking, beer-guzzling, womanizing sugar addict, more akin to the cavorting fallen angels of the non-biblical book of Enoch than to the glorious warrior of light and ter-

---

[2]Sex becomes the closest thing to a transcendent experience that humanists can approximate. Sex becomes a secular sacrament. This use of Christian spiritual images as humanistic metaphors to exalt humanity and this life over God and the next world is a common postmodern revision of cultural symbols. Unlike Platonism and humanism, true biblical spirituality is holistic, embracing the physical world as a worthy creation, and recognizing spiritual tension, not as separation of matter and spirit but as sinful nature and conscience convicted by the law of God (Gal 5:16-25).

ror that he really is in the book of Daniel.

Much like Seth in *City of Angels,* Michael devours the simplest pleasures of life, like a good piece of pie, the largest ball of twine in the world and the company of women. He appreciates it all in the manner that we often fail to because we are too absorbed in our own troubles. He is determined not to allow life to be what happens when he's busy making other plans.

FALLEN ANGELS

Another aspect of the spiritual realm that has garnered the attention of Hollywood in recent years is the notion of spiritual warfare. An interesting interpretation of angelic armed conflict is the low-budget *The Prophecy* (1995), which spawned two sequels as a result of its success. In this story Christopher Walken, playing the archangel Gabriel, is planning another "fall from heaven," like his predecessor Lucifer, because of his anger at God's "unjust" control of the universe. The problem is that the angels' rebellion allows them to snatch souls from people to keep them from entering into heaven, so God has to send in his man to stop it all. That man is a priest who has lost his faith and has become a cop (played by Elias Koteas).

Though much of the theology is not biblical, it renders some Bible-friendly images of disguised, sword-toting angels. It also forthrightly deals with the uncomfortable scriptural fact, frequently ignored by the pious, that angels have often been sent by God to bring death to multitudes of people.

The hero, in a state of unbelief, explains why he turned from God:

> Did you ever notice how in the Bible, whenever God needed to punish someone, or make an example, or whenever God needed a killing, he sent an angel? Did you ever wonder what a creature like that must be like? A whole existence spent praising your God, but always with one wing dipped in blood. Would you ever really want to see an angel?

This is a sobering truth that those who consider themselves "spiritual warriors" should reconsider in their headlong pursuit of all things angelic. Angels in the Bible are awesome creatures of power that often terrify human beings, making them fall to the ground on their faces in fear (see Gen 17:3, 17; Josh 5:14; Dan 8:17; 10:7).

Constantine, adapted by Kevin Brodbin and Frank Cappello from the comic book, is about an exorcist, John Constantine, with a special ability to see the spirit world, trapped in a battle between God and the devil over the souls of men. But Constantine is also dying of lung cancer, and according to Roman Catholic theology, he is damned for the mortal sin of committing suicide in his past. Because he came back to life, he now tries to outbalance those mortal wages and work his way back to heaven by sending demons back to hell. But his time is short, and as Gabriel the angel tells him, everything he's done, he's done for a selfish intent on earning his way to heaven. So God is not appeased. As the tagline says on the movie poster, "Hell wants him. Heaven won't take him. Earth needs him."

Every movie must be understood within the context of the culture that it is created within. And our postmodern society relativizes good and evil, trivializes faith, and reviles Christianity as hate speech because of its condemnation of sinners to hell. In this kind of environment, a movie like *Constantine* depicting a real spiritual world of angels and demons, a real God and a real Satan, with a real hell where people are really punished for their sins, can't be all bad.

And this world portrays the souls of men being fought over like a scene out of the visions of Daniel or Elisha. When a fallen angel complains that God is not fair because "murderers, papists and molesters" need only repent to be forgiven, you know a chord of salvation through faith has been truthfully struck. Even Constantine's own efforts at salvation through works is spurned by the archangel Gabriel. The movie represents the hero's journey from a cynical rejection of God as a spoiled kid without a plan, to a final confession of God as a sovereign who has "a plan for all of us."

On the dark side, the entire worldview of spiritual warfare in *Constantine* is a free-will nightmare of Manichean dualism, where God and the devil are near equal beings of power, who make a bet with each other. They can have no direct contact with men, in order to see who can win them by influence alone. This apparent Job-like wager is a far cry from the sovereign God of the Bible who declares the end from the beginning, even for the battle of Armageddon. The devil and his minions reign over hell and torture people in a medieval depiction of damnation, in contrast with the biblical portrait of them all (Satan included) being tormented in the lake of fire (Rev 20:10).[3]

Ghost Rider reiterates this Mephistopheles motif. Motorcycle acrobat Johnny Blaze (Nicolas Cage) makes a deal with the devil to save his father's life. In return, Johnny must roam the earth as the Ghost Rider, sucking souls into hell. He is given an opportunity to get out of his contract by helping the devil stop his evil son Blackheart from unleashing hell on earth. The Rider accomplishes his goal through an act of personal sacrifice.

Another film that, like *Constantine*, portrays faith as the true victor in spiritual warfare is *The Exorcist: The Beginning*, written by Alexi Hawley. This story purports to tell the historical origins of the personal spiritual struggle of Father Merrin, who was the priest in the original *The Exorcist*.

We see Merrin in an archaeological dig in East Africa, post-WWII. The dig unearths an ancient demon that Merrin must battle as it begins murdering people in the area. Unlike the original movie, this prequel suggests the futility of ritual and incantation when battling spiritual evil. At the climax of the movie, when facing a demon possessed woman, Merrin loses his exorcism ritual book and must resort to quoting Scripture from faith as his weapon of warfare. Believe it or not, this movie actually depicts mere faith as providing the death blow to demonic powers and principalities.

The Exorcism of Emily Rose, by Scott Derrickson, brings a more realistic approach to the question of spiritual warfare by bringing it into a modern courtroom where an attorney, played by Laura Linney, attempts to provide evidence for the existence of demons in order to exculpate a priest from the charge of murdering an allegedly possessed girl. But the story also gives credence to the possibility that the girl had epilepsy as opposed to spirits inhabiting her body, thus embodying the modern di-

---

[3]There is a voodoo witchdoctor who is portrayed as "neutral," trying to stay out of the spiritual barroom brawl. Contrarily, the Bible denounces witchcraft as an abomination (Deut 18:9-14) and denies the possibility of neutrality in relation to God (Mt 12:30).

lemma of natural-versus-supernatural explanations. While the movie makes both sides of the argument believable, the possession experiences are depicted as strongly demonic in spectacle, leaving the viewer with a distinct impression of a supernatural world, unexplainable by natural phenomena.

HEAVEN AND HELL

Eternal punishment for sins is one of the most unacceptable doctrines to the unbeliever. So a common way that unbelievers deal with heaven and hell is to turn them into symbols for earthly experience. An example of this translation of hell to earth is *Jacob's Ladder*. In *Jacob's Ladder* (an obvious biblical reference) by Bruce Joel Rubin, a returning Vietnam vet is plagued by demons that turn out to be metaphors for his own personal problems in need of resolution before he dies. This is a literalization of the pop psychology metaphor of "personal demons" that haunt us.

Rare is the movie that paints a biblical portrait of eternal life and eternal damnation. Such comedies as *Bill and Ted's Bogus Journey*, Woody Allen's *Deconstructing Harry, South Park: Bigger, Longer and Uncut, Little Nicky* and others mock heaven and hell or playfully use them for irreverent comedic purposes. And many horror movies use hell as a mere tool for exploitation of gore, violence and evil rather than as true moral warning. But there are a few mainstream movies that have attempted to face the eternal retribution spoken of in the Bible.

Ghost, by Bruce Joel Rubin, was one of the few movies in past years that depicted people actually being drawn down into hell for punishment. This in itself was a triumph in a relativistic culture that has championed the goodness of humankind and the rejection of moral judgment. Unfortunately, the New Age message of the film was that only "bad" criminals and murderers get hell, but "good" people like the hero get heaven. So the biblical truth that there is no one who is good enough to go to heaven on his or her own merits (Rom 3:12) is replaced by a works salvation of the goodness within a person.

Typically, hell is interpreted as a burning fire over which Satan reigns. Movies like *Spawn, Bedazzled, Constantine* and *Ghost Rider* picture God and the devil more in Zoroastrian terms of two nearly equal powers fighting it out, yin and yang-like, with the results in question. Satan is envisioned as the overlord of hell who will punish people in the flames with his great power. What is missed in all this battling of spiritual forces is the biblical revelation that Satan does not rule over hell and that he does not punish people in hell; God is in charge and he does the punishing. In fact, God is going to punish Satan in hell as well (Rev 20:10, 15).

KARMA AND REINCARNATION

Another way of redefining heaven and hell has been the use of karma and reincarnation. Using karma as a substitute for true heaven and hell is more acceptable to the modern mentality, which wants to deal with responsibility for actions but doesn't want to face true punishment for sinners in the hands of an angry God (see Rev 14:10-11).

Karma is the Eastern belief, culled from Hinduism and Buddhism, that we pay for our sins, or the wrong we've done, in an impersonal, cyclical, "What goes around, comes around" kind of way. The payment exacted upon the soul is reincarnation as a lower life form than the previous life in the attempt to "get it right" the next time. We carry the burden of our past into the future.

The purpose of reincarnation is to work off the penalty for our sins in a purgatory-like fashion. It is similar to the biblical notion of reaping what we sow from our sins (Gal 6:7), but with the added unbiblical qualification that we can work our way to heaven as we become better, more moral people through successive incarnations. Thus we each become our own savior, able to ultimately triumph over sin through our own goodness. We save ourselves.

In Albert Brooks's comedy *Defending Your Life* the hero dies and goes to Judgment City, where he must go through a trial (but "It's not really a trial," they say, avoiding the impression of crime) in order to see whether he is mature enough in spirit to go to heaven or whether he is destined to go back to earth to try again and get it right. In this story fear is the big factor in determining one's spiritual redemption. Brooks uses a "This was your life" concept of showing movies of the person's past behaviors as evidence for his "guilt" or "innocence."

As we see these movies of the hero's life, we find that his fate is based on his living too fearful of a life—too fearful to have defended himself against a bully as a child, too fearful to have invested money as a young man and too fearful to have fought for a better salary for himself as an adult, among others. These self-oriented points of judgment reduce the story to a parable of redemption through selfishness. If the hero was only more aggressive to get what he wanted in life, he would go to heaven.

What Dreams May Come, written by Ron Bass from Richard Matheson's novel, is an epic adventure through heaven and hell. The hero dies and goes to heaven. But his wife, his soul mate, is in such psychic pain from her loss (in addition to losing her two children in death as well) that she commits suicide. In the worldview of this movie, suicides go to a hell of their own making, "not because they were immoral or selfish," but because they violated the natural order of their process of spiritual growth. They create their own hell because they are too obsessed to connect with others.

The hero, played by Robin Williams, decides to go on a quest through hell to try to bring his beloved back. As he does, we are treated to a visual feast of torments worthy of Dante himself, similar to scenes out of C. S. Lewis's *The Great Divorce*. The hero finds redemption in self-sacrifice, choosing to stay in hell with his beloved rather than going to heaven without her. This knocks her out of her self-created head trip, and the two end up in heaven again, only to be reincarnated for another go at falling in love on earth.

REINCARNATION

Flatliners

Defending Your Life

Dead Again

What Dreams May Come

Down to Earth

The movie is filled with Eastern metaphysical musings about mind being the nature of reality and about physicality being only illusion. The heavens and hells people live in are creations of their own minds in a karmic universe. God is given one mention that reduces him to irrelevance. When asked by the newly dead hero where God is in all of this, the wise mentor (played by Cuba Gooding Jr.) tells him, "Oh, he's up there, somewhere, shouting down that he loves us, wondering why we can't hear him. Ya think?" Not only is God unseen and unheard, but that little "Ya think?" tacked on at the end announces God as a being without any substantial reality outside of one's subjective beliefs. An unseen, unheard, unknown God is really the same as no God at all.

An interesting alternative ending on the DVD more clearly reveals the intentions of the authors. The mother who committed suicide is about to return to earth to work through her bad karma: "There is a reason every religion in the world talks about atonement. Because we know inside we need to take responsibility for what we've done." Her return to earth is more therapy than punishment.

Flatliners, written by Peter Filardi, comes closer to the Christian notion of sin and repentance. Medical students secretly explore near-death experiences by stopping their hearts and reviving them. Sins from their past—sexual promiscuity, racism, hatred and bullying—begin to threaten their present reality. One of the characters decides to address childhood racist and hateful actions by making amends with a black woman from his grade school. His repentance dissolves the surreal attacks. Their redemptions lay in their repentance, a good example of one half of the equation of true redemption, though stopping short of the role of faith in God (see Acts 20:21; 26:20). Rather than portraying personal weaknesses *(Defending Your Life)* or poor self-esteem *(What Dreams May Come)* as humanity's problem, *Flatliners* addresses actual sin—but neglects to address God.

Movies can be a powerful means of communicating spiritual realities, good or bad, true or false, as our survey has illustrated. Whether antichrists, angels, demons, or heaven and hell, the spiritual curiosity of human beings cannot be ignored and finds its way to the big screen in plenty of mainstream movies. While many of these presentations are far from biblical, they can often become inspiration for a further study of Scripture to find out the truth of the matter.

WATCH AND LEARN

Watch one of the movies in this chapter with some friends. Discuss the interpretations of spirituality that you agree with and the interpretations you disagree with. How does the redemption portrayed coincide with biblical truth? Where does it depart from biblical truth?

DÉNOUEMENT

WATCHING MOVIES WITH EYES WIDE OPEN

In this book I have introduced you to the basic structure of storytelling that is used in screenwriting with the intent of sharpening your skills in discerning the worldviews and philosophies that are communicated through Hollywood movies. Those skills were applied to various specific worldviews, including existentialism, postmodernism, monism, Christianity and others, in order to illustrate how trends in thinking and society are reflected in and influenced by movies.

Though these principles of discernment are relevant for both adults and youth, many of the examples I have used are from movies that are R-rated or are more adult-oriented. In the same way that we allow alcohol or driving licenses in our culture only for adults who have reached a certain age of maturity, so I think discretion should be used in movies as to the maturity level necessary for a viewer. Various websites summarize the content of movies, so viewers can make informed decisions before they get to the theater. It is important to remember that not all movies are worthy of our time or attention, because all stories are not created equal.

DISCRETION AND BALANCE

Just as God permits the adult consumption of wine and strong drink (Deut 14:26; Jn 2:1-11) but not its abuse (Eph 5:18), so many movies are for mature viewers because of their content but should not be carelessly consumed without caution or self-reflection as the unwary cultural glutton does. As viewers, we must be sensitive to our own weaknesses and negative propensities. One person's sense of exploitation may simply illustrate his own prudery, while another person's tolerance may actually be her own indulgence in besetting sin. So we must be careful to draw personal lines that we will not cross, based upon what particular things affect us negatively when we are exposed to them in movies.

In the same way that alcoholics won't take a sip of alcohol because they know their weakness toward drunkenness, so adult viewers ought to know their weaknesses and avoid watching those movies or parts of movies that will draw them down spiritually rather than exhort them morally. Statements like "The sex and violence don't bother me" are not necessarily expressions of maturity. If a movie is exploitative with vice, it *ought* to bother the viewer, and if it doesn't, then that viewer is being deadened in his or her spirituality and humanity.

A LOVE-HATE RELATIONSHIP

One of the biggest hindrances to valuable discussion of movies is our tendency to "love" or "hate" a movie with such conviction that those who disagree with us are discouraged from communicating or sharing their own viewpoints. If the negative aspects we perceive in a film outweigh the positive aspects, we tend to ignore those positive aspects and reject the movie altogether. If the positive aspects outweigh the negative for us, then we tend to neglect those negatives and wholly endorse the movie with glowing praise. Phrases like "I hated that movie" or "I loved that movie" are often perceived by others as warnings to avoid discussion because of such strong conviction.

Even in writing this book I have struggled with this need for balance. Because of the constraint of space, I have tried to focus on movies that illustrate a particular point, good or bad, without examining counterpoints. One unintended result may be the appearance of unqualified approval or disapproval of a movie. Be careful not to jump to this conclusion. An analysis of a movie does not necessarily mean an *absolute* endorsement or rejection of watching that movie.

THE GOOD, THE BAD AND THE MEDIOCRE

If my intentions for this book have been successful, you will walk away from it with a more balanced appreciation for movies, both those you like and those you dislike. You will have the ability to appreciate the good and pinpoint what you think is bad. Movies, after all, are art, and they are therefore meant to stimulate thought and challenge preconceived notions. Sometimes, a movie that communicates a disagreeable theme or message can still be a worthy watch if it makes us think through and discuss important issues.

Talking about movies seems problematic at times because people take their perceptions so personally. If we love a movie that someone else hates, we tend to think the other is a pessimist and may dislike us as well. If we hate a movie that someone else loves, we tend to think the other may be overly optimistic and blissfully ignorant. And in both cases we wonder how blind the other could be not to have seen what we have seen. Sometimes we even question that person's character. This can lead to pride and condescension rather than conversation and discovery. How can we avoid this kind of communication barrier and engage in helpful dialogue about the movies we see?

PERSUADING VERSUS ARGUING

I have found that the approach most conducive to openness in discussion is to describe what I liked about a movie first, even if I "hated" the movie, and then to describe what I didn't like or disagreed with in its craft or content. Whether others hated a movie or loved it, they will be more likely to consider your perspective and welcome dialogue if you have shown a balance of perception and have focused on the positive first. And there's usually *something* good about every film, no matter how bad it is. Sometimes you just have to work harder to find that positive.

Of course this approach can be taken wrongly to an extreme. For instance, the discussion of the acting or directing in a pornographic film does not justify consuming such depravity. Discussing the realism of special effects in an immoral slasher film that exploits the destruction of human bodies can simply amount to a rationalization as well. Be careful: "All things are lawful for me, but not all things are profitable. . . . I will not be mastered by anything" (1 Cor 6:12).

This brings up a common complaint about the mixture of good and bad in movies. Rare is the film that can be fully embraced in all it communicates. Some people believe that since movies are such a mixture of truth and error in their worldviews and values, Christians should avoid watching them for the sake of holy living. They claim that allowing a little bit of "compromise" leads to the slippery slope of more and bigger compromise until one falls away from the faith (or at least falters in one's spiritual walk).

While there is merit in this argument regarding those who would subject themselves to things that they feel draw them away from God, let me redirect our thoughts to the first chapter of this book on sex, violence and profanity in the Bible. We must remember that not all exploration of sins within drama is exploitative or inherently sinful. Since the Bible itself explores human evil with great breadth and much detail, we cannot say that movies that do so are, without exception, exploitative.

The key is to ask some questions: Is this an educational approach to exposing evil? What are the context and consequences of the vice portrayed? Is it dehumanizing or humanizing? Does the movie celebrate evil, or does it ultimately condemn it? Is the sin displayed as an end in itself, or is it a part of the bigger picture that leads to redemption? Does the movie go overboard in detail, or is some detail necessary to emphasize the seriousness of our behavior? Only in this way can we avoid the extremes of cultural gluttony and cultural anorexia, which are both detrimental to our humanity as created in the image of God.

And we need not be afraid of being challenged by worldviews that contradict our own. Sometimes elements of our own worldview may not be true, and we need to be challenged to reexamine them, even from a viewpoint with which we ultimately disagree. Of course that takes humility and a lack of fear, two things that are too often in short supply in the Christian community.

The fact is, there is nothing perfect in this life. We live in a fallen world. Everything and everyone is tainted by sin, even those with whom we agree. Even Christian media are not exempt from imperfection. No Christian sermon, book or movie is completely unstained by our fallenness. But we do not cut off all contact with Christian culture because of this reality. We interact with it. So we should deal with "secular" culture as well, discerning the truth and error in art that radiate a "fallen splendor."

As Christians, we do not walk away from an unbeliever because he or she cusses or lives in open rebellion against God; we interact with that person in order to find common ground in our humanity and eventually offer redemption for sin. It is the same with the arts. Because all truth is ultimately God's truth, we can find what we think is true in a movie and dissect what we think is false. Sometimes the false or the evil becomes too much, and we walk out of the theater or fast-forward the video. This is inevitable. But our goal should be to interact with society with a view toward reform, not to retreat from society, for retreat leads to spiritual and social defeat.

THE APOSTLE PAUL'S EXAMPLE

In Acts 17 the apostle Paul models a redemptive interaction with culture. He addresses the pagans of his day (the Epicureans and Stoics) within the arena of the ideas of his day (the Areopagus). Paul was not afraid to engage those heathen ideas.

In some ways television, music and the movies are the modern arena of ideas. Many people are influenced in their worldview by the entertainment industry, whether willingly or unwittingly. Like Paul, we had best be informed about the media of communication in our culture.

Paul studied Greek culture and philosophy under Gamaliel (Acts 22:3).[1] He analyzed the religious altars of the Greeks (Acts 22:23) and made himself familiar with their deities so that he could find a point of

---

[1]"When we add to this the extensive knowledge of Greek literature and culture which is reflected in his letters, it is manifest that Paul was neither naïve nor obscurantist when it came to a knowledge of philosophy and Gentile thought" (Greg Bahnsen, *Always Ready: Directions for Defending the Faith*, ed. Robert Booth [Atlanta: American Vision, 1996], p. 241).

common connection with them. He respectfully quoted several Greek poets, including Epimenides, Aratus and Cleanthes (Acts 17:28), affirming that they had a partially true glimpse of God's full truth. Paul thus brought out of the Greek pagan beliefs a more accurate rendering of the truth by *interacting with* the culture, not by avoiding it or embracing it.[2]

It is at this point that I want to make a significant qualification to everything that has been written. When Christians learn about discerning worldviews in movies, there is a tendency to see movies only as a means to an end. An informed Christian will analyze a movie in order to "understand our culture" and share the gospel with that culture. In this sense, they only "use" movies without listening to them. They will reduce a movie to its ideas and entirely bypass experiential truths that it may communicate. Please consider this important caveat: I am not saying that moviegoing is a "figure out the worldview" game, as if that is all there is to it.

I believe that we should listen to movies. Let them challenge us, allow them to help us see the world through different eyes, let them help us experience human existence in ways that we haven't before. By entering into the story, we can experience a part of human existence and truth that we cannot reduce to abstract ideas or philosophy. It is not enough to merely recognize that *Stranger Than Fiction* presents an existentialist worldview that believes we find meaning in our monotonous lives by facing death and discovering transcendence in our everyday experiences. We must embrace what is true about that within our Christian worldview.

Yes, we must understand that without Christ, the attempt to find meaning or transcendence is impossible. But like Harold Crick, we too must face the fact that our lives are not in our control, that we are going to die and so must make the most of our short lives, including the appreciation of the little things in life as valuable. Like the pagan poetry

---

[2]Some might argue that Paul was acquainted with Greek culture *before* he became a Christian. Though this is likely true, Paul's history as a "Hebrew of Hebrews; . . . a Pharisee" (Phil 3:5) meant that he engaged the surrounding culture while maintaining a devout adherence to the law of God. Apparently he did not consider it a compromise to interact redemptively with his cultural environment.

that Paul referred to in Athens, *Stranger Than Fiction* may be a distorted and ultimately inadequate worldview compared with the Bible, but that does not make it worthless in the eyes of God. It still contains a partially true glimpse of God's full truth. We must embrace the truth we do find in movies like this and, like Paul, qualify it with our own understanding of the resurrected Christ.

WATCH AND LEARN

Invite friends to begin a movie discussion group. Try to pick movies that will be the least offensive for a wider appeal. Watch different kinds of movies each time, like a comedy, a foreign film, an art-house film, a "chick flick," a guy movie, a drama and so on. Have viewers read *Hollywood Worldviews* before they join.

Be a facilitator for the discussion. Ask questions like the following:

1. *The craft:* What did you like and not like about the craft and production of the film? What about the writing, directing, cinematography and acting?

2. *The story:* Whose story is this? What is the character arc and redemption of the hero? Discuss the arc with examples from the movie. What is the hero's inner flaw? What choice does the hero make to overcome the flaw? What is the theme or themes explored in the movie?

3. *The worldview:* What worldviews are explored in the film, and how are they honored or dishonored? What do you think the filmmakers are saying about the human condition and how we ought or ought not to live?

Index